QUEEN VICTORIA
AND THE BONAPARTES

Also by Theo Aronson

QUEEN VICTORIA
and the
BONAPARTES

—

THEO ARONSON

THE BOBBS-MERRILL COMPANY
Indianapolis / New York

THE BOBBS-MERRILL COMPANY, INC.
A Subsidiary of Howard W. Sams & Co., Inc.
Indianapolis · New York

Printed in Great Britain

To the memory of

JOHN MCINTOSH

Contents

PART ONE—'THESE GREAT MEETINGS OF SOVEREIGNS'

Chapter One: 'Such an extraordinary man'   3

Chapter Two: Spring at Windsor   21

Chapter Three: '*Vive le Hemperor!*'   38

Chapter Four: Summer at Saint Cloud   46

Chapter Five: 'The gayest of cities'   58

Chapter Six: 'Poor, dear, modest, unpretentious Osborne'   73

PART TWO—'THE SINISTER DESIGNS OF OUR NEIGHBOUR'

Chapter Seven: The Disenchantment   87

Chapter Eight: 'Grief and anxiety'   100

Chapter Nine: Separate Ways   108

Chapter Ten: Decline and Fall   121

PART THREE—'THIS TIME OF TERRIBLE TRIAL'

Chapter Eleven: Camden Place   137

Chapter Twelve: 'That same pleasing, gentle and gracious manner'   146

Chapter Thirteen: The Prince Imperial   160

Chapter Fourteen: Sorrow's Crown of Sorrow   171

Chapter Fifteen: 'In affectionate remembrance . . .'   181

PART FOUR—'MY DEAR SISTER, THE EMPRESS'

Chapter Sixteen: Victoria and Eugenie   199

Chapter Seventeen: Osborne, Balmoral and the Côte d'Azur   210

CONTENTS

Chapter Eighteen: *Entente Cordiale*   224

Epilogue   235

    Notes on Sources   241

    Bibliography   247

    Index   253

Illustrations

Between pages 116 *and* 117

Queen Victoria aged thirty-five
Louis Napoleon, Emperor of the French
The Empress Eugenie
Queen Victoria welcomes Napoleon III and the Empress
    Eugenie
The royal box at Covent Garden
Queen Victoria and Prince Albert in 1855
Queen Victoria invests Napoleon III
Princess Mathilde Bonaparte
Prince Napoleon
The State Visit to Paris
Queen Victoria in widowhood
The Empress Eugenie at the zenith of her career
The exiled Emperor Napoleon III
Bertie, Prince of Wales
Louis, the Prince Imperial
The scouting party before the Zulu attack
The cross erected by Queen Victoria
Queen Victoria and Princess Beatrice before the Prince Im-
    perial's coffin
The Empress Eugenie in later years

Acknowledgements

I must thank Her Majesty Queen Elizabeth II by whose gracious permission certain extracts from the Journals of Queen Victoria are here published for the first time. For arranging this, I am indebted to Sir Michael Adeane, Her Majesty the Queen's Private Secretary and Keeper of the Archives, and Mr Robert Mackworth-Young, Librarian at Windsor Castle.

For help, advice and information I must thank also the Countess of Longford, Miss E. H. Berridge, Miss A. T. Hadley, Mlle Louise Duval, Major D. Barr, Mr Anthony Dennison, M. Pierre Blanchard and Mr L. A. Short. I am grateful for all the help that I have received from the Bibliothèque Nationale, Paris; the Library of Congress, Washington; the British Museum, London; and the many libraries and newspaper libraries in London and Paris. Three recently published books which have proved especially valuable are *Victoria R.I.* by Elizabeth Longford, *The Empress Eugenie* by Harold Kurtz and *Napoleon III in England* by Ivor Guest.

My chief debt is to Mr Brian Roberts for his unfailing interest and expert advice during every stage of the writing of this book.

For permission to quote copyright material I am indebted to the publishers of the following books: *The Letters of Queen Victoria*, Second Series, edited by George Earle Buckle (John Murray, 1926); and *Leaves from a Journal*, edited by Nicolas Bentley (André Deutsch, 1961).

Part One
'These great meetings of Sovereigns'

CHAPTER ONE

'Such an extraordinary man'

1

'I must write a line to ask what you say to the *wonderful* proceedings at Paris, which really seem like a *story* in a book or a play!' wrote Queen Victoria to her uncle, King Leopold of the Belgians, on 4 December 1851. 'What is to be the result of it all?'

The '*wonderful* proceedings' to which the thirty-two-year-old Queen was referring with such schoolgirlish enthusiasm was the *coup d'état* by which Prince Louis Napoleon Bonaparte, President of the French Republic, had made himself dictator of France two days before.

The Prince President's seizure of power had come as a complete surprise to Queen Victoria. On the very day of his *coup d'état* she had been urging her Uncle Leopold to visit her at Osborne; the Belgian King's fears of some sort of upheaval in France had seemed to her exaggerated. 'I feel ashamed,' she now admitted, 'to have written so *positively* a few hours before that nothing would happen.'

The Queen should have known better. Louis Napoleon Bonaparte had always been one for the unexpected. And if there was one thing about which he had never left anyone in doubt, it was his determination to make himself master of France. Reticent in most things, he had never been reticent about his ambitions. These Victoria understood well enough. It was simply that she was not yet accustomed to the deviousness of his methods. In fact, Queen Victoria did not really know a great deal about Prince Louis Napoleon.

They had met only once. This had been in the days of Louis Napoleon's exile in England, when the Queen had attended an official breakfast in Fulham in aid of a somewhat unromantic cause: the erection of baths and wash-houses in the East End of London. Other than on this one public occasion, she had never set eyes on him. She was aware that he had been born during the halcyon days of the Great Napoleon's Empire; that his father had been the Emperor's disgruntled brother Louis and his mother the Empress Josephine's daughter by her first marriage—the seductively mannered Hortense de Beauharnais. She knew, too, that since the death of Napoleon's only son in 1832, Louis Napoleon had been a very active pretender to the throne of France. However, thus far, his attempts to re-establish his uncle's Empire had been not only unsuccessful, but faintly comic.

The first attempt, made in the year before Victoria's own accession to the British throne, had taken place at Strasbourg. At dawn on 30 October 1836, the twenty-eight-year-old Prince, heading a handful of loyal Bonapartists, had presented himself to the somewhat startled French garrison and exhorted them to march behind him to Paris. The garrison had refused to do any such thing. Most of the soldiers had not even believed that this unheroic-looking young man was the Great Napoleon's nephew. Prince Louis Napoleon had been arrested and sent to Paris, where King Louis Philippe, the current French sovereign, had decided to play down the incident by having the impetuous pretender shipped off to New York.

Within four months the Prince was back in Europe and within four years had made yet another attempt on the throne. In August 1840 (it had been the year of Queen Victoria's marriage) he had assembled a band of fellow conspirators and set off from England in a hired steamer, bound for Boulogne. To lend the expedition the right Napoleonic touch, a tame and somewhat bedraggled-looking eagle had been bought from a boy at the Gravesend docks and chained to the mast. This second attempt had proved no less disastrous than the first. Louis Napoleon had again failed to rouse the garrison to his cause and again he had been arrested. This time Louis Philippe's government had been determined to take no chances. Prince Louis Napoleon had been sentenced to perpetual imprisonment in the fortress of Ham, in northern France.

'How long,' the pretender had remarked dryly, 'does perpetuity last in France?'

4

For him, it had lasted six years. He had escaped from Ham, disguised as a workman, in 1846, and had once more taken up residence in England. From here, with somewhat more circumspection but no less determination, he had continued his imperialist intrigues.

Throughout these years of Bonapartist activity, Victoria's sympathies had been with King Louis Philippe. In this she had been backed up, to the hilt, by her husband, Prince Albert. Louis Napoleon might have cut the more romantic figure, but the stolid Orleans King, besides being France's chosen sovereign, was a friend of the English Queen. The two of them had exchanged visits and the term *entente cordiale*, signifying an understanding between Britain and France, was first bandied about during Louis Philippe's time; not until late in his reign did a coolness develop between the two sovereigns. Then, in addition to being friends, Victoria and Louis Philippe were related through the Coburgs. Amongst other connections, Victoria's adored Uncle Leopold was married to one of King Louis Philippe's daughters. Already the fact that England was so willing to harbour a conspirator such as Louis Napoleon was a source of amazement to the Queen's Continental relatives. Was he not, besides being an irresponsible trouble-maker, the nephew of England's greatest enemy—the dreaded Napoleon? Was not his aim to revive the military glories of the Napoleonic Empire; to upset the balance of Europe, so carefully restored by the victors after Waterloo?

Louis Napoleon's chance had come, quite suddenly, in February 1848. What he had been unable to achieve through his colourful sallies against the Orleans regime was accomplished by the French themselves: King Louis Philippe was overthrown by revolution. His flight to England was followed by the proclamation of a Republic. The news threw Victoria and Albert into a state of apprehension ('All [that] our poor relations have gone through is worthy only of a *dreadful* romance,' she exclaimed) and Louis Napoleon into a froth of excitement. 'The Republic is proclaimed,' he cried, 'it is for me to be its master.' However, the years of adversity had taught him patience and it was not until the new Republic had passed through some months of turbulence that he made the first moves to achieve his ambition.

A President of the Republic was to be elected by universal suffrage: he put his name forward as a candidate.

At this stage Queen Victoria began to take Louis Napoleon's pretensions more seriously. That he would be elected to the Presidency seemed certain (the name he bore guaranteed this), but that this softly spoken, somewhat starry-eyed adventurer with the waxed moustaches would prove to be anything more than a flash in the French political pan seemed extremely doubtful. Victoria's Prime Minister, Lord John Russell, imagined that Louis Napoleon might play the part of Richard Cromwell: by his weakness he would pave the way for the restoration of the monarchy. This was the Queen's own wish. 'In France there really ought to be a Monarchy before long, *qui que ce soit*,' she told her Uncle Leopold.

'Louis Napoleon's election seems certain,' she wrote on another occasion, 'and I own I wish for it as I think it will lead to something else.' Even the dethroned and exiled King Louis Philippe was in favour of Louis Napoleon's candidature.

The result of the presidential election put something of a damper on these pleasurable royal speculations. Louis Napoleon's majority was immense: he had polled the votes of almost three-quarters of the electorate. To Frenchmen thirsting, some for glory, some for order and some for an embodiment of the continuing spirit of the Great Revolution, the name Napoleon had meant far more than all the electioneering promises of his rivals. On 20 December 1848 the forty-year-old Prince Louis Napoleon Bonaparte was proclaimed President of the French Republic.

'The success of Louis Napoleon is an extraordinary event . . .' wrote the Queen to King Leopold, adding with characteristic sagacity, that 'it will, however, perhaps be more difficult to get rid of him again than one at *first* may imagine'.

Victoria was right. Once Louis Napoleon had been elected President he set about, at first imperceptibly and then more boldly, consolidating his position. Not until he had been President of France for three years, during which time his popularity increased enormously, did he feel ready to make the next move. On 2 December 1851—the anniversary of Austerlitz and of the first Napoleon's coronation—he staged his *coup d'état*. Overnight he established himself as complete master of France.

It was this bold stroke that prompted Queen Victoria to dash off those ecstatic lines to her Uncle Leopold, asking for his opinion of the *wonderful* proceedings at Paris'.

As always, King Leopold's answer was carefully considered. 'As yet one cannot form an opinion,' he wrote, 'but I am inclined to think that Louis Bonaparte will succeed.'

2

One of the strengths of Queen Victoria's character was that her impulsiveness was tempered by her sound common sense. No matter how emotional her initial response, in the end her reason usually prevailed. This was true of her reaction to Louis Napoleon's *coup d'état*. Once the first flush of excitement had worn off, she counselled calm. She hoped that King Louis Philippe's family would neither 'move a limb nor say a word' and that her government would remain entirely passive in its dealings with France. The *coup d'état* was to be neither condemned nor approved of; 'a strict line of neutrality and passiveness' was to be followed by Britain. With Victoria's sound advice, the Prime Minister, Lord John Russell, was in complete accord.

But the Queen had reckoned without her *bête noire*—the Foreign Secretary, Lord Palmerston. The jaunty Palmerston, without waiting for instructions, gave the *coup d'état* his full approval. In private conversation and with not a word to his colleagues, he assured the French Ambassador (Count Walewski, the Great Napoleon's illegitimate son by Marie Walewska) that Louis Napoleon's assumption of power had his 'entire approbation'. Particularly galling to Victoria and Albert was the fact that they heard of Palmerston's sanctioning of the *coup* in a roundabout fashion. Lady Normanby, wife of the British Ambassador in Paris, who disliked Palmerston as heartily as did the royal couple, was related to one of Prince Albert's private secretaries; it was in a vehement letter from Lady Normanby to this secretary that Queen Victoria first read of Palmerston's *reckless conduct*'. She could not believe it. The French government must be *pretending* that Palmerston had given his approval, she protested. But they were not. When the truth of Palmerston's indiscretion was confirmed, the Queen made such a fuss that the Prime Minister was obliged to demand his resignation as Foreign Secretary. It was given on 20 December 1851.

Victoria was overjoyed. For years she and Albert had been at loggerheads with the volatile Lord Palmerston. To be rid of him now was looked upon as a considerable achievement. 'I have the greatest pleasure in announcing to you a piece of news which I know will give you as much satisfaction and relief as it does to us, and will do to the *whole* world,' she wrote effusively to her Uncle Leopold. '*Lord Palmerston is no longer Foreign Secretary.* . . .'

That particular battle won, the Queen could turn her attention to its cause. In truth, it had been the hated Palmerston's championing of the *coup*, more than the *coup* itself, which Victoria had minded. While it had appalled some of her subjects, others had—like the Queen—accepted it more philosophically. What else could one expect from the French? After all, in a nationwide plebiscite held three weeks after the *coup*, some seven and a half out of eight million voters gave their approval to Louis Napoleon's seizure of power. It was not, of course, the sort of thing that one would like to see happening in England, but for fickle France, which had undergone six changes of regime in as many decades, it was not nearly so outrageous.

The great thing, claimed Queen Victoria, was to keep cool and not *provoke* Louis Napoleon. When her Prime Minister, Lord John Russell, assured Count Walewski that what England desired was 'the happiness and welfare of France', she expressed wholehearted approval. In a private letter to King Leopold (who tended to be more fidgety about the matter) she was more explicit.

'We shall try and keep on the best of terms with the President,' she wrote, 'who is extremely sensitive and susceptible, but for whom, I must say, I have never had any *personal* hostility.'

Yet, for all this, the Queen remained on her guard. She was, after all, dealing with a Napoleon. One of Louis Napoleon's first acts after the *coup* came as a sharp reminder of this. He forced the sale of all the property belonging to the Orleans family in France and confiscated King Louis Philippe's private fortune, thus robbing the King's sons of their inheritance. Although the proceeds were used for the most praiseworthy purpose—the erection of amenities for the poor—the dictatorial act earned him widespread condemnation. His political enemies referred to it, by an untranslatable pun, as *le premier vol de l'aigle*. Victoria called the move 'too dreadful and monstrous' and Albert, always more ready than his wife to think the worst of Louis Napoleon, labelled it 'a crime that cries to Heaven'.

Such scares set Britain looking to her defences. There was even some wild talk of a French plan to invade England and carry off the Queen from Osborne by a *coup de main*. What precisely Louis Napoleon planned to do with her, having captured her, was never explained.

Victoria refused to be panicked. On the whole, she believed in the President's peaceful intentions; yet, she admitted to King Leopold, 'with such an extraordinary man as Louis Napoleon, one can never be for one instant safe'.

Exactly how extraordinary a man he was, she was beginning to find out. A few weeks after the *coup d'état*, the worldly Lord Cowley replaced Lord Normanby as British Ambassador in Paris, and from Cowley's reports Victoria was able to learn something of Louis Napoleon's personality. He seemed a complete enigma. Lord Cowley professed himself utterly baffled. 'To fathom the thoughts or divine the intentions of that one individual, the Prince President of France, would sorely try the powers of the most clear-sighted,' he complained to the Queen's close associate, the Dean of Windsor.

In a dispatch to the new Foreign Secretary, Lord Malmesbury, Cowley embroidered on this theme. The President's personality seemed to be 'a strange mixture of good and evil', he wrote. 'Few approach him who are not charmed by his manners. The patience with which he listens to those who differ from him is remarkable. I am told that an angry word never escapes him. . . .'

That the Queen should be intrigued by this sphinx-like figure is understandable. Before long she was dropping hints to Lord Malmesbury that she found Lord Cowley's reports from Paris a little too dry, too lacking in intimate information about the Prince President and his circle. The Ambassador duly enlivened his dispatches, even to the extent of reporting on Louis Napoleon's private life. Thus the Queen was no doubt informed when the bachelor President—an accomplished philanderer—finally rid himself of his English mistress, Miss Howard. 'Miss H. is, I believe,' wrote Cowley to Malmesbury, 'at last *congédiée.*'

As the year following the *coup d'état* unfolded and it became increasingly obvious that Louis Napoleon was planning to restore the Empire, Victoria came to accept the inevitable. To England's Queen, any monarchy would be better than no monarchy at all. She might titter, in private, at some of the stories that were circulating about his ambitions (one concerned an imperial crown, suspended from a triumphal arch and surmounted by the inscription '*Il l'a bien mérité*'; the crown had been removed, leaving only the inscription and the dangling rope), but her official reactions were always sensible.

The question of Louis Napoleon's future title was a case in point. He planned to style himself Napoleon III, in recognition of the Great Napoleon's only son who had died in exile in 1832. This infuriated Europe's more legitimate sovereigns. How dare this adventurer, elected to power, regard the Bonapartes as an established royal dynasty? They would refuse to recognize him. But Queen Victoria would have no truck with such pigheadedness. She impressed Lord Malmesbury with the importance of Britain's *not* giving her Continental allies an undertaking that she would join them in refusing to acknowledge Napoleon III. 'Objectionable as this appellation no doubt is,' she wrote, 'it may hardly be worth offending France and her Ruler by refusing to recognize it. . . .' The rest of them had no means, she added practically, of forcing Louis Napoleon to do anything that he did not want to do, 'nor would any diplomatic form of obtaining an assurance from him give us any guarantee of his not doing after all exactly what he pleases'.

In this, she was proved correct. On 2 December 1852—again on the anniversaries of Austerlitz and Napoleon I's coronation—Louis Napoleon Bonaparte was proclaimed Napoleon III, Emperor of the French. A plebiscite on the question had given him an even bigger majority than for his *coup d'état.*

The proclamation sent a flurry of alarm through the Courts of Europe. Had not the Powers at the Congress of Vienna pledged that no Bonaparte should again sit on the throne of France? Would the restoration of the Empire not lead to a hankering after the military glories of the first Napoleon's day? 'We are here in the awkward position of persons in hot climates,' complained King Leopold to his niece of this brand-new Napoleon, 'who find themselves in company, for instance in their beds, with a snake; they must *not move, because that irritates* the creature, but they can hardly remain as they are, without a fair chance of being bitten.' The Tsar of Russia, unable to ignore the fact that Louis Napoleon had been proclaimed Emperor, could yet not bring himself to treat this parvenu as a legitimate sovereign. He compromised by addressing him, after a delay of several weeks, not by means of the accepted *Sire, mon frère,* but as *notre très cher ami.*

To this studied insult the new Emperor replied, with characteristic dryness, that whereas one put up with one's 'brothers', one chose one's 'friends'.

Queen Victoria showed herself more accommodating. She lost no time in accrediting her ambassador to Napoleon III and in addressing him as 'my good Brother, the Emperor of the French'. In her formal letter of recognition, she assured him of her 'invariable attachment and esteem' and of her 'sentiments of sincere friendship'. She signed herself 'Your Imperial Majesty's good Sister, VICTORIA R.'

To the Queen, this was merely the language of diplomacy; into the fulsome phrases, Napoleon III was ready to read a great deal more.

3

'I am delighted, my lord,' said the Emperor Napoleon III to the British Ambassador, Lord Cowley, 'that England has been the first Power to recognize me.'

He was indeed delighted. His life-long ambition—the restoration of the Great Napoleon's Empire—having been realized, this new Napoleon was determined to avoid the rock on which

11

the First Empire had foundered: Napoleon I's rivalry with England. This was one feature of his illustrious ancestor's reign which he planned not to emulate.

For Napoleon III, such a friendship would be perfectly natural. He was very fond of England. London had been his home during several long periods of exile and he had always felt thoroughly at ease in English society. He appreciated the orderliness, the steadfastness and the freedom of the British way of life. Even his long-standing mistress, the recently pensioned-off Miss Howard, had been English. As Prince President, he had made a point of expressing his admiration for British institutions; ambassadors, and British statesmen visiting Paris, were forever reporting yet another of Louis Napoleon's comments on the excellence of all things English. At the first ball of the Second Empire, the Emperor chose Lady Cowley as his partner in the opening *quadrille d'honneur*.

That such praise of England should reach the ear of Queen Victoria was both inevitable and intentional. For Napoleon III had decided that in order to establish an *entente* with England, he must court England's Queen. He was always a great believer in the conducting of affairs on a personal rather than an official level. Victoria's prompt acceptance of him as her 'good Brother' had encouraged him; he now launched into his scheme for allying himself to her more closely still. He chose the classic approach to a royal alliance: a royal marriage.

For the forty-four-year-old Emperor, the finding of a suitable bride was not going to be a simple matter. Few princesses of the first rank would be eager to link themselves to this parvenu monarch. He was therefore obliged to cast about among Europe's lesser royalties for an Empress. When negotiations for the hand of a Swedish princess had collapsed, his choice fell on Princess Adelaide of Hohenlohe-Langenburg. The seventeen-year-old Princess might not be the member of a reigning House but she had one decided advantage: she was Queen Victoria's niece. Her mother was the Queen's half-sister—daughter of Queen Victoria's mother's first marriage. As such, Princess Adelaide would be a catch indeed.

Napoleon III approached the project with customary circumspection. He could not afford a public rebuff from Queen

Victoria. Count Walewski was directed to sound out Lord Malmesbury on the matter. The Emperor, said Walewski to Malmesbury, was eager to form a union which would 'tighten the bonds of friendship between England and France'; would the Queen therefore object to the tightening of them by a marriage between Napoleon III and Princess Adelaide? Lord Malmesbury dutifully passed the inquiry on to the Queen.

Victoria was thrown into a quandary. If she were to refuse, she told her Prime Minister, she would be accused of being influenced by 'personal feelings of animosity against the Emperor, or by mistaken friendship for the Orleans family, or misplaced family pride, etc., etc.'; if she accepted, it would seem as though she were turning her back on her Continental allies to bolster Napoleon III's regime. It would have been better, she said a trifle sharply, if she had not been approached directly on the matter.

Her instincts were to refuse the offer. Official acceptance of Louis Napoleon had not meant personal approval and it certainly did not entail his inclusion in her family circle. He was far too exotic a bird for the Coburg aviary. The Queen might not have been fully informed on the Emperor's libertinism but she certainly knew something of it. Princess Adelaide happened to be staying with her at Windsor at the time and the physical presence of this unspoilt creature ('so pretty, so young, distinguished and ladylike') must have rendered the idea of the proposed match with the licentious Emperor more distasteful still.

And then there was the question of Napoleon III's future. How long was he likely to last? As the Queen remarked to Lord Malmesbury, the fate of royal consorts in France since 1789 was hardly such as to inspire confidence in the match.

On the other hand, Victoria did not reject the idea of the marriage completely. It would certainly be a splendid position for Princess Adelaide; in fact, the girl was likely to be so 'dazzled' by the prospect that the Queen decided against telling her anything about it for the moment. She and Prince Albert discussed it at considerable length with Lord Malmesbury; they 'talked of the marriage reasonably', noted the Foreign Secretary, 'and weighed the *pros* and *cons*'.

13

The problem was temporarily side-stepped by Victoria suggesting, in an unofficial capacity (through Lord Malmesbury back to Count Walewski) that the matter be decided by the Princess and her parents but that, as they were Protestants, she did not think their acceptance very likely.

This was meant as a face-saving rebuff for the Emperor, but the unsubtle Walewski refused to see it as such. He was determined to go to Langenburg to beard the Princess's parents. The announcement of his imminent arrival flung the Hohenlohes into a state of panic. Letters flew between Langenburg, Windsor and Brussels (Uncle Leopold, always on the lookout for yet another crown to add to the Coburg collection, considered this one too uncertain) with no one wanting to be responsible for the final refusal. 'Oh! if we could but say "No" at once . . .' wailed the girl's mother.

The matter was settled by the Emperor himself. When Walewski arrived in Paris *en route* to Langenburg, he was astounded to hear that his master was paying court to someone else. When Walewski urged the Emperor to wait for an official answer from Princess Adelaide's parents, Napoleon reluctantly agreed to do so. Fortunately, the answer was already on its way. Equally fortunately, it was a refusal.

It must have been towards the end of the Hohenlohe marriage negotiations that Queen Victoria first heard of the Emperor's infatuation with a certain Mademoiselle de Montijo. Lord Cowley was certainly very full of it. In letter after letter to London, he made much of Napoleon III's obsession with the beautiful, red-haired Spanish countess. According to the cynical Cowley, Eugenie de Montijo was simply a flashy *femme du monde*, bent on trapping the Emperor into marriage. In this she was being actively encouraged by her mother—an ambitious busybody, well known in international society.

By the middle of January 1853, with the Second Empire barely six weeks old, Cowley was able to report the success of the united efforts of the Montijo ladies. 'The great one has been captured by an adventuress,' ran the lip-smacking phrases. 'To hear the way in which men and women talk of their future Empress is astounding. Things have been repeated to me, which the Emperor has said of her, and others which have been said

14

to him, which it would be impossible to commit to paper. In fact she has played her game with him so well, that he can get her in no other way but marriage, and it is to gratify his passions that he marries her. . . .'

Victoria could have no complaints now about the dreariness of her Ambassador's reports.

It was from highly coloured accounts such as these that Queen Victoria was obliged to form her opinion of the future Empress Eugenie. She learned that Eugenie's father had been the Count de Montijo, a grandee of Spain, and her mother—less illustriously—the daughter of a wine merchant in Malaga, by name Kirkpatrick. Eugenie's youth (she was now twenty-six) had been spent, it appeared, in flitting from one country to another in the company of her worldly mother; with her eldest daughter successfully married off to the Duke of Alba, the Countess de Montijo had been determined on an even more illustrious marriage for the flamboyant Eugenie. It was no wonder that Queen Victoria saw the future Empress as a showy *intrigante* ('beautiful, clever, very coquette, passionate and wild' was Victoria's description); a fitting match for the somewhat spurious Emperor.

The Queen might even have heard the rumour that Eugenie had been fathered by none other than the latest British Foreign Secretary, the urbane Lord Clarendon. Clarendon, as English Minister in Madrid during the 1830s, was said to have been the Countess de Montijo's lover. Indeed, it was known that Napoleon III had recently tackled the Countess on the subject. 'Sire, it cannot be true,' was the Countess de Montijo's indignant denial, 'the dates do not correspond.'

Less than a month after the collapse of the plans for an approach to Princess Adelaide, Napoleon III married Eugenie de Montijo in the garishly decorated Cathedral of Notre Dame. The lyrical letter which Lady Augusta Bruce wrote from Paris to Victoria's mother, the Duchess of Kent, describing the wedding, was no doubt eagerly read by the Queen herself. That the Emperor was passionately in love with his new Empress, Lady Augusta had no doubt; his normally inscrutable expression was positively radiant. For the Empress herself, Lady Augusta had nothing but praise.

'Her beautifully chisled features and marble complexion, her nobly *set-on* head, her exquisitely proportioned figure and graceful carriage were most striking, and the whole was like a Poet's Vision! I believe she is equally beautiful when seen close, but at a distance at which we saw her the effect was something more than that of a lovely picture, it was aerial, ideal. . . .'

In the course of this rapturous description Lady Augusta also made mention of the Empress's engaging manners and extreme nervousness. She was obviously not quite the brazen adventuress of Queen Victoria's first imaginings. In a letter to her Uncle Leopold, written a few days after the wedding, the Queen admitted that 'the description of the young Empress's character is an interesting one and also agrees with what I had heard from those who know her well. It may be in her power to do much good—and I hope she may. Her character is made to captivate a man, I should say—particularly one like the Emperor.'

Whatever the advantages of Napoleon's marriage to Eugenie, it did not bring him any closer to his longed-for alliance with Great Britain. Indeed, now that he had married a parvenue, acceptable to neither European royalty nor the French *haute monde*, it was more than ever advisable that he associate himself with England's unquestionably royal and highly respectable sovereign. In the autumn of 1853 reports were put about in France that the Queen was about to invite the Emperor to Windsor. One of Napoleon's ministers consulted with Lord Cowley on the subject; the puzzled Lord Cowley wrote off to Lord Clarendon, the new Foreign Secretary; Clarendon appealed to the Queen.

Victoria's answer left no room for doubt.

'The Queen hastens to answer Lord Clarendon's letter,' she wrote, 'and wishes him to inform Lord Cowley that there never was the slightest idea of *inviting* the Emperor of the French and that Lord Cowley should take care that it should be clearly understood that there was and would be no intention of the kind, so that there should be no doubt on the subject. The Queen feels sure that the Emperor has had these reports put in himself.'

Those 'bonds of friendship between England and France' remained as slack as ever.

4

And then gradually, during the next few months, the bonds began to tighten. What Napoleon III had been unable to achieve by diplomacy came about through the threat of war. Britain and France were drawn into a military alliance to defend Turkey against Russia. An Anglo-French convention was signed, and by March 1854 their combined armies were on their way to wage war against Russia in the Crimea. Less than forty years after Waterloo, a British sovereign and a Napoleonic emperor were fighting together as allies. To the French Emperor this was all highly gratifying, but to Queen Victoria it was scarcely credible. What, she wondered, would her grand-father, King George III, have said; he who used to stamp about the terrace of Windsor Castle demanding of the Eton boys, 'I hope you hate the French'? As it was, one of the Queen's older generals had the regrettable habit of always referring to the enemy in the Crimea as 'the French'.

The sovereigns of the two countries might be political allies, but Queen Victoria still saw no reason why they should be anything more. She simply could not bring herself to trust Napoleon III. When the easy-going Lord Clarendon advised the Queen's cousin, the Duke of Cambridge, *en route* to the Crimea, to accept an invitation to stay as Napoleon's guest at the Tuileries, Victoria was furious. She would have thought, she protested, that her allowing the Duke of Cambridge to go to Paris at all would have been enough; now here was Lord Clarendon urging the Duke to accept Napoleon's invitation, 'because the *Emperor wished it*'.

'The Queen must and *will* protest, for she cannot mix up personal friendship with a political Alliance,' she fumed. 'The former is the *result* of the *experience* of years of mutual friend-ship, and cannot be *carried by storm.* . . .'

The Duke of Cambridge stayed, therefore, at the British Embassy and not at the Tuileries.

The truth was that both she and Prince Albert, as upholders

of the system of constitutional monarchy, were hesitant about identifying themselves, for the sake of expediency, with a despot such as Napoleon III. Other than their joint enmity towards Russia, Napoleon III's France and Victoria's England had very little in common. Once the war in the Crimea was over, the royal couple might find themselves seriously compromised by their friendship with Napoleon III's Catholic, illiberal and unstable regime.

But as muddle succeeded muddle in the Crimea, it was thought that some sort of show of solidarity between the Allies might not be out of place. Napoleon invited Prince Albert to visit him at the military camp at Boulogne for a few days in early September 1854. Albert accepted.

The visit was a great success. The Emperor exercised his considerable charm to such an extent that even the normally impervious Albert succumbed. Far from being a tyrant, Napoleon III revealed himself to Albert as a man of almost gentle disposition—calm, indolent, humorous. He looked neither as old nor as pale as in his portraits (the obliging Winterhalter had endowed him with the required air of majesty) and he was much gayer than was generally supposed. Albert's brother, Duke Ernest of Saxe-Coburg, described the Emperor as 'a German savant rather than a Sovereign of France', and both brothers were delighted at the ease with which the Emperor spoke German and the readiness with which he recited Schiller. Prince Albert might deplore Napoleon's lack of musical appreciation, his incessant cigarette-smoking and the general *ton de garnison* of the imperial entourage, but he welcomed the frankness with which his host discussed any topic and the attention with which he listened to Albert's wordy advice. Napoleon was astounded to hear that the Queen read every foreign report; Albert was equally astounded to hear that the Emperor did not. Ever conspiratorial, Napoleon III relied on private agents reporting on his diplomats rather than on the diplomats themselves. Albert, in his patronizing but incisive way, judged the Emperor to be a rather amateur politician; a mixer-together of 'very sound and many crude notions'. His visit could not fail to be a 'source of great satisfaction' to Napoleon, decided Prince Albert.

While Prince Albert returned home to write a ponderous memorandum on the visit, Napoleon employed his time in a more advantageous fashion. He bombarded the Queen with praise of her husband. To Victoria such flattery, whether from the Emperor direct or via Walewski and Clarendon, sounded sweet indeed. The Emperor, reported Clarendon smoothly, 'had spoken with enthusiasm of the Prince, saying that in all his experience he had never met with a person possessing such various and profound knowledge, or who communicated it with the same frankness. His Majesty added that he had never learned so much in so short a time, and was grateful.'

To the gratified Queen, none of this sounded excessive.

Having heaped on the flattery, the Emperor got down to business. He was determined to be received by the Queen of England. During the visit to Boulogne Prince Albert had said something about the possibility of the Emperor and Empress visiting Windsor; Lord Clarendon, on Walewski's behalf, now pressed for a more definite invitation. The Emperor would be 'delighted to avail himself of the Queen's gracious kindness; nothing would give him so much pleasure. . . .'

Victoria, refusing to be tied down, wrote back saying that the Emperor could come if he liked. The middle of November would suit her best. But Napoleon could not agree that November would be a good time. A 'better time would be later, so as to show the friendship had suffered no diminution'.

Victoria reacted sharply. 'The Emperor Napoleon's answer to Lord Cowley with reference to this visit to England . . . is almost a refusal now, and has not improved our position. The Queen would wish that no anxiety should be shown to obtain the visit, and that it is quite clear to the Emperor that he will be *le bienvenu* at any time. His reception here ought to be a boon to him and not a boon to us.'

The stalemate was broken, with dramatic suddenness, early the following year. Napoleon III announced his intention of going to the Crimea to take personal command of his armies. With the campaign having been bogged down for months, the Emperor was anxious to make a *grande geste*; to strike a spectacularly Napoleonic blow for his Empire. The news appalled the British government. The Queen was particularly upset.

What if the French troops, led by their Emperor, were to win a glorious victory and so steal the British thunder? 'This,' she exclaimed, 'we *never* could bear.'

With such reasoning Lord Palmerston—whom the political whirligig had now brought to the position of Prime Minister— was in complete accord. Lord Clarendon was dispatched hot-foot to France to try to dissuade the Emperor from his rash decision. Finding Napoleon ready to listen to reason but unable to convince him himself, Clarendon thought that a State Visit by Napoleon to England might do the trick. Where British diplomacy had failed, British royalty might well succeed.

This suited the Emperor very well. He let Lord Cowley know that a visit to Windsor soon after Easter would be convenient. The British government leapt at the opportunity. A State Visit was arranged to take place from 16 to 21 April 1855.

Even now the Queen could not entirely reconcile herself to the coming visit. A few days before the imperial couple were due to arrive, Victoria received Queen Marie Amélie, widow of King Louis Philippe (the King had died, in exile at Claremont, a few years before) and Victoria found herself deeply disturbed by the ex-Queen's visit. It made her, she said, 'so sad to see her drive away in a plain coach with four miserable post-horses, and to think that this was the Queen of the French, who, six years ago, was surrounded by the pomp and grandeur which now belong to others; that in three more days the Emperor of the French would be received with all possible respect, pomp, and éclat, and that this same reception attended her late husband here. Now *all* is swept away; another dynasty reigns in that fickle country! The contrast was painful in the extreme. . . .'

A little after noon on Monday 16 April, the *Pélican*, carrying the Emperor and Empress of the French, emerged through a thick fog to draw up alongside the landing-stage at Dover. To the thunder of guns and the cheering of a dense crowd, the imperial couple stepped ashore. The Emperor was wearing the blue tunic and red trousers of a French general; the Empress a plaid dress under a pale grey coat. Prince Albert, in uniform, stepped forward to greet them.

The Queen was waiting at Windsor.

CHAPTER TWO

Spring at Windsor

1

Queen Victoria had been in a nervous state for days. 'These great meetings of Sovereigns, surrounded by very exciting accompaniments, are always very agitating,' she wrote on the day of the Emperor's arrival. The Queen, for all the apparent assurance of her manner, was naturally shy; she always dreaded meeting strangers. It was true that by now she realized that Napoleon III was not the ogre of her earlier imaginings: Prince Albert's meeting with him had finally dispelled any such notion. Nor had the Empress Eugenie proved to be the *femme fatale* of Lord Cowley's first reports. In fact, she had a reputation for chastity; Victoria had been gratified to hear that Eugenie admired the high moral tone of the English Court. None the less, the visit of this somewhat unconventional couple was bound to bring some strain.

Preparations had been in hand for weeks at Windsor. On the day before the arrival, Victoria, Albert and seven of their children walked to the stables to inspect the Emperor's fourteen magnificent horses, shipped over from France, and to chat to the various grooms. The Queen was pleased to discover that one of the grooms—the head groom—was an Englishman and another a German. The first had been with the Emperor during his years of exile in England; the second had accompanied him on his two unsuccessful assaults on Strasbourg and Boulogne.

Returning to the castle, the royal party toured the newly decorated suite of rooms, all delighting in the crimson, green and purple hangings and upholsteries; the *pièce de résistance* seems to have been the imperial bed with its violet satin curtains, its green bedhead embroidered with a golden eagle and its feather-crowned canopy. Already the imperial apartments were filling up with luggage and swarming with servants.

On Monday, while Albert went down to Dover to meet the guests, the Queen battled to organize her clothes ('such trouble with my toilettes, dresses, bonnets, caps, mantillas etc., etc., of every sort and kind') and then took the excited children on a drive through Windsor's lavishly decorated streets. The five-year-old Prince Arthur could hardly contain himself; he had questions about everything. At five o'clock the Queen went to change into a pale blue dress with 'shaded trimmings' and an hour later she entered the Grand Hall, where the entire Court and the officers of State and the Household stood assembled. All were in the stiff splendour of levee dress. Lining the walls of the Hall and forming a guard of honour on the Grand Staircase were the scarlet-uniformed Yeomen of the Guard.

Surrounded by various members of her family—the fifteen-year-old Princess Royal, the fourteen-year-old Prince of Wales, her cousin the Duke of Cambridge and her half-brother, Prince Charles of Leiningen—the Queen took up her position.

The guests were to have arrived at the castle soon after six o'clock, but their triumphant progress through London had slowed them down. Not until a quarter to seven did the Queen hear that they had left Paddington Station. This period of waiting seemed '*very* long', she said. It was almost dark before the distant thudding of a gun announced that the train had been sighted. A few minutes more and what had at first been a barely distinguishable sound of approaching horses grew louder and louder until the Quadrangle outside rang with noise. A line of carriages, escorted by a detachment of Life Guards, was swinging towards the Grand Entrance. There was a sudden blare of trumpets and the band drawn up in the Quadrangle burst into the anthem of the Second Empire—*Partant pour la Syrie*. A second or two before the carriages drew up at the entrance, the Queen, followed by her family, emerged from the main door and advanced to meet her guests.

'I cannot say what indescribable emotions filled me, how much it felt like a wonderful dream!' wrote Victoria of this moment of meeting the Emperor and Empress of the French. Napoleon kissed her hand and she kissed him on both cheeks.

He was 'extremely short' she noticed, 'but with a head and bust which ought to belong to a much taller man'. She then embraced 'the very gentle, graceful, and evidently very nervous Empress'. She presented her two eldest children—Vicky and Bertie—and her cousin and half-brother. With Eugenie on the arm of Albert and Victoria on the arm of Napoleon, they mounted the Grand Staircase between the rows of motionless Yeomen and made their way to the Throne Room.

Here were collected five of Victoria's other children (Prince Leopold was still a baby), to whom the Emperor and Empress were presented and to whom they were, says Victoria, very kind. Then on to the Reception Room, where Victoria presented her ladies to the Empress, Albert his gentlemen to the Emperor and, to complete the pattern of introductions, the imperial guests presented their suite to the English Court. Victoria and Albert led their guests to their rooms and hurried back to their own to change for dinner.

'Everything,' wrote Victoria with satisfaction and relief, 'had gone off beautifully.'

Her sense of gratification was not shared in the imperial apartments. The Empress was near despair. While she was frantically changing out of her travelling-clothes in order to be dressed in time for dinner, it was discovered that her trunks had not yet arrived. They had been held up somewhere between Dover and Windsor. Most of her jewellery and all her sumptuous dresses were lying neatly packed, fifty miles away, with no possible chance of retrieving them before the following day. For Eugenie, renowned for her *chic*, this was a disaster. And, to top it all, her hairdresser, Félix, had likewise been mislaid in the general confusion of the arrival.

When, still in her *peignoir* and on the verge of tears, Eugenie explained her predicament to Napoleon, he suggested that she plead fatigue and excuse herself from dinner.

But after a few minutes Eugenie's naturally buoyant nature re-asserted itself. She was, after all, very much a woman of the world, accustomed to the vicissitudes of travel. While her maids of honour were still bemoaning the misfortune, she made up her mind about what was to be done. She borrowed a simple grey dress trimmed with pink ribbon from one of her ladies and had it hastily altered to fit her slender figure. Then, with the help of her women, she dressed her lustrous red-gold hair almost as professionally as the distraught Félix (at the moment reaching Windsor) would have done. Finally, not quite satisfied with the effect, she snatched a handful of huge pink chrysanthemums from the vase of her dressing-table and arranged them in a wreath about her head.

By the time one of her gentlemen arrived to tell her the reason for Félix's absence, she was smiling again. 'I hope he will not kill himself with despair,' she laughed. 'My ladies have almost replaced him.'

Thus simply dressed, the Empress joined the Emperor in the Rubens Room to wait for the Queen. When Victoria and Albert arrived to fetch them for dinner, the Queen was charmed. Such simplicity, such lack of ostentation endeared Eugenie to Victoria immediately. Beside the elegant Empress, the dumpy Queen in her lavishly trimmed yellow dress and flashing jewels must have made a poor second, but there was no hint of jealousy in Victoria's description of her guest. 'The profile and the line of the throat and shoulders are very beautiful,' she enthused, 'the expression charming and gentle, quite delightful. The pictures of Winterhalter are very like her. The hair light brown, the face very pale, the mouth and teeth lovely.'

Two of the Empress's ladies, noted the Queen innocently, could not appear at dinner as their things had not yet arrived.

If Victoria was charmed with the Empress at first sight, she found herself being fascinated by the Emperor at first hearing. With those hooded eyes, that hooked nose, those cat's-whisker mustachios and that top-heavy body, he might not be considered conventionally handsome, but his manner was certainly very engaging. On first meeting her, he had spoken, in his relaxed fashion, of his pleasure at seeing her and of his admiration for Windsor Castle. Now, at dinner, his conversation had an even more soothing effect. 'We got on extremely well at dinner,' she wrote, 'and my great agitation seemed to go off very early; the Emperor is so very quiet: his voice is low and soft, and *il ne fait pas de phrases*'. There was, admitted the Queen in a letter to her Uncle Leopold the following day, 'great fascination in the quiet, frank manner of the Emperor....'

Napoleon III, not for the first time in his life, was beginning to win a heart.

2

Throughout her long life, there was one type of man to whom Queen Victoria was irresistibly drawn. Such men were always exotics: they were unconventional, mysterious, colourful, rakish and sensual. More often than not there was something of the dashing, devil-may-care air of the Regency about them; to the prosaic, materialistic world of Victoria's own age, they brought something of the romantic atmosphere of an earlier period. They aroused in the plump, plain, sensible Queen an undercurrent of excitement. When she was with them she could not help feeling that she was playing—in the most innocent way imaginable—with fire.

At the age of sixteen, the young Victoria's imagination had been stirred by occasional glimpses of just such a man. He was her second cousin, the notorious Duke Charles of Brunswick. Although she was not allowed to exchange one word with him, there is no doubt that she found this dark, handsome, sensuous-looking gallant wildly attractive.

A year or two later she fell under the spell of an older, but no less seductive, figure: the worldly, witty Lord Melbourne, her first Prime Minister. Everything about him enchanted her: his *insouciant* manner, his amusing conversation, his adventurous past, even his blue-grey eyes and wind-ruffled hair. Another Prime Minister, Benjamin Disraeli, was to prove even more fascinating. Something *outré*, almost Oriental, about this smooth-tongued charmer was to play havoc with the Queen's emotions.

Less bizarre, but no less romantic, were the clutch of Battenberg princes who appeared on the scene in the 1880s. With their dark good looks and swashbuckling behaviour, they would be very much to Victoria's taste; 'Court Battenbergism' they would call the Queen's ardent championship of these flamboyant princes. And in her old age it would be to her exotic Indian servant, Abdul Karim, known as the Munshi, that

25

Queen Victoria would be drawn and whom she was to defend in the face of the outspoken disapproval of her family and Household.

All this is not to say that Prince Albert, who did not belong to the category, could not satisfy her emotionally (or, for that matter, physically); nor that the honest-to-goodness John Brown did not meet her particular needs. It was simply that these two dependable personalities could not set her imagination aflame to the same extent as the others.

In many ways, the Emperor Napoleon III epitomized the type to which she was always attracted. He looked like a buccaneer. His past had been both glamorous and scandalous. His manner was attentive and intimate. His glance was impenetrable. There was an indefinable aura of mystery about him. He was, in addition, a highly accomplished seducer. It was no wonder that Queen Victoria found him so captivating.

'She was charmed with the Emperor,' the suave Lord Clarendon said afterwards to the diarist Charles Greville, 'who made love to her, which he did with a tact which proved quite successful. He began this when he was in England, and the Queen was mightily tickled by it, for she had never been made love to in her life, and never had conversed with a man of the world on a footing of equality; and as his love-making was of a character to flatter her vanity without alarming her virtue or modesty, she enjoyed the novelty of it without scruple or fear. . . .'

Lord Clarendon's assessment is a shade too superficial. This was not the first time that the Queen had been made love to (Prince Albert had proved himself quite capable of that) nor did Napoleon III make love to her in even the generally accepted nineteenth-century sense of the phrase. But he certainly set out to fascinate, flatter and, indeed, flirt with her. He had done a great deal of groundwork before the visit and was by now completely *au fait* with her past, her preferences and her personality. To Victoria, accustomed to Albert's frank and artless manner, Napoleon's interest and attentions were flattering in the extreme. It was 'very extraordinary and unaccountable,' she afterwards said to Lord Clarendon with charming naïveté, how the Emperor seemed to know everything about her since she had been twelve years old: what she had done, where she had been, even what she had worn.

Queen Victoria, on the other hand, was no fool. Had the Emperor been nothing more than a charlatan, she would have been very quick to discover it. The fact that he set out, consciously, to impress and captivate her did not mean that he was not impressive nor captivating. He was both these things, and many more; if his advances to the Queen were carefully calculated, they were not forced. Disraeli, many years later, was to use the same tactics.

Once she had come to appreciate Napoleon's real worth, the Queen allowed herself to meet him more than half-way. She was ripe for a mild, almost unconscious flirtation such as he was offering her. Although she was devoted to Albert, she had been married to him for some fifteen years and the high-spirited, pleasure-loving Hanoverian princess had not been completely submerged by his serious and scholarly nature. Women interested Albert very little; he was fond of Victoria but he tended to take her for granted. And by this time he was far too preoccupied to waste his days with the honeyed phrases of love-making. For the thirty-five-year-old Victoria, with her less disciplined temperament, a periodic flash of emotional colour was a necessity. Thus when Napoleon, with his dreamy eyes and dangerous reputation, began his subtle advances, she abandoned herself to his flattering attentions.

This skilful courtship was conducted along the most innocuous lines; it never went beyond the exchange of confidences. But then Victoria had seldom exchanged confidences with a man like Napoleon III: everything he spoke about seemed tinged with romance or adventure. He told her how deeply impressed he had been at the sight of her, *une jeune personne*, opening Parliament for the first time, eighteen years before. Had she known, he wondered, that he had acted as a special constable in London during the Chartist riots of 1848? He spoke of the occasion on which he had spent forty pounds for a box simply to see her pay a State Visit to the theatre. He told her of how he had once been locked up in a London park for two hours because he had forgotten the time.

Victoria listened and was enthralled. She found these glimpses of his relatively humble past particularly intriguing. It seemed to her almost incredible that only six years ago this powerful sovereign had been living in exile in England, poor and almost unknown. He now behaved, she thought, as though he had been an Emperor for most of his life.

The Emperor, she noted on the fifth day of the visit, 'is *very* fascinating; he is so quiet and gentle, and has such a soft pleasant voice. He is besides so simple and plain-spoken in all he says, and so devoid of all phrases, and has a good deal of poetry, romance, and *Schwärmerei* in his composition, which makes him peculiarly attractive. He is a most extraordinary, mysterious man, whom one feels excessively interested in watching and knowing. . . . All he says is the result of deep reflection; and he sees in trifles and ordinary occurrences meanings and forebodings which no one else would find out.'

Napoleon's gentlemanly flirtation was by no means confined to the murmuring of pleasantries and mysteries into Victoria's ear; it also took the form of pleasing those near and dear to her. He was forever kissing and patting and chatting to her numerous children, and Victoria was particularly touched by the way her own favourite, Prince Arthur, was always singled out for attention. He was so unhappy, Napoleon smilingly told her one day, because the Empress had lost her heart to Prince Arthur. On another occasion he delighted the mother by presenting the children with a tableful of presents which he had brought over for them.

In his dealings with Albert, too, the Emperor's manner could not be faulted. He seemed to become less French and more German, less polished and more philosophical, when he was with Victoria's husband. He trudged dutifully around Albert's model farm at Windsor and was quite likely, in some quiet moment of the day, to break into German *Studentenlieder*, which he professed to admire so greatly. He had been educated, he took care to remind his host, in Bavaria.

'The Emperor is as *unlike a Frenchman* as possible,' claimed Victoria, 'being much more *German* than French in character.'

However, Albert was not so easily won over. The earnest, liberal-minded Prince could never quite shake off his distrust of this jumped-up despot. In that wordy memorandum, drawn up after his first meeting with Napoleon at Boulogne, Albert had made clear his deep suspicion of the Emperor's dictatorial methods. 'Having deprived the people of every active participation in the Government, and having reduced them to mere passive spectators, he is bound to keep up the "spectacle", and as at fireworks, whenever a pause takes place between the different displays, the public immediately grows impatient.' The harm which Napoleon's constant searching for spectacles to divert his people would do to the peace of Europe, was something which Albert greatly feared.

The Emperor's visit to Windsor did, however, bring forth one of the Prince's rare flashes of humour. 'I shall have to have precautions taken in the Crypt of St George's Chapel,' quipped Albert on this visit to England by a Bonaparte, 'to see that George III does not turn in his grave!'

But on the surface, all was harmony. Napoleon, in his appreciation of those whom Victoria valued, even remembered Uncle Leopold. To Brussels, from where King Leopold was watching the proceedings with a particularly jaundiced eye, the Queen was able to report that the Emperor had spoken very highly of him. To Berlin, she wrote to her friend, Princess Augusta of Prussia, to say that the Emperor had referred to her as 'a most excellent person'.

For Windsor, for England, for the British way of life, Napoleon had nothing but praise. '*L'Angleterre, c'est admirable,*' he breathed on one occasion, and on another, 'What a difference in your country, where everything is lasting and solid.' He was even in raptures about the greenness of the English grass.

'In short,' noted the gratified Queen, 'everything that is English he admires so much.'

3

The Empress Eugenie's conquest had been almost as complete. The Queen was in ecstasies about her. But whereas Napoleon had set out, deliberately, to win over the Queen, Eugenie managed it almost unconsciously. Like Victoria herself, Eugenie was incapable of dissembling; there was no hint of deceit or guile in her nature. Her manner was utterly natural.

Nevertheless, Victoria's first—and enduring—impression of Eugenie was slightly inaccurate. To the Queen, the Empress was always a beautiful, lively, delicate, gentle and self-effacing creature. Beautiful and lively Eugenie certainly was, but not even her most dedicated apologist could describe her as delicate, gentle or self-effacing. Although the Empress was never the ambitious, reactionary, war-mongering virago that her critics were afterwards to make her out to be, she was a woman of strong opinions and assertive manners. Her vitality was exceptional.

But it is understandable that Eugenie should have created a somewhat different impression at Windsor in that spring of 1855. She was very young, still in her twenties, and had been an Empress for just over two years. Previous to that, she had had precious little contact with royalty, having been raised in a quite different *milieu*. She had not been accepted by the old French aristocracy—the *faubourg Saint-Germain*—let alone by the reigning Continental families, and was still looked upon as a showy, shallow *arriviste* with ideas above her station. It was no wonder that she should feel unsure of herself. Nor, with her high regard for legitimate monarchies, could she help standing in awe of so long-established and respected a monarch as the Queen of England. With so much depending on the success of this visit, the parvenue Empress would have been on her best behaviour. In addition, Eugenie's public manner, even at the zenith of her career, tended to be rather diffident; this would have been accentuated during her visit to this strange and self-confident Court.

This was why Victoria could say of the Empress that 'naturally, she felt the *gene* of her position, from not having been brought up to it', but that 'her manner is the most perfect thing I have ever seen—so gentle and graceful and kind . . . and so modest and retiring withal.'

Whenever there was time to spare during these crowded days, Victoria would settle down for a little *tête-à-tête* with the Empress. Although there was only seven years' difference in their ages, the contrast between them was pronounced. Eugenie would be wearing some simple dress, uncluttered by any ornament, with her copper-coloured hair drawn well back from her lovely face. This simplicity would set off to perfection the translucency of her skin and the blue-green of her heavy-lidded, down-slanting eyes. Although very sparing in her use of cosmetics, she always outlined her pale eyes in heavy black; this characteristic pencilling became known as 'the Empress's signature'. Beside her Victoria, with her florid complexion and her rabbity mouth, looked like nothing so much as a middle-aged, badly-dressed housewife. On the other hand, Eugenie could not compete with the dignity and authority of the Queen's bearing; she could not rival that assured sense of majesty.

The Empress, who was naturally talkative (her 'Spanish liveliness and vivacity', the Queen called it) soon felt more at ease with her hostess, and their talk ranged from new settings for old jewellery to the conduct of the Crimean War. The prime reason for the State Visit—to dissuade the Emperor from going to the Crimea—was very much on Victoria's mind and she lost no time in raising the subject with the Empress. Eugenie was all for his going. She was sure that he would give the Queen good reasons for his decision.

For one thing, explained Eugenie, it was necessary for the Emperor to repair the damage done to the imperial image by his wayward cousin, Prince Napoleon. Prince Napoleon, better known as Plon-Plon, was the son of the Great Napoleon's youngest brother Jerome, ex-King of Westphalia. In order to cover himself with glory, claimed Eugenie, Plon-Plon had gone out to the Crimea, from where he had promptly returned, having merely covered himself in ridicule. It was up to Napoleon III to try to cut a more heroic dynastic figure. On the other hand, as neither Plon-Plon nor his father were to be trusted, the Emperor dare not leave them behind in Paris while he went off to the Crimea. Plon-Plon, Napoleon was to tell the Queen on a later occasion, was clever and capable, but impulsive and totally lacking in direction.

Victoria and Eugenie spoke also about the Empress's native Spain, of the unhappy life of Spain's oversexed Queen, Isabel II, and of the constant danger to royalty from assassins. 'She is full of courage and spirit,' enthused the Queen, 'and yet so gentle; with such innocence and *enjouement*, that the *ensemble* is most

31

charming. With all this great liveliness, she has the prettiest and most modest manner.'

About Eugenie's looks the Queen was in raptures. Time after time, with a wealth of underlinings and capital letters, she would make enthusiastic note of Eugenie's dresses (the trunks, of course, had arrived by then) and of her beauty. During the day there were simple dresses of blue or grey silk; at night there were breath-taking creations of white tulle. The vastness of the skirts worn by the Empress and her ladies interested Victoria's somewhat unfashionable Court immensely. Lady Clarendon considered them 'quite remarkable, a complete return to the old fashion of hoops'. There was a ball one evening in the Waterloo Gallery ('Really to think that I, the grand-daughter of George III, should dance with the Emperor Napoleon, nephew of our great enemy, now my dearest and most intimate ally, in the Waterloo room too . . .' exclaimed the Queen) and Eugenie, dressed in a crinoline of white net, with pearls about her neck and in her hair, drew gasps of admiration.

'*N'est-elle pas délicieuse?*' whispered Victoria to someone as the Empress glided by.

The Duchess of Cambridge's verdict was a little less lyrical. 'She is no Empress and no Princess,' she said, 'but just a charming woman and *comme il faut.*'

Even Albert, usually so impervious to feminine charm, had nothing but praise for Eugenie. On one occasion, when the Empress appeared in a flounced dress of pale green silk with a small white bonnet set well back on her head, Albert was full of admiration. 'Altogether I am delighted to see how much he likes and admires her,' wrote Victoria, 'as it is so seldom that I see him do so with *any* woman.'

'Albert,' she noted in some surprise after the visit was over, 'got on famously with the Empress.'

4

The State Visit to England was divided into two parts: four days were to be spent at Windsor and three in London. The high spots of the stay at Windsor were a military review in

Windsor Great Park and the investing of the Emperor with the Order of the Garter.

Queen Victoria, who dearly loved her soldiers, considered the review 'a most brilliant, and beautiful, and exciting affair'. As the royal party set out, the Quadrangle of the castle was alive with sound and colour: gleaming carriages, jingling accoutrements, fluttering feathers, caparisoned horses, grooms in scarlet, *piqueurs* in green and gold, and everything bathed in superb spring sunshine. The Queen drove down the Long Walk in a phaeton with the Empress sitting beside her and the Princess Royal, the Prince of Wales and little Prince Arthur sitting opposite. In front, around, and behind her carriage jogged scores of splendidly uniformed men. The Emperor, riding a high-spirited chestnut horse, rode beside her, leaning down now and then to speak to her as they went along. 'He rides extremely well,' enthused the Queen, 'and looks well on horseback, as he sits high.' Only the size and enthusiasm of the crowd lining the Long Walk alarmed her: Napoleon was so exposed.

But no misadventure marred the afternoon's enjoyment. The Queen found it all so exciting: the blaring bands, the trundling guns, the dust, the shouts, the glitter. There was even Lord Cardigan on the horse that he had recently ridden during the Charge of the Light Brigade. Not least of the excitements was the fact that the Emperor managed to find several opportunities, between inspections, taking of salutes and watching of manœuvres, to come cantering over to the royal carriage for a word with the Queen.

After the National Anthem had been played and the colours dipped in salute, the carriage procession passed slowly along the ranks and then returned home in the chill spring dusk. 'The enthusiasm, the crowd of excited people and riders, were quite indescribable,' noted the Queen. 'I never remember any excitement like it. It was at moments almost alarming, and there were numbers of terrified ladies standing on the road, clasping one another for fear of being ridden over. . . .'

It was all, she claimed, a great triumph.

The Investiture the following day was no less successful. However, it was a much more solemn occasion. The Queen, wearing her sumptuous Garter robes with customary ease and dignity, entered the Throne Room with Prince Albert and the great officers of State. She took her seat at the head of a long polished table and watched the entry of the Knights Companion of the Order. When they were seated at the table, the Chancellor read out the statute ordaining that the Emperor be declared a Knight of the Order. Prince Albert and the Duke of Cambridge then went to fetch the Emperor.

As Napoleon, who, according to one witness, 'did not appear to advantage in his white silk tights and stockings', entered the Throne Room, the Queen and the Knights rose to receive him. She announced that he had been elected a Knight of the Most Noble Order, and the Garter King of Arms came forward with the Garter and knelt before her. Albert buckled the Garter on to the Emperor's leg and Napoleon then placed his foot on a cushion to allow the Queen to pull the Garter through the knot. 'The Queen,' commented Lord Clarendon cynically, 'fumbled *ostensibly*, as she always does, to show her unfamiliarity with the slightly indiscreet article of male attire.'

That accomplished, Victoria kissed the Emperor on both cheeks and, taking the blue ribbon, completed the Investiture. During this part of the ceremonial her fumblings were unintentional, for it was the Emperor who presented his right, instead of his left, shoulder. 'We were *all* nervous, including myself,' admitted the Queen.

As the Queen and the Emperor passed out of the room at the close of the ceremony, he was heard to remark to her, in his wry, half-smiling manner, 'At last, I am a gentleman.'

5

Queen Victoria's busy pen somehow found time, during this round of ceremonial, to make comment on the imperial entourage. When Louis Napoleon had assumed the imperial title in 1852, he had found the assembling of a Court appropriate to his new dignity no easy matter. The *faubourg Saint-Germain* had remained firmly aloof, and Napoleon had been obliged to draw his courtiers from the remnants of Napoleon I's parvenu aristocracy and the *nouveaux riches*. The resulting assembly was a mixture of once-famous names—Murat, Ney, Flahaut—and of almost limitless fortunes. The imperial Court thus tended to be, if not actually vulgar, just a little too dashing and a little too smart. Those handsome, flamboyantly mannered men and those vivacious, superbly dressed women were far too free and easy for more conservative tastes; they were certainly a very different breed from the fossilized, convention-ridden courtiers of St Petersburg, Vienna and Berlin. Even the less hide-bound Court of St James's found their behaviour somewhat startling at times. At Windsor the *demoiselles d'honneur* would leave their bedroom doors wide open while they dressed, shouting gay conversation from room to room. Even the Empress was seen to perch casually on the edge of a table on occasion. Prince Albert, while admitting that Napoleon's Court was 'strictly kept', complained that 'the gentlemen composing his entourage are not distinguished by birth, manner or education'.

But Victoria, bemused by Napoleon's charm and always a stage removed from the lax activities of his suite, had no criticism to make. The ladies were all quiet, ladylike and pleasing and the men charming, gentlemanlike and clever.

It was extremely gratifying for the Queen to discover that not all Napoleon's entourage shared their master's enthusiasm for the idea of his taking personal command of his armies in the Crimea. Marshal Vaillant (a 'charming, amusing, clever and honest old man') was very much against it. The Emperor's reputation could not risk a military defeat, nor would it be safe for him to absent himself from France for long. With this reasoning Colonel Fleury, the Emperor's aide-de-camp, agreed. 'The structure is still not secure enough,' was his frank comment on the Second Empire. Both men begged the Queen to do what she could to change the Emperor's mind.

But the Emperor was not to be dissuaded. During the course of several councils of war, convoked to discuss military strategy in the Crimea, Napoleon remained firm. He was all for breaking the Crimean stalemate by a 'vigorous diversion' led by himself. On all other aspects of the campaign, the French and English attending the councils were in accord.

The Queen was quite content to leave the conducting of these war councils to Prince Albert. Not only did she not attend them but she hesitated to interfere in any way. On one occasion, when the discussions were being held in the Emperor's apartments, they went on so long that Victoria was afraid that they would all be late for luncheon. She went to discuss the matter with the Empress, who, equally concerned, let Lord Cowley know how late it was. When the men still did not appear, Eugenie urged the Queen to go and call them herself.

'I dare not go in, but Your Majesty can; that is your concern,' said Eugenie.

In the light of the Empress Eugenie's future involvement in affairs of State, her reticence at this stage of her career is interesting.

The Queen knocked and entered the council chamber. She asked the company what they should do about luncheon. They assured her that they would come at once. But they did not and, after a further wait, the ladies lunched alone.

By the end of the State Visit an agreement had been drawn up. But whether or not the Emperor would go out to the Crimea was left unresolved. Not until after he had returned to France did Napoleon decide against going. A pistol, fired at him while he was out riding in the Champs Elysées, helped make up his mind: he could not risk either his life or a prolonged absence from his capital.

Victoria attended the final council of war at which formal agreement was reached between the Allies. Napoleon had previously assured the Queen that, without Albert, nothing would have been achieved. Seated on a sofa beside the Emperor, Victoria pronounced the meeting to be one of the most interesting things she had ever attended and one which she would not have missed for the world. An earlier memorandum, written by Prince Albert, formed the basis of the agreement. This had first been summarized, then worked on by Napoleon and finally drawn up by Prince Albert. The Emperor made his observations, noted the Queen, 'in that very calm, quiet way, which has such a wonderful effect on everyone'.

On Thursday, 19 April, the fourth day of the visit, the entire party left Windsor Castle for Buckingham Palace, where the last three days were to be spent.

'I cannot say *why*,' wrote the Queen, 'but their departure made me so melancholy. I was near crying. Passing through the rooms, the hall, and down the stairs, with all its state guards, and the fine old yeomen, the very melancholy tune which *Partant pour la Syrie* is, the feeling that all about which there had been so much excitement, trouble, anxiety, and expectation, was past, the doubtfulness of the future—all made me, I know not why, quite *wehmüthig*. . . .'

They drove into London, in a procession of nine carriages escorted by a detachment of Household Cavalry, through an immense and wildly cheering crowd.

CHAPTER THREE

'*Vive le Hemperor!*'

1

Queen Victoria's new-found passion for the Emperor of the French was not shared by quite all her subjects. There were a great many Englishmen who bitterly resented this fêting of Napoleon III. To them, he was still the bloody tyrant who had murdered democracy in France. Denied the Queen's opportunities for conversion, their dislike and distrust of Napoleon remained as strong as hers had once been. The London *Times*, edited by J. T. Delane, fulminated against him almost continuously. The historian Froude wrote about the 'sinister phenomenon' of the Emperor's visit and claimed that 'outside the privileged circles who wanted order preserved, and security to property, and safe enjoyment of idle luxury, Louis Napoleon had no friends amongst us'. He was, thought Froude, 'an ugly object in the eyes of those who believed in some sort of Providence'.

As for Thomas Carlyle, he could hardly contain his disgust for the hospitality being lavished on Napoleon by the Queen. The 'soi-disant august pair' he slightingly called the Emperor and Empress.

'Louis Napoleon has not been shot hitherto. That is the best that can be said,' wrote Carlyle. 'He gathers great crowds about him but his reception from the hip-hip-hurrahing classes is not warm at all. On Monday, just before they arrived, I came (in omnibus) down Piccadilly. Two thin and thinnest rows of abject looking human wretches I had ever seen or dreamt of— lame, crook-backed, dwarfish, dirty-shirted, with the air of pick-pockets and City jackals, not a *gent* hardly among them, much less any vestige of a gentleman—were drawn up in St James Street to Hyde Park Corner to receive the august pair.

I looked at them with a shuddering thankfulness that they were not drawn up to receive *me*.'

Carlyle's reference to the fact that the Emperor had not yet been shot at was more than just a jibe by a jaundiced opponent. The possibility of an attack by an assassin was by no means remote. During the nineteenth century, death by assassination was very much a royal risk. Already, by 1855, Queen Victoria's own life had been threatened on several occasions. Sometimes a maniac would fire a pistol into her carriage; at others her assailants managed to get closer than that. One man was arrested in Buckingham Palace itself; another—an eccentric officer—struck her across the forehead with a cane while she was out walking. If he could but get hold of her, declared an attacker after his arrest, he would tear her to pieces.

But whereas most of the Queen's would-be assassins were cranks, Napoleon's were far more likely to be political enemies. There had been some talk, at Windsor, of the various French refugees who had fled Paris after the *coup d'état* and were now living in London. They had never made any secret of their determination to kill the Emperor. Conspiracies one could deal with, Napoleon had told Victoria, but when a fanatic chose to attack and sacrifice his own life, there was little or nothing that one could do.

This was why, throughout the period that the imperial couple was in London, the Queen was in a state of constant anxiety. Whereas, at Windsor, much of the ceremonial had taken place safely indoors, in London the royal party was on almost continuous show. The streets of the capital were crowded to see the spectacular carriage processions pass by. Hardly had the Emperor and Empress arrived at Buckingham Palace on the morning of Thursday, 19 April, than they were obliged to set out, with an escort of Household Cavalry, for a State luncheon at the Guildhall. Amongst the crowds lining the route moved throngs of British detectives and especially imported French secret police. One nasty moment was experienced when Captain Fraser, the cavalryman riding closest to the carriage, saw a roughly dressed man run alongside the carriage and put his hand on the door. Several times the Captain ordered him off. The man ignored him. Increasingly worried, the Captain ran his sword through the man's hat and flung it into the crowd. Still the man kept pace with the carriage. Exasperated, the Captain kicked him violently in the small of his back. Undaunted, the man clung on. It was at this moment that one of the footmen leaned forward and, nodding towards the hanger-on, enlightened the harassed cavalryman. 'The head of the detectives, sir,' he explained in an agitated whisper.

For the rest all went well. 'Whilst we were at luncheon,' wrote the Queen in her Journal later that day, 'we heard that the Imperial Couple had reached the City in safety, a great relief. . . .'

From the Guildhall the Emperor and Empress drove to the French Embassy for a diplomatic levee, and that evening the entire royal party attended a command performance of *Fidelio* at Covent Garden. 'Never did I see such enormous crowds at night, all in the highest good humour,' wrote the Queen. 'We literally drove through a sea of human beings, cheering and pressing near the carriage. The streets were really beautifully illuminated. . . .' Napoleon pointed out to the ever-attentive Queen that the initials of the two royal couples, Napoleon and Eugenie, and Victoria and Albert—so frequently displayed along the processional route—spelt NEVA. As the enemy capital, St Petersburg, stood on the River Neva, the Emperor considered this to be highly significant. It was the sort of quasi-mystical observation on the part of Napoleon III which Victoria found so impressive.

Within the Opera House their reception was no less enthusiastic. The Empress, in her white tulle crinoline edged with white marabou feathers, looked magnificent; beside her the Queen, in a blue and gold dress, a diadem of diamonds and a necklace of huge Indian rubies, looked her usual opulently inelegant self. But it was noticed that whereas Victoria seated herself without taking her eyes off the applauding audience, the parvenue Eugenie looked round to make sure of her chair before sitting down.

The Queen spent the entire performance in happy conversation with the Emperor. Her appreciation of what was happening on stage seemed confined to the finale, when the curtain

40

rose to reveal the band of Her Majesty's Foot Guards blaring out the two national anthems. This had 'a very fine effect', thought the Queen.

On the following day (it was Napoleon III's forty-seventh birthday) they all drove out to Sydenham to see the Crystal Palace. As the public had been excluded from the building, they were able to stroll about undisturbed in the glass-tempered sunlight, gazing approvingly at the giant palms, the second-rate statuary and the high-flung fountains. Eugenie, looking exquisite in a lilac dress and a white bonnet, professed herself enchanted at a replica of the Alhambra; 'she is so fond of her own country', noted the Queen. However, the Empress soon tired of the seemingly endless drag through the halls and Prince Albert ordered a bath chair to be brought for her. She was delighted with the little vehicle; whereupon Albert, with unusual gallantry, arranged to buy it for her.

While Eugenie was charming Prince Albert, Napoleon was enthralling Queen Victoria. They sat beside each other at luncheon in the private apartments of the Crystal Palace, and never had her admiration of his many-faceted personality been higher. He was so *very* fascinating, she thought. By the end of the day, she reckoned that they had spent over ten hours in each other's company; not for one moment had she been anything less than enchanted.

By the time they had finished luncheon, the building had once again been opened to the public, and the royal party had to pass through a crowd of over thirty thousand cheering people. The Queen found it a considerable ordeal. Never having conquered her own fear of an attempted assassination, she was even more apprehensive for the Emperor's sake. 'I felt as I walked on the Emperor's arm, that I was possibly a protection for him. All thoughts of nervousness for myself were past. I thought only of him. . . .'

Her fears proved groundless. At no stage was the State Visit marred by either attempted assassinations nor hostile demonstrations. The weather remained superb ('which, it seems', noted the Queen, 'is generally the case with the Emperor . . . as well as with me') and the crowds enthusiastic. Even the normally acidulous Charles Greville had to admit that the

Emperor's reception had been tumultuous. 'Wherever and whenever they have appeared, they have been greeted by enormous multitudes and prodigious acclamation . . .', he wrote. 'I am glad the success of the visit has been so great.'

With this, the Queen was in full agreement. 'Everywhere a most enthusiastic reception, hearty in the extreme,' was her summing-up. She was always amused to hear the lusty cry, in cockney French, of *'Vive le Hemperor!'*

2

Friday evening was the last of the visit. Some four hundred guests had been invited to a concert at the Palace. The programme consisted mainly of operatic arias which the Queen pronounced good but which Napoleon, with the best will in the world, could not pretend to be enjoying. 'He does not care at all for music,' observed Victoria. Out of deference to his tastes, she had the programme kept short, with a break for presentations and supper between the two parts. Nevertheless the Emperor, with his left leg stuck well out to display his Order of the Garter, sat through it all uncomplainingly. They even managed, said the Queen, to discuss 'several important subjects' during the course of it. In fact, the two of them seem to have chatted with as much animation through this concert as they had through *Fidelio* the night before.

So *causant* was Napoleon's mood, wrote the Queen afterwards, that had the concert been longer, he would have been inclined 'to converse upon many *more* delicate subjects even. . . .'

During the supper break, the Emperor introduced the Queen to Baron Georges Haussmann, *Préfet de la Seine*, under whose direction Second Empire Paris was being refashioned. Haussmann expressed the hope that the Queen would soon visit the French capital. Napoleon, who had already pressed the Queen to come, was rather annoyed at his *Préfet's* presumption ('they are such fools in France' he sighed), but Victoria assured them that she would be delighted. It was not for her alone, she had previously explained tactfully to the autocratic Emperor, to decide such matters.

Throughout the concert, it was noticed that the fifteen-year-old Princess Royal could not take her eyes off the Empress. She 'simply devoured her', reported Countess von Bernstorff. By now the precocious and highly emotional Vicky had developed an almost embarrassing crush on the ravishing Eugenie; she raved about the Empress, said the Queen. Eugenie had given Vicky a little jewel-studded watch the day before, and the gift had sent the girl into ecstasies. Indeed, in the months ahead, during which time Vicky was to be courted by Prince Frederick Wilhelm of Prussia, she would declare herself unable to decide whether it was he or the Empress whom she loved best.

Vicky's schoolgirlish adoration is understandable. For one thing Eugenie, who had a decided weakness for pretty girls, warmed to such obvious devotion; for another, she epitomized an adolescent's dream of sophisticated beauty. The Empress was looking particularly lovely that evening. Her white net dress was trimmed with bunches of white lilac and there was more lilac, a-sparkle with diamonds, in her red-gold hair. 'She looked so simple and so elegant,' said the Queen. 'I wish I could make a sketch of her as she was.'

Victoria wore a blue dress, lavishly trimmed with lace, her large Indian rubies and two feathers in her hair.

They parted company well after midnight with Napoleon saying how grieved he was that this should be their last evening together and Eugenie looking so 'low and sad'.

Saturday morning found them all looking lower and sadder still. After breakfast, hosts and guests prepared to take leave of each other. The albums were brought out and in each was inscribed some sentimental verse or phrase. Towards eleven the Queen led her guests out of the gloom of the Palace into the sunshine of the Courtyard, where the carriages were waiting. Prince Albert and the Duke of Cambridge were to accompany the Emperor and Empress to Dover. For the last time Napoleon implored the Queen to come over to Paris that summer. She promised that she would make every effort to do so.

As the moment of leave-taking drew near, the royal children burst into tears. This set Eugenie off. She flung herself into the Queen's arms, begging her to come soon to Paris; only that possibility would make their imminent separation easier to bear. Napoleon and Victoria embraced each other twice. The Queen could hardly hold back her tears.

The band broke into *Partant pour la Syrie* (the Queen had heard it fourteen times on Thursday) and the procession moved off. The strains of the anthem, which Victoria always considered rather mournful, simply increased her feeling of desolation. Turning abruptly away from the departing carriages, she ran upstairs, her brood of sobbing children close on her heels. Reaching the salon which her guests had recently quitted, she hurried to the window for a last look at the swiftly disappearing procession. The Emperor and Empress, seeing her at the window, turned round, rose and waved a last farewell. For a long time Victoria stood at the window, watching and waving, until the carriages with their jogging, glittering escort of Household Cavalry could be seen no more.

3

'And thus this visit, this great event, has passed, as, alas! everything does in this world,' wrote the Queen. 'It is a dream— a brilliant, successful, and pleasant dream, the recollection of which is firmly fixed in my mind. On all it has left a pleasant, satisfactory impression. It went off so beautifully, not a hitch nor *contretemps*, fine weather, everything smiling; the nation enthusiastic, and happy in the firm and intimate alliance and union of two great countries. . . .'

A week later, in a conscientiously written memorandum, the Queen outlined the advantages of the Emperor's visit. Given Napoleon III's position and personality—an autocrat of strong personal feelings—a warm *domestic* reception, such as had been given him by Victoria and Albert, would make a lasting impression on his mind. 'As he is France in his sole person,' wrote the Queen, friendship with him was of the utmost importance. While he remained friendly with Victoria, France would remain friendly with Britain. He would also appreciate the fact that Victoria was the only European royalty who had thus far treated him as a fellow sovereign; therefore he would tend to discuss his problems with her, as an equal, rather than with his courtiers or servants. It was thus up to her, she maintained, 'to *keep* him in the right course, and to protect him against the extreme flightiness, changeableness, and to a certain extent want of honesty of his own servants and nation'. She must always keep open a *personal* channel for frank and honest communication between them. An alliance between Victoria and Napoleon would ensure the continued alliance between Britain and France.

For the Emperor personally, her enthusiasm knew no bounds.

'That he *is* a very *extraordinary* man, with great qualities there can be *no* doubt—I might almost say a mysterious man. He is evidently possessed of *indomitable courage, unflinching firmness of purpose, self-reliance, perseverance,* and *great secrecy*; to this should be added, a great reliance on what he calls his *Star,* and a belief in omens and incidents as connected with his future destiny, which is almost romantic—and at the same time he is endowed with wonderful *self-control,* great *calmness,* even *gentleness* and with a *power of fascination,* the effect of which upon all those who become more intimately acquainted with him is *most sensibly* felt.'

Napoleon had made his conquest.

CHAPTER FOUR

Summer at Saint Cloud

1

No sooner had Napoleon III arrived home than he began working towards a return visit by the Queen. It would be as well to take immediate advantage of the sympathetic atmosphere prevailing between Windsor and the Tuileries. There was to be an *Exposition Universelle* in Paris that summer; the Emperor invited the Queen and Prince Albert to attend it.

This time Victoria needed no cajoling. Lord Clarendon, remembering the 'undisguised repugnance' of the Queen to the idea of the Emperor's visit in April, was amused at the enthusiasm with which she now leapt at the chance of a journey to Paris. A date was set for a ten-day stay in mid-August.

Between them, and not without a certain sardonic amusement, Lords Clarendon and Cowley organized the Queen's part in the forthcoming State Visit. She and Prince Albert would be accompanied by a party of eight (it was finally stretched to thirteen) and of their numerous children, they would bring only the two eldest—Vicky and Bertie. 'H.M. thinks that a long train of bambinos would *prêter au ridicule* and lead to jokes about the *ménage anglais* as well as to ill-natured remarks about the Empress who has no children,' wrote Clarendon.

The Queen need have had no fears on the score of the Empress's infertility. Not many weeks had passed before the agitated French Ambassador dragged Clarendon out of a cabinet meeting to tell him that the Empress Eugenie was *enceinte*. Would Lord Clarendon go at once to Osborne to acquaint the Queen with this momentous news? Clarendon, to whom the idea of a pregnant sovereign was no novelty, assured the Frenchman that this would not be necessary. A letter to Her Majesty would do as well.

Victoria was delighted to hear it. She insisted, via Clarendon and Cowley, that the Empress take every precaution during the coming royal visit. She would be quite *miserable* if the Empress were to exert herself for their sakes.

Early in July the Emperor's suggested programme of entertainments was presented to the Queen for approval. Victoria was all enthusiasm. She had one reservation only. If, on the fifth day, she was expected to view the Exhibition, tour the Louvre *and* attend a ball at the Hôtel de Ville, she would be quite 'unfitted for any exertion the following day'. The day's arrangements were duly changed.

There remained other problems. One concerned the question of precedence. Prince Albert's rank was causing the French Court considerable concern; it was so vague. He had not yet been created Prince Consort; was he or was he not entitled to take precedence over princes of the blood—especially when that blood was the far from blue Bonaparte blood? Early in his reign, the Emperor had divided his clamorous family into two distinct sections. One was known as the *famille civile* and the other as the *famille impériale*. The former, which had no rights of succession, was made up of the various female, disinherited and doubtfully legitimate branches; the latter of the Emperor, the Empress, ex-King Jerome of Westphalia and his two children—Plon-Plon and Mathilde. Did Jerome and his children rank above Albert?

The Queen was all for the Emperor pleasing himself on this question; the Emperor was all for pleasing the Queen. But the vain and feckless old Jerome was not prepared to please anyone. He had no intention, he announced, of playing second fiddle to a Coburg princeling. Nor, as a brother of the Great Napoleon, could he see his way clear to assisting in this fêting of England's Queen. He therefore refused to attend any public ceremonies. He would plead illness and make for Le Havre. And this is what he did. Only on the last day of the Queen's stay was he induced to return to Paris to pay his respects in private. Even this grudging gesture had to be rendered worth his while by the long-suffering Emperor; 'the old wretch,' says the diarist Viel-Castel, 'does nothing without a money bribe. Like a cabman, he must be paid according to the distance.'

47

Then there was the question of the sort of piece which the Queen might wish to see during a proposed evening of theatrical entertainment. The choice threw Lord Cowley into something of a quandary. He ventured to suggest some light comedies, although 'they go, of course, a little near the wind'. Victoria's answer left him in no doubt. 'Respecting the performances, the Queen does not care whether they are laughable or not,' instructed Clarendon, 'but what she *does* care for, however, *very much*, is that they should be *quite proper* and free from équivoques, to which she could on no account take her children. . . .'

Yet when the abashed Lord Cowley admitted to his diffidence in raising such matters, Clarendon reassured him: 'all she cares about is to know *everything*'.

The imperial visit to England had been especially planned to last from a Monday to a Saturday so as to save the Emperor's Catholic Court from having to spend a Sunday in England. The Queen, however, would be spending not only one, but two Sundays in France. Would British sabbatarian feelings be outraged if she attended a concert on one of the Sundays? The Queen was sure that they would not. As far as devotions were concerned, the English Court would attend private services in their own apartments. On this question also, Victoria knew her own mind. Lord Cowley was to give the chaplain a hint on what Her Majesty most admired in a sermon. It was brevity.

On Saturday, 18 August 1855, with all arrangements finalized, the royal party set sail in the *Victoria and Albert* bound for Boulogne.

The Emperor Napoleon III, surrounded by his officers, was on the quayside to meet them. The scene, said the Queen, was brilliant, the sunshine broiling. As Victoria walked down the gangplank, Napoleon hurried up to greet her and, meeting halfway, the couple embraced twice. He then led her ashore 'amidst acclamations, salutes, and every sound of joy and respect'.

From then on it was all enchantment. Victoria allowed nothing to spoil her enjoyment. The heat in the train to Paris might be unbearable, the dust choking and the countryside uninteresting, but she was beside herself with excitement. At every halt there were addresses of welcome by perspiring *préfets*, bunches of flowers from curtseying schoolgirls, and shouts of '*Vive la Reine d'Angleterre!*' from superbly uniformed troops. Gradually the countryside became prettier, leafier and more populous until finally, as the sun was setting, the train steamed into Paris. On the lavishly decorated platform of the Gare de Strasbourg stood the Emperor's cousin, Plon-Plon, looking, as another royal visitor once said, 'like a worn-out *basso profundo* from some obscure Italian opera house'. The royal party took their places in a waiting carriage and the procession began its journey through Paris to the Palace of Saint Cloud, where the Queen would be staying.

Nothing, said Victoria of this moment when the cortège swung out of the station into the Boulevard de Strasbourg, could give any idea of the splendour of the scene that faced her.

Although it would be an exaggeration to say that Napoleon III had actually rebuilt Paris for the Queen's reception, his plans for the aggrandizing of his capital were well under way by the time she entered it in August 1855. No city in Europe looked more magnificent. The crowded medieval town was being transformed into an imperial metropolis—a matchless city of tree-lined boulevards, triumphal arches and grandiose squares. Nor were the Emperor's schemes solely aesthetic. During his visit to England Napoleon had told the Queen that this refashioning of his capital was meant to serve a more practical purpose as well: it would cut down the chances of a successful rising by the mob. Those spectacularly broad avenues would allow for a detachment of cavalry to sweep through them; those smoothly macadamized surfaces would prevent the tearing up of paving stones '*pour en faire des barricades*'; those immense exhibition buildings would house companies of troops.

But such disturbing considerations were far from Victoria's mind as she drove through Paris that summer evening. In honour of her arrival, the transformed city had been especially decorated as well, and the eager-eyed Queen passed through a forest of flags, banners, oriflammes, Venetian masts, mock-marble columns and plaster statues. There was even a life-sized portrait of herself wrought, for some obscure reason, in human hair. Figures bearing the proud names of Civilization, Industry,

Concord and Justice stood heroically grouped on mammoth plinths. Every thousand yards or so, vast archways of imitation marble, rich in statues, garlands and coats of arms, spanned the wide boulevards. Everywhere enormous Napoleonic eagles glittered gold in the swiftly setting sun.

The open carriage, with its jogging escort, drove through vociferous crowds down the Boulevard de Strasbourg, around the Place de la Concorde, up the Champs Elysées, under the Arc de Triomphe, through the Bois de Boulogne and on to Saint Cloud. 'In all this blaze of light from lamps, torches, amidst the roar of cannon, and bands, and drums, and cheers, we reached the Palace,' wrote the Queen.

Here Victoria and Eugenie were reunited. Having embraced the Empress, Victoria turned to Plon-Plon's sister, the statuesque and unconventional Princess Mathilde. There had been some speculation among the spectators as to whether the Queen would kiss the Princess, for it was common knowledge that Mathilde was living with a man not her husband. Victoria embraced her warmly and unhesitatingly. Eugenie then led her guests up the staircase lined with *Cent Gardes*, in the full splendour of their sky-blue tunics and silver cuirasses, to their apartments. 'I felt quite bewildered, but enchanted,' wrote the Queen. 'It was like a fairy tale, and everything so beautiful!'

In describing her impressions of the triumphant arrival to her Uncle Leopold, Victoria could hardly contain her excitement. 'Our entrance into Paris was a scene which was *quite feenhaft*, and which could hardly be seen anywhere else; was quite *overpowering*—splendidly decorated—illuminated—immensely crowded—and 60,000 troops out. . . .'

Her reception, she was assured, was 'much greater and more enthusiastic even' than those given to Napoleon I on his return from his victories.

2

Napoleon III proved to be an even better host than a guest. Queen Victoria was delighted by his efforts to ensure her comfort. The suite of rooms assigned to Victoria and Albert—

once the apartments of Queen Marie-Antoinette—had been redecorated at great expense in white and gold. The Queen's room had been designed to resemble, as much as possible, her own at Buckingham Palace. The zealous decorators had even gone so far as to saw the legs off an exquisitely proportioned table lest it prove too high for the diminutive Queen. In spite of this and other, less reprehensible, efforts, the Empress is reported to have burst into tears on inspecting the rooms before Victoria's arrival: she had considered them so much less pretty than the original ones. A frantic crowding-in of additional pieces of furniture had followed until, as one of the Queen's ladies reported, there was simply no more room in which to put it.

But Victoria was thrilled with the result. 'I have such a home feeling!' she exclaimed in answer to the Emperor's solicitous inquiries.

If Napoleon was the perfect host, Victoria was no less the perfect guest. Everything was charming. Despite her having been given a 'home feeling', she had to admit that it was all very different from England. Saint Cloud seemed so delightfully foreign: those *outside* shutters, those clipped avenues, those orange trees, that luminous atmosphere, that view of distant Paris, so white and glittery. The coffee was excellent and the cornices, gilded in *three* different shades of gold, quite splendid. The furniture was 'so well stuffed', noted the Queen, 'that by lying a little while on the sofa, you are completely rested'.

She found the demeanour of the imperial Court equally comforting. She had half expected things to be a little amateur, a little flashy even, but there was hardly a trace of any parvenu origins to be noticed. 'Everything is beautifully *monté* at Court,' she reported to King Leopold, 'very quiet and in excellent order: I must say we are both much struck with the difference between this and the poor King's [Louis Philippe's] time, when the noise, confusion and bustle were great.'

It was all very well for the Queen to make a gratified note of the absence of any confusion; it was quite a different matter as far as the members of her suite were concerned. Whereas all the energies of the French Court were directed towards making Victoria's visit as smooth an operation as possible, her ladies tended to come up against nothing but confusion. According to Lady Bruce, the muddle concerning luggage and attendants was beyond description. When the ladies reached Saint Cloud, feeling 'filthy, disgusting, tired, done up and half asleep', their boxes had not yet arrived and they had only twenty minutes in which to dress for dinner.

This was merely an introduction to what Lady Bruce called the strange customs of that 'barbarous land'. It seems that an army of footmen had been assigned to look after the suite. So eager were these attendants to be of service that the poor ladies were robbed of all peace or privacy. *'Je ne quitte pas la porte de Madame la Marquise,'* promised one of the footmen allotted to Mary Bulteel, afterwards Lady Ponsonby. He proved to be as good as his word. Not only did he never leave her door, but, as it boasted neither lock nor bolt and as he was apt to come bustling into her room without warning, she never felt safe from him. Bathing became a form of torture for her. Only by sitting in her tub with her eyes glued to the door, and by leaping out of the water the minute she noticed the handle beginning to turn, and by then flinging her full weight against the door, could she manage to keep him at bay. At other times when she was being less watchful, her shrieks of *'N'entrez pas, n'entrez pas!'* made no impression. He would come darting into the room, smiling blandly, to assure her that it was essential that he explain something or other to Madame la Marquise.

The footmen had obviously been forewarned of the odd British habit of frequent bathing. Mary Bulteel claims that had she ordered cans of hot water a dozen, instead of merely a couple, of times a day, her attendant would have registered no surprise. 'I hope the tubs may introduce a new era,' wrote Lady Bruce, 'but till last account, the British custom seemed to have struck no root in the ungrateful soil.'

The service at mealtimes, which Victoria considered so excellent, was obviously far less professional at the ladies' end of the table. At any moment a large, white-gloved hand was likely to be seen gathering up crumbs in a 'primitive' manner and it was not unknown for truffles to be served with the fingers if they proved too rebellious for a spoon. A con-

fused scuffling behind one's chair, as five or six scurrying footmen crossed paths, usually led to an hysterical hissing of
the word '*Imbécile!*' It was an expression which Mary Bulteel
found becoming increasingly useful as the visit progressed.

Another member of the Queen's suite, Lady Churchill,
was horrified to find herself facing three wine glasses at *breakfast*. She was consequently obliged to explain the difference
between breakfast and luncheon to the uncomprehending
French. '*Manger de nouveau, toujours manger,*' they sighed,
marvelling at the British ability to eat three large meals a day.

'Can you not hear them,' snorted Lady Bruce, 'and eating
each time double at least what we do!'

But no such chauvinistic criticism ever escaped Victoria's
lips. To her, all the arrangements were perfection. As the first
day of the visit was a Sunday, Napoleon had decreed that it be
spent as an 'English' Sunday. This meant that the day was
devoted to walks, drives and a church service. And this allowed
ample opportunity, of course, for the Emperor to take up once
more the threads of his subtle courtship. He saw to it that he
was alone with Victoria as they drove in the phaeton through
the dappled sunshine of the tree-lined avenues of Saint Cloud;
it was on his arm that the Queen strolled through the formal
gardens of the Palace after luncheon; it was on her side of the
barouche that Napoleon rode his horse when they all went for a
drive in the newly laid-out Bois de Boulogne. And within no
time she had once more fallen under his spell. Even she was at
a loss for adjectives to do justice to his many qualities. To King
Leopold she reported, 'He *is* very *fascinating*, with that great
quiet and gentleness.' To Baron Stockmar, 'He is so simple, so
naif, never making *des phrases*, or paying compliments—so full
of tact, good taste, high breeding. . . .'

On and on ran the royal pen until the recipients of Victoria's
letters must have wondered whether Napoleon were some sort
of magician or whether Victoria had indeed fallen in love. 'For
the Emperor personally I have conceived a real affection,'
admitted the Queen to Stockmar and went on to say that
Napoleon had 'the power of attaching those to him who come
near him, which is quite incredible'.

This infatuation for the Emperor of the French must have

alarmed poor Stockmar considerably. A close association between Britain and France certainly did not fit in with his particular plans. What he and the two other members of that earnest Coburg triumvirate—Prince Albert and King Leopold— were dreaming of was an alliance between Britain and Prussia. Injected with generous doses of British liberalism and British prestige, Prussia was to lead Germany to a united, democratic future. This enlightened greater Germany would replace the present cluster of reactionary kingdoms, principalities and grand duchies that went to make up the *Deutscher Bund*. Headed by Prussia and allied to Britain, Germany would be a model constitutional state. As such, it would be utterly opposed to the despotism and militarism of Napoleon III.

And now here was England's Queen, not only allied to fickle France, but clearly obsessed by its machiavellian Emperor. So uneasy, in fact, did the Prussians become about the Anglo-French alliance, that Princess Augusta of Prussia wrote off to the Queen to ask if there was any truth in the rumour that the British officers had been made to efface the name 'Waterloo' from their clasps and medals.

Victoria's answer was characteristic. 'Most certainly not,' she replied sharply, 'it is there and there it will remain, and we hope ere long Sebastapol may be added.'

There was one little point of dissension which Victoria and Napoleon were able to settle quite happily during the visit. This concerned the Orleans family. In the course of the State Visit to England, Napoleon, appreciating Victoria's sympathy for the fallen dynasty, had made a point of asking after them. He had even sent a message, through Victoria, to the widowed Queen Marie-Amélie. Encouraged by this gesture, Victoria now raised the question of her relationship with the Orleans family. She felt that she must make no secret of her feelings of friendliness towards them. The Emperor was all understanding. He, in turn, explained his reasons for the confiscation of their property. 'A curious conversation,' noted the Queen in her Journal, 'but which I was greatly relieved to have had; for, with my feelings of sincerity, I could not bear that there should have been anything between us . . . I was very anxious to get this out, and not to have that untouchable ground between us.'

The Queen, reporting these talks to King Leopold, declared that the Emperor 'had shown great tact and good feeling about all this, and spoke without any bitterness of the King'. As though to set the seal on this harmonious exchange, they all drove out to visit the various places connected with the Orleans family. On the first Sunday they went to Neuilly to see the ruins of Louis Philippe's favourite summer residence; on another occasion they visited the chapel of St Ferdinand, erected in memory of the King's eldest son, who had been killed in a carriage accident.

The great château at Neuilly had been burned down during the revolution of 1848. It now presented, thought the Queen, 'a most melancholy picture of decay'. The royal party wandered around the desolate, grass-grown ruins which, more than anything else, seemed to bear witness to the impermanence of affairs in France. Albert, who had been Louis Philippe's guest at the château nineteen years before, was particularly struck by this aspect. 'You may imagine what a strange impression so many changes must have produced . . .' he wrote to his step-mother. 'All this is vanished as if before the wind.'

During their visit to the chapel of St Ferdinand, built on the spot where the young Duke d'Orleans had died, Victoria was able to indulge her preoccupation with death to the full. She and Albert moved about the dimly lit chapel, musing about the fate of the poor Orleans family and admiring the second-rate carvings by Triquetti. As the royal party left the chapel, a woman came forward to sell them two medals. One bore the head of the late Duke d'Orleans; the other that of his son, the Count de Paris—present Orleans pretender. Napoleon bought them for Victoria as souvenirs. How strange, thought the Queen, that the *Emperor* should be buying her these medals, especially when that of the Count de Paris carried an inscription to the effect that the Orleans pretender was 'the hope of France'.

Knowing that her pilgrimage would please the former Queen Marie-Amélie, Victoria wrote to King Leopold, telling him all about it. She asked him to let the Queen know that she had been thinking of her and her family and how much she admired the late King's 'great works at Versailles which have been left *quite intact*'.

'Indeed,' added Victoria, unable to keep off the old refrain for long, 'the Emperor (as in everything) has shown *great* tact and good feeling. . . .'

3

'The dear Empress, who was all kindness and goodness, whom we are all very fond of, we saw comparatively but little of,' wrote Victoria to King Leopold after the visit, 'as for *really* and *certainly very* good reasons she must take great care of herself.'

The Queen's discretion was somewhat excessive. By now all Europe—and certainly King Leopold—must have known that Eugenie was pregnant. Indeed, Lord Clarendon, who accompanied the Queen, complained that the Empress could speak to Victoria's ladies 'of nothing but her condition'. As Eugenie was not to give birth until mid-March the following year, she could only have been two months pregnant, but Napoleon was determined that she should run no risks. She had already had several miscarriages. Thus, during the royal visit, she made very few public appearances.

As far as it affected Queen Victoria, the Empress's withdrawal from public life could not have been more opportune. Although there was never a suggestion of jealousy in the Queen's feelings towards the Empress, Victoria could not hope to show off to advantage beside Eugenie. Miss Marion Ellice, writing from Paris to Lady de Rothschild, summed up the situation by saying, 'How *fortunate* that the Empress should be unable to accompany the Queen everywhere—she is so beautiful and so graceful!'

But even though she was spared comparison with Eugenie, Victoria did not escape criticism for the dowdiness of her clothes. The Queen was wearing 'an abominable white bonnet with big white feathers of the most ungraceful description', reported Marion Ellice on one occasion, and on another Princess Mathilde was appalled to see the Queen setting out with a huge home-made handbag on which was embroidered a multi-coloured parrot. The embroidery was the handiwork of one of her daughters, explained the Queen with disarming pride to the astounded Princess.

Even that bluff old soldier, General Canrobert, fresh from the trenches in the Crimea, expressed bewilderment at the Queen's 'shocking toilette'. She looked so extraordinarily old-fashioned: those massive, over-trimmed bonnets, those enormous satin reticules, those short, relatively narrow skirts, those low-heeled pumps with black ribbons tied around the ankle. Her colours, not one of which matched the others, were all crude.

Nor was such criticism confined to strangers. The Queen's own suite, usually so loyal to their mistress, admitted to feeling ashamed of her lack of dress sense. 'I regret to say that the Queen was badly dressed on these occasions, in early Victorian gowns, with a *penchant* for a "lilac cravat" as she called it,' wrote Mary Bulteel afterwards. On the one occasion that the normally tactful Napoleon III could bring himself to compliment the Queen on a dress, he asked if it had been made in England. No, she admitted cheerfully—in Paris, especially for that evening.

But for all that, Victoria, unlike Eugenie, looked unmistakably royal. General Canrobert, having dealt with her appearance, had to admit that what most impressed him was her 'dignified air'. There was, he realized, some intangible aura about her which set her apart from others; she had a definite stamp of greatness. 'The unaccountable dignity of her short stature, and *bienveillance* of manner have walked into their hearts,' claimed the usually cynical Lord Clarendon. One evening, when the royal party visited the opera, Mary Bulteel reported that the Empress, who looked lovely, was 'hesitant, gauche in her manner, and ignorant of what to do when they reached the door of the royal box'. Victoria, on the other hand, stepped forward without a moment's hesitation and walked right to the front of the box. There she stood, acknowledging the tumultuous applause of the crowd below. Although Eugenie's looks and dress were matchless, it was Victoria who won the praise.

'The blessed one!' exclaimed Lady Bruce. 'She is only too good for them, that is the feeling one has, but certainly the impression she made is remarkable.' Of course, added her ladyship with fine British patronage, 'impressions with them are fleeting. . . .'

CHAPTER FIVE

'The gayest of cities'

1

'Tomorrow,' wrote Prince Albert at the end of their first Sunday at Saint Cloud, 'the Parisian campaign begins.' And indeed, on Monday festivities began in earnest. From then on the round of public engagements was unceasing.

One of the main reasons for Victoria's State Visit to Paris was that she might attend the *Exposition Universelle*. Accordingly, on Monday morning, she visited the *Palais des Beaux Arts*. Here she was received by Plon-Plon in his capacity as President of the Exhibition. With him as escort, and leaning on the arm of the Emperor, Victoria trailed through the glass-roofed palace. Behind walked Albert, Vicky, Bertie and the rest of the party. With their typically mid-nineteenth-century taste, the visitors tended to stroll past the paintings by Ingres and Delacroix and to linger in front of the vast canvasses by Decamps, Meissonier and Horace Vernet. When they reached the Winterhalters, even their lingering slowed down and chairs were fetched so that they might give full attention to the syrupy offerings of this popular Court painter. Winterhalter's tall, imperious-looking image of the Emperor bore very little resemblance to the short, friendly figure by the Queen's side, and his conventionally pretty portrait of the Empress missed her essentially heroic beauty. But Victoria sat for some minutes in enraptured silence in front of them and then, perhaps lest any inferior works spoil the impression, the royal party took their leave.

When a compatriot asked Vicky, the Princess Royal, which of the pictures she liked best, her answer was prompt. 'The English ones, *of course*.'

The *Exposition* was dutifully visited twice more during that week. Again on the arm of Napoleon, Victoria, looking radiantly happy, moved slowly from hall to hall, inspecting, commenting, admiring. She was particularly impressed by the *productions des manufactures royales* (*'quite* magnificent') and bought herself '*one* small object' in Sèvres porcelain. Napoleon, on the other hand, presented Albert with a particularly large piece of Sèvres. It represented, claims the Queen, the Exhibition of 1851. 'Albert was much pleased,' she says, 'for it is a *chef-d'oeuvre* in every sense of the word.'

Two aspects of Victoria's behaviour during this State Visit were especially striking: one was her almost boundless energy, the other her unfeigned enjoyment of things. Time and again she manifested these two admirable and endearing characteristics. She would not even allow the heat, which was, she admitted, like a 'furnace', to spoil her pleasure. One afternoon, following an exhausting morning at the *Exposition,* she spent several hours driving through the streets of Paris. The huge, good-natured crowd roared its approval as she sat in the merciless sunshine, responding gaily and tirelessly to the cheers. She, in turn, registered her approval of Paris and the Parisians. 'Everything so gay, so bright, and though very hot, the air so clear and light. The absence of smoke keeps everything so white and bright, and this in Paris, with much gilding about the shops, green shutters etc., produces a brilliancy of effect which is quite incredible . . .' she enthused.

On passing the Conciergerie, Napoleon informed her that that was where he had been imprisoned after one of his attempts to overthrow the Orleans regime. 'Strange, incredible contrast, to be driving with us as Emperor through the streets of the town in triumph!' exclaimed the Queen.

Another day they all attended a *déjeuner champêtre* at Versailles. The Empress, who had a cult of Marie-Antoinette, received them in one of the pseudo-rustic cottages built by that 'poor unhappy Queen'. The ghosts of the *ancien régime* seemed to have had no adverse effect on the spirits of the rather bourgeois-looking group, and luncheon was a cheerful affair. After the meal, Victoria, not wanting to waste a moment, unpacked her painting things and settled down to sketch the brilliantly uniformed soldiers standing about in the leaf-filtered sunlight. The effect, she said, was 'the prettiest possible'.

In fact, Napoleon's soldiers fascinated the Queen. One morning, while the conscientious Albert again visited the *Exposition*, Victoria remained painting at Saint Cloud; again her subjects were the Emperor's splendid troops. Victoria adored soldiers and those of the Second Empire were particularly decorative. 'While dressing,' she wrote one day, 'I stopped to look at the *Cent Gardes*, very like our Life Guards—magnificent men of six feet upwards—riding by; and then hearing a charming sort of *fanfare*, I ran to another window, and saw a body of Zouaves marching up, preceded by buglers. They look so handsome, and walk so lightly.'

When she had finished sketching the Zouaves that morning, she started a letter to her Uncle Leopold. 'I am *delighted, enchanted, amused* and *interested*, and think I never saw anything more *beautiful* and gay than Paris—or more splendid than all the Palaces. Our reception is *most* gratifying—for it is enthusiastic and really kind in the highest degree. . . . How beautiful and enjoyable is this place!'

That afternoon Victoria and the Emperor rejoined Prince Albert at the Tuileries (he was 'somewhat impatient at our non-appearance') and went on to visit the Louvre. In spite of the almost suffocating heat, the Queen insisted on a thorough inspection of the paintings. Lord Clarendon, who was obliged to trail along behind her, complained that 'no Royal Person ever yet known or to be known in history comes up to her in *indefatigability*'. One fat member of the entourage, tightly uniformed and sweating profusely, whispered to the hardly less exhausted Clarendon, 'I would give everything—everything—including the Venus de Milo—for a glass of lemonade.' Even Napoleon, towards the end, was seen to be 'going in great distress'.

When the tour was finally over and Clarendon expressed to the Queen the gallant hope that she was not more tired than she looked, she replied, with ineffable sweetness, that she was not in the least tired.

It was almost seven o'clock by the time the footsore party returned to the Tuileries. Even now, while she was meant to be resting before going on to the great ball at the Hôtel de Ville, Victoria put the time to good use by filling in her Journal.

At nine o'clock they drove in state to the Hôtel de Ville. Dressed with her usual cheerful want of taste in a white silk ball gown, covered with lace and embroidered with geraniums, flashing—as one journal put it—'at every possible point with diamonds', and with the Koh-i-noor sparkling in her diadem, Victoria ascended the staircase and took up her position on the dais in the ballroom. Despite the fact that there were some eight thousand guests packed into the room and that the heat was almost unbearable, she enjoyed herself immensely. In the ordinary way this suffocating atmosphere, made worse by the heady scent of thousands upon thousands of massed flowers, would have been too much for the Queen. Now either Paris or the Emperor, or both, seemed to have made her oblivious of her usual allergy. 'The heat is very great,' she had reported to her uncle that morning but had added, with a touch of defiance, that 'the air is certainly *lighter* than ours—and I have no headache'.

Victoria's vigorous dancing amazed the onlookers. One Frenchman was moved to compare it favourably with the fighting prowess of her soldiers. And when she was not dancing, she would be walking around the rooms on the Emperor's arm, smiling and nodding at the guests. It was well after midnight when they reached Saint Cloud.

Yet no matter how late she went to bed, the Queen slept fitfully. She was always far too stimulated.

2

During the State Visit the Queen came to learn something more about those two other Bonapartes—Napoleon III's cousins, Plon-Plon and Mathilde.

Unlike the Emperor, Plon-Plon and Mathilde looked undeniably Bonaparte. Both had the dark-eyed, cameo-complexioned, Italianate look of the Great Napoleon. Princess Mathilde carried herself with a certain plump dignity; Plon-Plon looked like a bloated version of the first Emperor.

At the start of his reign, Napoleon III—in his anxiety for links with the British royal family—had proposed a match between Plon-Plon and Queen Victoria's cousin: the fat and jolly Princess Mary of Cambridge. The proposal had been promptly nipped in the bud by Victoria. Instead, Princess Mary married the Duke of Teck and became the mother of the future Queen Mary, consort of King George V.

Now, on meeting Plon-Plon in the flesh, Victoria took an almost instant dislike to him. She had heard, from both Napoleon and Eugenie, that he was headstrong and irresponsible; she was now to experience personally his contrariness and lack of good manners. 'Prince Napoleon not very gracious,' was her terse comment after spending the morning in his company at the *Exposition*. After her second visit she complained that he was 'very gruff and contradictory as usual'. One day, when seated beside her at luncheon, he insisted on bringing up the subject of 'the workers'—whose cause he claimed to champion—as often as possible. 'He seems to take pleasure in saying something disagreeable and biting, particularly to the Emperor, and with a smile which is quite satanic,' noted the Queen.

But there was more to Plon-Plon than met the eye. He was no fool. An intelligent, eloquent and idealistic liberal, he was anxious to see a democratization of his cousin's regime. His views were sound; it was simply that he had such a deplorable way of airing them. He was forever criticizing, attacking and undermining; he was incapable of inspiring trust or commanding sympathy. And as the Queen was obliged to judge only by what she saw and heard, she assumed him to be no more than an ill-natured and tactless boor.

She was none the less forced, '*à contre-coeur*' as she put it, to invest him with the Order of the Bath. His manner, she noted on that occasion, 'was rude and disagreeable in the highest degree'.

Princess Mathilde, on the other hand, she found 'very civil'. The truth was that Mathilde, who could be every bit as outspoken as her brother Plon-Plon, was on her best behaviour during the Queen's visit. She even managed to please Victoria by being especially kind to Bertie, the Prince of Wales. But the Queen was well aware of the Princess's unconventional, indeed scandalous, private life. Separated from her husband, the Russian Prince Demidoff, Mathilde lived quite openly with a painter by the name of Nieuwerkerque. Even her cultural enthusiasms, which supplied the regime with a much needed intellectual aura and earned her the soubriquet of *Notre Dame des Arts*, could not compensate for this breach of code.

The Empress Eugenie found the presence of this forthright and independent-minded pair particularly irksome. 'I had a good deal of conversation with the dear Empress, who is good, clever, and sensible, as well as lovely and attractive,' wrote the Queen on one occasion. 'The first part of the conversation was about Prince Napoleon and Princess Mathilde, and their being such a difficulty and such a disadvantage to them.'

Lord Clarendon, whose quips were always guaranteed to send the Queen's ladies into fits of deliciously shocked laughter, referred to the surly Plon-Plon and the plump Mathilde as 'the assassin and the cook'.

3

In the year 1840, King Louis Philippe, then in the tenth year of his reign, had decided to have the body of Napoleon I brought back to Paris from Saint Helena. This move had been part of his plan for the adding of a little Napoleonic glamour to his own lack-lustre regime. Already, to win for himself this reflected glory, King Louis Philippe had had the Emperor's statue hoisted atop the Vendôme column, his Arc de Triomphe completed and part of Versailles turned into a museum to house the imperial battle pictures. As an ultimate gesture, he had decreed that the body of the late Emperor be brought back in state to Paris. Permission had been granted by a cynical Lord Palmerston and no less a person than the Prince de Joinville, one of the King's own sons, had been dispatched to Saint Helena to fetch the remains.

On 15 December 1840, a monstrously ornate funeral car, drawn by sixteen richly caparisoned horses, had trundled Napoleon's coffin through the cold and crowded streets of Paris. After a seemingly endless funeral service, the remains had been laid to rest on a vast catafalque beneath the dome of les Invalides. To allow for the erection of this catafalque, the altar had been removed from the church. 'And why not?' the watching Thackeray had quipped. 'Who is God here but Napoleon?'

The remains safely deposited, King Louis Philippe had returned to the Tuileries, highly satisfied with the day's work. In fact, he had had very little cause for self-congratulation. The much publicized return of Napoleon's coffin had simply served as a nail in his own. Louis Philippe's careful fostering of the Bonaparte legend made possible the return of a Bonaparte to the throne of France. For when, after the revolution of 1848, Louis Napoleon had presented himself as a candidate for the Presidency, the French people, remembering the much vaunted glories of Napoleon's reign, had cast their votes for this new Napoleon. They had hoped that he would bring back the splendours of the First Empire.

Now, in the year 1855, it seemed as though he had. This State Visit by Queen Victoria was certainly very splendid. And one of its highlights was the Queen's visit, late one afternoon, to the Hôtel des Invalides, to see these very remains. To many, her gesture was little short of amazing: for the fact that the Queen of England was going to pay homage at the tomb of Napoleon, once England's greatest enemy, marked an extraordinary turn of events. It never ceased to astound Victoria herself. 'There I stood,' she afterwards wrote, 'at the arm of Napoleon III, his nephew, before the coffin of England's bitterest foe; I, the grand-daughter of that King who hated him most, and who most vigorously opposed him, and this very nephew, who bears his name, being my nearest and dearest ally!'

Napoleon's coffin had been moved from that flamboyant catafalque and now lay in one of the side-chapels beneath the Dome. A special crypt was being constructed for the illustrious remains, but, as this had not yet been completed, it was in its temporary resting-place that Victoria saw the coffin. Passing the circular, balustraded opening in the floor of the building, the Queen leaned over to look down into the crypt which would one day house the body. Napoleon III, in a characteristic aside, remarked that it looked rather like a huge reservoir. However, such flippancies ceased when the party actually reached the chapel.

The coffin was covered with a violet velvet pall which glittered all over with golden bees. Around the chapel stood veterans of the First Empire, holding flaming torches. In their glancing light Victoria could discern, at the foot of the coffin, those three sacred dynastic relics: the hat Napoleon had worn at Eylau, the sword he had used at Austerlitz and the plaque of the *Légion d'Honneur*. The Queen stood in homage before these treasured remains. It was a solemn moment, rendered still more dramatic by the fact that a storm was brewing, making the atmosphere within the tomb tense and oppressive.

The royal group—Victoria, Albert, their two children, the Emperor, Prince Napoleon and Princess Mathilde—stood for several minutes in silence. Then the Queen, deeply moved, turned to the young Prince of Wales and, putting a hand on his shoulder, said, 'Kneel down before the tomb of the Great Napoleon.' Dutifully, Bertie knelt down.

At that moment the storm broke. The thunder crashed about the chapel walls, echoing and re-echoing around the vaults. Flashes of lightning whitened the glare of torches and the mounting hiss of rain filled the air. All combined to give the scene an almost supernatural aura; to crown it, an organ burst into a thunderous rendering of *God save the Queen*.

'Strange and wonderful indeed!' exclaimed Victoria.

But the moment passed, the Prince of Wales scrambled to his feet and the party hurried out to their carriage through the driving rain.

'It seems as if,' noted Victoria in her diary, 'in this tribute of respect to a departed and great foe, old enmities and rivalries were wiped out, and the seal of heaven placed upon that bond of amity which is now happily established between two great nations! May Heaven bless and prosper it!'

4

Prince Albert's mood was not nearly as euphoric as his wife's. He was undoubtedly enjoying his stay in Paris but he could still not overcome his reservations about Napoleon III's regime. For this serious-minded, methodical Prince, devoted to the ideals of peace and orderly progress, the Second Empire was far too showy, too militant, too loosely rooted. He was deeply impressed by the improvements to Paris, he was intensely interested in the *Exposition*, he was even ready to believe, to a certain extent, in the Emperor's professed love of peace. But he remained uneasy. He could not share Victoria's uncritical enthusiasm for the French alliance.

Yet even he could not help being charmed by the Emperor personally. 'I have frequently talked with Albert,' wrote Victoria, 'who is naturally much calmer, and particularly much less taken by people, much less under *personal* influence than I am. He quite admits that it is extraordinary how very much attached one becomes to him when one lives with the Emperor, quite at one's ease and intimately, as we have done during the last ten days. . . .'

The Emperor, she went on to say, 'is so fond of Albert, appreciating him so thoroughly, and shows him so much confidence'. Indeed, when the visit was over, Napoleon wrote to tell Albert of his great esteem for his character and of his friendship for his person. 'Of this you must be convinced,' continued Napoleon, 'for we know by intuition those who love us.'

In the face of such unreserved admiration, even the cautious Prince Albert was obliged to melt.

There was no hint of restraint in the response of the Prince's children to the charms of their host and hostess. Vicky and Bertie were besotted with the imperial pair: Vicky with the Empress and Bertie with the Emperor. The Princess Royal's *Schwärmerei* for Eugenie, which had unfolded in England, was now in full flower. 'Vicky is never tired of praising the beauty, kindness and goodness of the Empress . . .' wrote Victoria.

As for Bertie, the Emperor Napoleon was introducing him to a whole new world. On one of the first days of the visit, the Emperor had whisked the boy off for a drive through the streets of Paris; afterwards they had strolled together on the terrace of the Tuileries. Napoleon III, who loved children, knew exactly how to treat a boy like the Prince of Wales. Bertie, so accustomed to the humourless, heavy-handed ways of his father and his tutors, found himself responding immediately. Prince Albert was so set on moulding his son in his own image, of turning him into a model sovereign, that the young Prince's life had become a ceaseless round of instruction. Even his brief periods of relaxation were conducted under a critical and usually disapproving eye.

Poor Bertie just could not match up to his parents' expectations. He was a likeable enough lad with a flair for languages but he was by no means brilliant and by no means a saint. His mother and father made no secret of their disappointment.

And now here, in the person of the Emperor of the French, was a man who accepted him for what he was. Here was someone who seemed to take an unashamed delight in those things in which Bertie delighted; who loved show and colour and movement; who lived, quite naturally and unashamedly, for pleasure. To the young Prince, whose life had always been narrow, repressed and dedicated to self-improvement, Napoleon's tolerance, ease of manner and sense of enjoyment were a revelation. This, surely, was how life was meant to be lived.

Bertie looked up at the relaxed, cigar-smoking man who strolled beside him on the terrace and said, quite simply, 'You have a nice country. I would like to be your son.'

Indeed, Bertie was so happy and consequently making himself so agreeable, that even Prince Albert was satisfied. 'They [Vicky and Bertie] have made themselves general favourites,' wrote Albert to Stockmar, 'especially the Prince of Wales, *qui est si gentil*. As the French are sarcastic and not readily partial to strangers, this is so much more important.'

It was during this visit to Paris that Bertie's great love of France was born. The beauty of the French capital, the liveliness of the French people, the *bonhomie* of the French Emperor, the elegance of the French Empress, made an indelible impression on his young, pleasure-hungry nature. From now on it would be towards France, rather than towards Germany (so beloved by the rest of his family), that his personality was to be orientated. From the time of this first visit to Paris until the establishment, almost fifty years later, of the *entente cordiale*, he never ceased to work for an understanding between the two countries.

5

On the last evening but one there was a great ball at Versailles. 'Of the splendour of the fête at Versailles, I can really give no impression, for it exceeded all imagination!' enthused the Queen. But this did not, for one moment, prevent her from trying. She was as eloquent as ever in detailing its multiple glories: the garlands of flowers, the blaze of chandeliers, the cascades of fireworks and the brilliance of the Galerie des Glaces itself. This was one of the few occasions on which the Empress Eugenie appeared in public. She was wearing a white dress, trimmed with diamonds, and with yet more diamonds in her hair. She looked, thought Victoria, like a fairy queen or nymph.

'How beautiful you are!' exclaimed Napoleon to his wife as they met at the head of the stairs.

Between dances various guests were presented to the Queen. Among them was the Prussian Minister at Frankfurt, Herr von Bismarck. As he was destined to play so significant a role in future years, Bismarck's presence at this ball seems almost providential. The lives of Queen Victoria, the Princess Royal (future German Empress), the Prince of Wales, Napoleon III and the Empress Eugenie were all to be bound up with this massive white-uniformed figure. Some fifteen years hence, in this very Galerie des Glaces and on the ruins of the Second Empire, Bismarck would proclaim the German Reich. On this summer evening in 1855, his presence was not unlike that of the bad fairy at the christening party.

Not until after two in the morning did the royalties arrive back at Saint Cloud. In their exhausted, exulted state they stayed up for another hour, loath to go to bed and so put an end to a magical evening.

'It's terrible that there's only one more night,' sighed the Emperor. Victoria, in full agreement, begged him to come soon again to England. 'Most certainly!' he answered.

'But you will come back, won't you?' asked Napoleon. 'Now that we know each other, we can visit each other at Windsor or Fontainebleau without any ceremony, can't we?'

This would give her great pleasure, said Victoria. Laughingly she assured him that she would come back the following year as an ordinary traveller. Jumping out of the train with her bag in her hand, she would take a cab and present herself at the Tuileries to beg some dinner.

Here was Queen Victoria at her most endearing: a frank, charming and happy young woman, very much in love with life and—unwittingly—more than half in love with Napoleon III. As she sat chatting to the Emperor, every turn of her head, every move of her hands, would have set her diamonds a-sparkle. No one, seeing her flushed face, her bright eyes and her sweet smile could have doubted that she was enjoying herself to the full. It was so seldom that Victoria was able to relax with anyone other than the members of her family. And few were able to put her at her ease as completely as this softly-spoken, worldly man sitting beside her.

That very morning the two of them had experienced one of those moments of complete and enjoyable *rapport*. They had all driven through the forest of Saint Germain to the hunting-lodge of La Muette for luncheon. On their arrival, a party of young girls, dressed in white and shepherded by the village *turé*, came forward to greet the Queen. Before handing over the customary nosegay, the leading girl launched into a speech of welcome. It was interminable. Watched by the anxious *curé*, who had obviously composed the speech, she piped on and on— about the Royal Visit, the Anglo-French alliance, the *Exposition* and other appropriate subjects. Suddenly she stopped. She had forgotten the words. Victoria and Napoleon, hoping to save her further embarrassment (and themselves further tedium) thanked her and tried to take the posy from her. She refused to give it up. She was determined to finish the speech.

'Wait,' she insisted, 'I'll remember.'

The Queen and Emperor, only just managing to keep straight faces, duly waited.

Suddenly she was off again. Bravely she gabbled on until she broke down a second time. On this occasion the anguished *curé* tried to intervene by shouting out a frantic '*Vive la Reine d'Angleterre!*'

But the girl would not be cheated of the full text. For a third time she started up, ending on a confused and resounding chant of *'Vive la Reine d'Angleterre, vive sa Demoiselle, vive son Prince Albert, vive l'Empereur, vive l'Impératrice'* and finally, for good measure, *'vive tout le monde!'*

Not until the girls had been marched off by the clucking *curé* did Victoria and Napoleon allow themselves to burst into peals of laughter. And the Queen's laugh was always to be unashamedly hearty, even in her old age.

But, of course, Napoleon's accomplishments did not end with this putting of the normally nervous Queen at her ease. As valuable was his ability to create a heady, almost erotic atmosphere; it was an atmosphere to which her passionate, highly excitable nature was quick to respond. No wonder that she claimed that she would always look back on this visit to the Emperor as one of the most memorable periods of her life. Nor is it surprising that, for days after she got back to England, she felt 'dreadfully bewildered, excited, and unable to do anything but think and talk of everything. . . .'

Only once during this hectic week did Victoria experience a slight clouding-over of her happiness. This was late one after-noon while she was snatching a few moments' rest between the end of one function and the start of the next. Quite suddenly, sitting alone in the Empress's drawing-room at the Tuileries, she was overcome with a feeling of desolation. Whether it was due, as she claimed, to the band playing in the garden outside, or whether it was simply a reaction from the excitement of the last few days, she felt, for a little while, quite *'wehmüthig* and melancholy'. Her reflections that evening have a strangely prophetic ring. 'All so gay—the people cheering the Emperor as he walked up and down in the little garden—and yet how recently has blood flowed, and a whole dynasty been swept away. How uncertain is everything still! All is so beautiful here; all seems now so prosperous; the Emperor seems so fit for his place, and yet how little security one feels for the future! All depends on him and on his too precious life! These reflec-tions crowded on my mind, and smote upon my heart. . . .'

6

All too soon Monday, the dreaded day of departure, came around. Sad as was the prospect of parting for Victoria, it was every bit as sad for her two children. While their parents were preparing to leave, Vicky and Bertie slipped in to see the Empress. They begged her to persuade their mother and father to leave them behind. Eugenie, masking her amusement and, no doubt, her satisfaction, told them that it was impossible. Their parents could not manage without them.

'Not do without us!' exclaimed the Prince of Wales. 'Don't fancy that, for there are six more of us at home, and they don't want us.'

But the Empress, in her charming way, was firm, and the two disappointed children were obliged to get ready for the journey home. 'Vicky was melted in tears, *selon son habitude,*' noted the Queen as they left.

Victoria and her family took leave of the Empress at the Tuileries ('she was in tears, much grieved at parting . . . most truly and sincerely do I wish her all possible happiness') and then, accompanied by the Emperor, drove in state to the station. 'Alas! it was our last view of that gay, brilliant town, where we have been so kindly received, and for which I shall ever have an affectionate feeling.'

The Emperor travelled with them to Boulogne. Also in the railway carriage was Plon-Plon. He seems to have behaved quite pleasantly, which Victoria pronounced fortunate, 'considering that we had him for five hours with us in the carriage'.

Boulogne was the scene of yet more festivities, and not until eleven that night did they board the *Victoria and Albert.* Napoleon, who was to accompany them a little way out to sea, led the Queen on board. 'We glided out of the harbour,' she wrote, 'I with a heavy heart. . . .'

After a while the Emperor had to take his leave and board his own yacht for the return to Boulogne. It was an emotional and much dreaded moment for Victoria. Standing on the moonlit deck, with the lights of Boulogne twinkling in the distance and the flash of fireworks searing the sky, the Queen embraced

71

the Emperor. '*Vous reviendrez?*' he asked. She assured him that she would. He then shook hands warmly with Prince Albert and the children. They all followed him to the ladder and here, once more, Victoria squeezed his hand and embraced him. '*Encore une fois, adieu, Sire!*' she said.

She leaned over the rail to watch him climb down into the barge which was to carry him to his yacht. As the little boat pulled away, Napoleon called out to her, '*Adieu Madame; au revoir!*'

'*Je l'espère bien,*' cried the Queen in return.

She stood by the rail, watching the barge being rowed across the glittering sea, with no sound other than the splash of the oars to break the silence. She saw the Emperor climb aboard his own yacht and watched as it slipped away in the darkness. For a long time she stood waving her handkerchief until all hope of Napoleon seeing her had gone; 'and then *all* was still—all over . . .' she said.

She did not get to bed until a quarter to two; 'low, bewildered and excited'. The night that she left France, she afterwards admitted to Lady Cowley, she felt 'so unhappy'.

And on the very day that she arrived back home, she instructed Lord Clarendon to ask Lord Cowley to collect everything that the Emperor had 'said, thought or written about the visit and *herself*'. Nothing would be too small or too insignificant.

CHAPTER SIX

'Poor, dear, modest, unpretentious Osborne'

1

Queen Victoria returned to England believing firmly in the durability of the French alliance. That it would prove to be more than a temporary military partnership against Russia she had no doubt. The warmth of her reception from 'so *difficile* a people as the French was indeed *most* gratifying and most promising for the future'. In short, she assured her sceptical Uncle Leopold, 'the *complete* Union of the two countries is stamped and sealed in the most satisfactory and solid manner, for it is not *only* a Union of the two Governments—the two Sovereigns—it is that of the *two Nations!*'

The fall of Sebastopol to the combined armies a few weeks later seemed to knit the allies more closely together. Victoria's thoughts, as she stood by the celebratory bonfire blazing at Balmoral (Albert described the rejoicings as 'a veritable Witch's dance supported by whisky'), were as much for the Emperor of the French as for her own soldiers. 'This event will delight my brother and faithful ally—and *friend*, Napoleon III—I may add for we really are *great friends* . . .' she enthused.

The capture of Sebastopol brought the end of the Crimean War in sight. Although Britain, now that her belligerence was thoroughly aroused, was prepared to continue the struggle, Napoleon was anxious to make peace. He realized that France could not afford to wage war much longer. It was thus he who opened and guided the complicated and protracted peace negotiations. The Congress of Paris was very much his creation. There was a suspicion, amongst the British, that Napoleon III intended to make use of this Peace Congress to put certain of his own pet theories into practice. For one thing, he was known to favour aspiring nationalities. Would he not try to 'resettle the map' of Europe by suggesting a revision of the 1815 Treaty of Vienna? Prince Albert certainly thought so. Any such plan, confided the Queen to Lord Palmerston, would be very unwise. 'We have every interest not to bring about a European Congress *pour la Révision des Traités*, which many people suspect the Emperor wishes to turn the present Conference into,' she declared.

Although Napoleon did not 'resettle the map', the Peace of Paris, signed in the spring of 1856, was a great personal triumph. That the Emperor could persuade Britain to accept the terms was due, not only to his understanding with Palmerston, Clarendon and Cowley, but also to his friendship with the Queen. The long and affectionate letters which passed between Windsor and the Tuileries helped iron out many of the difficulties. Victoria might complain, in private, that the peace was premature and not really favourable to Britain, but she could not help congratulating Napoleon on his skilful handling of a delicate situation. He, in his turn, was lavish in his praise of Britain's conciliatory attitude. The Peace of Paris was a tribute, he assured Lord Clarendon, to Anglo-French understanding.

Lord Palmerston was less euphoric. 'The fact is,' he announced bluntly, 'that in our alliance with France we are riding a runaway horse, and must always be on our guard: but a runaway horse is best kept in by a light hand and an easy snaffle.'

There was further cause for an affectionate exchange of letters between the sovereigns during that spring of 1856. On 16 March the Empress Eugenie gave birth to a son. It had been an extraordinarily difficult delivery. Victoria was told how the normally impassive Emperor's eyes had filled with tears on describing his wife's sufferings. Napoleon had been deeply touched, reported the Foreign Secretary, by the Queen's letters of congratulation. Indeed, the Emperor lost no time in thanking Victoria personally. His wish, he wrote with customary adroitness, was that his newly born son might resemble Victoria's favourite child, 'dear little Prince Arthur', and that the Prince

74

Imperial would develop the 'rare qualities' of the Queen's own children. 'I hope,' he continued, 'my son will inherit my feelings of sincere friendship for the Royal Family of England and of affectionate esteem for the great English nation.'

Of the many hopes of Napoleon III for his son, this was one of the few which were to be realized.

It was in the months following Napoleon's double triumph—the Peace of Paris and the birth of an heir—that the Anglo-French alliance began showing the first signs of strain.

Hardly had the Peace Treaty been signed than it appeared as though the Emperor was aiming at an alliance with the recent enemy, Russia. The possibility alarmed the British government considerably. Napoleon III's appointment of yet another of his illegitimate relations—the Count de Morny, natural son of the Emperor's mother, Queen Hortense, who had died some years before—as Ambassador to St Petersburg seemed to justify British apprehensions. Morny was known to be pro-Russian. The anti-Russian Princess Augusta of Prussia (wife of the future German Emperor) wrote Queen Victoria a highly confidential and exceedingly agitated letter in which she claimed that Morny was being sent to Russia for the express purpose of putting an end to the Anglo-French *entente*. The lavish reception, in Paris, of the Tsar's brother, the Grand Duke Constantine, did nothing to allay such suspicions. Time and again France seemed to be siding with Russia on various issues arising out of the Peace Treaty, and there was a rumour that the French and Russian Emperors planned to meet, *à la* Tilsit, in Stuttgart in September 1857.

Queen Victoria, uneasy at the turn which events seemed to be taking, wrote several letters to the Empress Eugenie on the subject. She was assured by the Empress that there was nothing to fear. Lord Clarendon, too, was able to put the Queen's mind at rest by reporting, on excellent authority, that 'the Emperor is as staunch as ever to the Alliance, and that he believes that all his personal interests as well as those of France are bound up with England'.

Victoria's first stirrings of disenchantment with the Emperor must have been further encouraged by rumours of his infatuation for a nineteen-year-old Italian beauty, the Countess de

Castiglione. The Countess was to be the first of the many mistresses who were to make the Empress Eugenie's married life so embarrassingly difficult. Lord Cowley was forever passing on tit-bits about Napoleon's latest affair. The Emperor once absented himself from a fête for a *whole* evening, reported the Ambassador, by spending it in 'certain dark walks' with the ravishing Countess. At a later stage, Napoleon would set out to visit her each evening between eleven and midnight; 'how long he stays,' wrote Cowley with a hint of regret, 'I cannot tell you'.

For Victoria, who had so recently been the object of the Emperor's admiring, if innocent, attentions, such information could not have been especially flattering.

Yet when the Countess de Castiglione spent some weeks in London during the 1857 season and was seen at a ball by the Queen, Victoria was all admiration. 'A sensation was caused by the appearance of the beautiful Countess Castiglione (the Emperor Napoleon's great admiration),' she noted, 'really a perfect beauty, tall, with a wonderful figure, shoulders, arms, a lovely face and features, and a sweet smile—very distinguée looking.'

The slightly deteriorating relations between the two sovereigns were hardly improved by a sudden request from the Emperor's cousin, the detestable Plon-Plon, that he be received at Osborne. Plon-Plon, who was planning a visit to Manchester in the summer of 1857, felt it only right and proper that he be allowed to pay his respects to the Queen. With this reasoning Victoria failed to agree. However, Lord Cowley was prepared to plead Plon-Plon's cause. One never knew what might happen in France, he argued; with the Prince Imperial still a babe in arms, it was quite possible that Plon-Plon might become the ruler overnight. Showing, as always, good sense, Victoria agreed to the visit but insisted that it be kept as short as possible. There would be nothing for someone like Plon-Plon to *do* at Osborne, she complained. Yet when Plon-Plon suggested that he simply land on the Isle of Wight, pay his respects and make off again, she would not hear of it. He must make a short stay.

In fact, the visit was something of a success. Plon-Plon obviously put himself out to be polite, and both Victoria and Albert were pleasantly surprised by his behaviour. The Queen was able to assure the Foreign Secretary that Prince Napoleon had been 'most courteous and civil and his conversation very sensible'.

Conscious of the slight slackening of those 'bonds of friendship' between France and Britain, Napoleon now decided that it was time for another meeting between the sovereigns. The French Ambassador, in conversation with Lord Clarendon, spoke of the Emperor's earnest desire to come to England on a private visit 'in order to *éclairer* his own ideas, to guide his policy, and to prevent by personal communication with the Queen, his Royal Highness and Her Majesty's Government the dissidences and *mésintelligences* which the Emperor thinks will arise from want of such communications'.

The Queen, Prince Albert assured Clarendon the following day, was quite ready to do whatever was best for the public interest. They would therefore be quite prepared to receive the Emperor, with or without the Empress, informally at Osborne. 'I have no doubt,' continued Albert in the same, somewhat lukewarm strain, 'that good will arise from a renewed intercourse with the Emperor; the only thing one may perhaps be afraid of is the possibility of his wishing to gain us over to his views with regard to a redistribution of Europe, and [he] may be disappointed at our not being able to assent to his plans and aspirations.'

It was therefore agreed that the Emperor and Empress should visit Osborne from 6 to 10 August 1857. As this was a period during which the Queen was normally in residence, as well as the 'best yachting season', it was imagined that the imperial visit would appear less *forcé*. In fact, the timing of the visit could not have been more opportune. A dispute in the Balkans, which seriously threatened the Anglo-French alliance, came to a head during August. The presence of the Emperor in England did a great deal towards solving it.

2

In contrast to the State Visit of 1855, this four-day stay at Osborne was extremely informal. Although the Queen's description of the house—that vast, Italianate pile—as 'poor, dear, modest, unpretentious Osborne', was a shade fanciful, the tone of the visit was decidedly domestic. With the exception of a dance held in a marquee and a couple of large dinner parties, there was nothing in the way of formal entertaining. The party amused themselves by walking or driving about the estate and by sight-seeing on the island. They explored Carisbrooke Castle, they sailed up the Solent, they trudged around Albert's model farm, they drove, in char-à-bancs, to Ryde. The Empress wore simple cambric and muslin dresses; the Emperor was never in uniform. A great deal of time was spent in the company of the royal children. 'They were much admired, including our dear little pet, Beatrice,' wrote the Queen. At that stage Princess Beatrice, the ninth and last of Victoria's children, was only four months old. The weather, for much of the time, was 'abominable', so that the Queen's Journal notes a succession of postponed outings and of scurryings-in out of the rain.

Yet the royalties seem to have enjoyed these unsophisticated amusements immensely. The island, despite grey skies, was looking its tranquil, summery best; the sea was alive with yachts assembled for the regatta. The Queen was able to make the satisfactory entry in her Journal that they were 'all very merry—none more so than the Empress'.

Indeed, it was Eugenie who seems to have made the strongest impression on Victoria during this visit. She was obviously enchanted by her. In contrast, the Queen seemed to have rather less to say about the Emperor. It was not that she was disappointed in his manner in any way; it was simply that the emphasis seemed to have shifted. Whereas before she could never find enough superlatives to do justice to his many qualities, she now seemed to be taking him for granted and to be discovering Eugenie's many fascinations. Napoleon's liaison with the Countess de Castiglione might have had something to do with this. So devoted to her own, unquestionably faithful husband, Victoria could not help but disapprove of the Emperor's infidelity. Yet it is unlikely that the Empress was suffering from anything worse than a loss of face; as Eugenie had never been deeply in love with her husband, her pride rather than her heart would have felt the hurt.

'Nothing escapes the dear Empress,' wrote the Queen, 'whatever it is seemed to interest and please her. She really is quite charming, so lovely, so graceful, so merry, so natural, clever and lively and full of conversation. . . .'

Thus it was Eugenie who was the darling of Osborne during that stay of 1857. Avoiding breakfast in the Queen's draughty rooms (Victoria always insisted on open windows, no matter how squally the weather) the Empress would come down later, dressed in one of those pastel colours which she was making so fashionable. While Napoleon, Albert and their attendant ministers met in conference, the two women would sit chatting together in what Victoria insisted on calling 'our simple rooms'. Their talk seems to have been as much political as domestic.

After luncheon, which was usually attended by the Queen's elder children, the two of them would venture out for a walk or to plant a tree. Often they were driven back indoors by the rain. More conversation would follow, and it was usually five o'clock before Napoleon and Albert emerged from their political talks. Then the entire party would set out for a drive, after which they would separate in order to dress for dinner. For this Eugenie might appear in a white organdie crinoline, embroidered all over with imperial violets and with more violets arranged in a wreath in her hair, to captivate the company with her looks and her vivacity.

'Much general conversation,' noted Victoria of one of these dinner parties, 'much enlivened by the Empress's cleverness and originality.'

Eugenie had undoubtedly matured. Whereas during the previous visit she had been a new and very nervous sovereign, unsure of her position and in awe of England's Queen, she was now beginning to gain more confidence. Indeed, from this time on, self-confidence was to be the one quality which Eugenie would never lack. Contrary to what a great many people assumed, the Empress was more than just a spirited beauty with a flair for fashion. She had married Napoleon with a very lofty conception of their joint obligation towards France, and the years were bringing an increasing awareness of her position and responsibilities. Far from being the frivolous *Reine Crinoline* of popular imagination, she was a woman of lively intelligence and strong political interests. During the last few years her gradual involvement in affairs of State had increased her self-assurance; this, in turn, had given her additional poise. She was readier to express her opinions now; readier to lead or take over the conversation. As yet this confidence was in no way offensive; it merely gave her an air of authority.

The Queen was quick to notice the change. The adjectives with which she had described Eugenie during the first visit—modest, gentle and nervous—now gave way to such words as clever, lively and accomplished. She pronounced the Empress to be 'very well-informed and read, much more serious than people give her credit for—understanding all the questions of the day'. Eugenie's opinions always made very good sense; Napoleon, thought the Queen, would do well to follow her advice. Victoria went on to say that Albert 'is excessively fond of her, and I think few, if any Princess has pleased him as much'.

This might, indeed, have been one of the reasons for Victoria's championship of Eugenie. Albert had never really trusted Napoleon and, now that minor disagreements had broken out between their two countries, he was beginning to trust him even less. Of Eugenie, on the other hand, he was very fond and he quite often found himself in accord with her views. Like Albert, Eugenie disapproved of the rumoured Franco-Russian rapprochement and did not really share her husband's faith in the theory of 'completed nationalities'. Her outlook was more conservative, her manner less devious than his. Albert, reported Victoria to King Leopold, was the Empress's 'great ally'. And as Victoria usually looked to her husband for guidance, her attitude towards the imperial couple was beginning to echo his.

When the visit was over and the Queen was answering Napoleon's letter of thanks, she tactfully but firmly advised him to take notice of his wife's opinions. 'In a position so isolated as ours,' she wrote, 'we can find no greater consolation, no support more sure, than the sympathy and counsel of him or her who is called to share our lot in life, and the dear Empress, with her generous impulses, is your guardian angel, as the Prince is my true friend.'

Even more ardent than Victoria's championship of the Empress was that of Vicky, the sixteen-year-old Princess Royal.

Since last meeting the imperial couple in Paris in 1855, Vicky had become engaged to Prince Frederick Wilhelm of Prussia. The engagement seems to have led to no corresponding diminution of her adoration for the Empress. She could hardly bear to be out of her company. 'She is my *beau idéal* of a woman and I am quite enchanted with her,' she gushed. The Empress had asked Vicky to plait her a hat; 'I am busy at it now,' announced the enraptured girl; 'it gives me great pleasure to be able to do something for her and to think of her whilst doing it.' If her heart had not already been carried off, admitted Vicky to her fiancé, the Empress Eugenie would certainly have stolen it.

What the amiable Fritz's views were on having the Empress of the French as a rival one does not know.

Eugenie was all understanding. She gave Vicky some much needed advice on the subject of clothes. 'I'm telling you this because I want you to sparkle in Berlin,' she explained. She hoped that Vicky's marriage would be a happy one. 'You will come and see us, won't you?' she asked. 'I love to see a happy woman.'

But Vicky was almost more concerned with Eugenie's future than her own. 'What will be her fate! God grant that it may be a happy one,' she exclaimed. Unsuspected by the Princess, Eugenie's unhappy fate was to be closely bound up with her own.

3

The talks between Napoleon and Albert were going surprisingly well. With Lords Palmerston and Clarendon representing Britain and Counts de Persigny and Walewski supporting the Emperor, the difficulties were sorted out fairly satisfactorily. 'Good things were done, and bad ones averted at Osborne,' noted Lord Clarendon afterwards. 'A very black cloud hung over the alliance when the Emperor came here; but all was sunshine before he departed.'

There were two main problems under discussion. One was the trouble in the Balkans and the other Napoleon III's perennial—

the 1815 Treaty. The first was a very complicated issue. It concerned two little Balkan countries, once provinces of Turkey, which France was now eager to unite under a foreign prince. As the inhabitants of these two principalities (which were eventually to form Rumania) were Latins, Napoleon was especially interested in their future. Their union was opposed by Britain, who suspected that Russia was only too anxious to turn the proposed state into a satellite for use against Turkey.

Elections on the question of unification had been held in one of the principalities, and the result had been against it. France, suspecting trickery on the part of Turkey, had demanded that the election results be annulled. In this she was backed up by Russia and opposed by Britain.

This was how matters stood when the Emperor visited Osborne. After several long discussions, a compromise was reached. To satisfy French prestige, the election results *would* be annulled, but new elections would be held immediately after. When these results—which, presumably, would also be against union—were announced, the matter would be dropped and a commercial treaty between the two countries inaugurated. This way Napoleon would achieve union of a sort (although he begged Albert not to let the full story leak out, as 'the honour of France' might suffer) and everyone expressed satisfaction.

'All so thankful he had come, which has prevented further mischief,' was Victoria's blunt comment on Napoleon's contribution to the solution.

On the matter of the 1815 Treaty it was more difficult to effect a compromise. Napoleon complained that Britain always turned a deaf ear when France brought up the question of a revision of the treaties; indeed, Palmerston tended to be downright rude on occasion. Albert explained that the treaties, however inadequate they might be, had at least given Europe forty years of peace after twenty-five of war. Any attempt to revise them now might result in renewed bloodshed. Napoleon assured him that he had no wish to cause any upheaval but that there were some changes which could be made with safety. However, Albert remained firm and the Emperor did not press things too far. To him Britain's friendship was more valuable than any revision of treaties. Might it not be better, mused

Napoleon, if he turned his attention away from Europe and concentrated on Africa? He might make the Mediterranean, if not actually '*un lac français*', as Napoleon I had wished, '*un lac européen*', with Spain, Sardinia, Austria, England and France each helping themselves to a country on the North African coast. Such a project might well provide France with an outlet for her 'turbulent spirits', while rendering 'great benefit to the world'.

Such high-handed proposals must have made Albert's blood run cold. But he listened politely and felt confirmed in his opinion of the Emperor. However, he did speak up to suggest that Napoleon begin to delegate some of his powers by appointing a Prime Minister. With this Napoleon agreed; but where, he asked with some justification, would one find the man?

Although these discussions were all somewhat inconclusive, they were at least amiable; the Anglo-French *entente* seemed as secure as ever. 'All, Persigny and the Ministers, so pleased at the result of the visit, including Lord Palmerston, who had been very much *aigri*,' noted a relieved Queen Victoria. Prince Albert lost no time in penning a lengthy memorandum on the talks, a copy of which he dictated to the Princess Royal as a lesson in political science.

Lord Palmerston, complimenting the Queen on Prince Albert's contribution towards the satisfactory outcome, explained that 'the Prince can say many things we cannot'.

'Very naturally,' was Victoria's prompt rejoinder.

4

So they parted on the best of terms. Leave-taking was preceded by the usual exchange of gifts and by the usual floods of tears in the royal nursery. The usual compliments ('*les plus charmants enfants*') led to Victoria's usual assertion that all the children were devoted to the imperial couple. 'They quite adore the Empress, and would do anything for her,' she declared. There were the usual promises to see each other again very soon. The band struck up *Partant pour la Syrie*, which always made Victoria feel sad, and everyone drove down to the pier. Victoria,

Albert, their three eldest children and their Court boarded the imperial yacht, *La Reine Hortense,* and inspected it thoroughly. 'Not large or commodious,' was Victoria's verdict. Having said their last farewells, they were rowed back to the shore. With the French sailors shouting *'Vive la Reine d'Angleterre'* and the Empress waving her white handkerchief again and again, the imperial yacht steamed away. The royal party returned to Osborne, feeling 'rather *désoeuvrée'.*

'The Emperor and Empress so kind and civil, and so thoroughly pleasant and amiable,' noted Victoria. 'I know of no royalties who are less *gênant.'*

Although not as ecstatic as previously about the Emperor, Victoria was still well enough pleased with him. Lord Clarendon, commenting on the letter of thanks which Napoleon wrote to the Queen on his return, declared it to be 'about the best expressed and gentlemanlike letter I have ever read'.

Part Two
'The sinister designs of our neighbour'

CHAPTER SEVEN

The Disenchantment

1

On the night of 14 January 1858, Queen Victoria, recently arrived at Buckingham Palace to welcome the first of the guests for the Princess Royal's wedding, heard some startling news from Paris. The Emperor and Empress of the French had narrowly escaped assassination. Prince Albert's brother, Duke Ernest of Saxe-Coburg, arriving direct from the French capital the following day, was able to give her an eye-witness account of the horrifying event. The imperial couple had been driving in state to the opera when three bombs had been flung at their carriage. Although the explosions had killed ten people and wounded over a hundred others, the Emperor and Empress had escaped serious injury. There were slight cuts on their faces from splintering glass and Eugenie's white dress had been splattered with blood. Her calm, Duke Ernest told the Queen, had been exceptional. 'Don't bother about us,' she had said quietly to the frantic police, 'such things are our profession. Look after the wounded.' They had entered the opera house to be given a wild ovation by the audience and had remained in their box, noted the admiring Victoria, 'through the whole performance'.

The Queen immediately telegraphed her congratulations on their miraculous escape and the Empress answered by declaring that as the Emperor and herself were the only ones in the carriage to escape injury, 'the hand of Providence' had made itself 'clearly felt'.

Napoleon's reply was more down-to-earth. 'In the first flush of excitement,' he wrote, 'the French are determined to find accomplices everywhere. I find it hard to resist the demands for extreme measures which I am asked to take. . . .'

87

Not only was he finding it hard to resist such demands, he was finding it all but impossible. And the incident, serious enough in itself, was to spark off a series of even more disastrous events which would end by straining the English alliance to the limits.

When the arrests were made it was discovered that the bomb throwers, led by an Italian by the name of Orsini, had all come from England. The plot had been hatched in London and the bombs made in Birmingham. Thus, despite the fact that the reasons for the attack were all tied up with a campaign for the liberation of Italy from foreign rule, it was against England that the wrath of France was chiefly directed. The Emperor's half-brother, the Count de Morny, back from Russia and now President of the Chamber of Deputies, railed publicly against the refuge given by England to this 'nest of vipers'. In fiery addresses of congratulation to Napoleon on his escape (many of which were published in the official *Moniteur*) army officers openly insulted the British government for granting political asylum to the Empire's enemies.

'I could not believe,' commented Charles Greville dryly, 'that those hot and enthusiastic expressions were to be taken entirely as proofs of a passionate attachment to the Emperor's person, but that these were outbreaks of that hatred of England which sometimes slumbered but never died.'

The feeling was reciprocal. Queen Victoria reported that the British were 'very indignant here at the conduct of the French officers, and at the offensive insinuations against this country. . . .'

While, in France, Napoleon was coerced into passing harsh legislation in the cause of public safety, from England he asked for an assurance that political refugees would be treated with more strictness in future. To this Palmerston acquiesced by introducing a bill to make conspiracy to murder a felony. Parliament, all a-flame with national pride, refused to be dictated to by France and the government was forced to resign. Not for the first time had Lord Palmerston's championing of Napoleon III landed him in hot water. He was succeeded by Lord Derby, heading a short-lived Tory government.

To add further insult to injury, Dr Bernard, a London-based French refugee who had been arrested for his complicity in the

Orsini bomb-throwing plot, was acquitted by a British jury, despite the judge's obvious belief that he was guilty. This blatant partisanship infuriated the French and upset both the Emperor and the Empress considerably. Queen Victoria herself was indignant at the jury's lack of impartiality. Dr Bernard's 'unfortunate acquittal', she declared to Lord Cowley, was entirely due to 'the cowardice of the Jury and the shameful behaviour of the public'.

With the fall of Palmerston's ministry things quietened down a little. Lord Malmesbury, the new Foreign Secretary, was able to assure the Queen that 'much of the excitement that prevailed on the *other* side of the water is subsiding . . . in this country, if our differences with France are settled, it is probable that the popular jealousy of foreign interference will be killed; but at least for some time it will show foreign Courts how dangerous it is *even to criticise* our *domestic* Institutions'. A few days later Disraeli, now Chancellor of the Exchequer, reported that his announcement in the House, about the 'painful misconceptions' between England and France having terminated in an honourable and friendly spirit, had met with cheers.

But the Orsini affair had yet more momentous results than this Anglo-French rift. What it did was to re-open the whole Italian question.

For many years Italy had been controlled by several reactionary powers—the Bourbons of Naples in the south, the Papacy in the centre and the Austrians in the north. And for years nationally minded Italians had worked for the liberation of their country. In the 1820s a secret society known as the Carbonari had dedicated itself to the regeneration of Italy; amongst its sympathizers had been the young Louis Napoleon. His association with the movement had been short-lived but it had made an indelible impression on him; the liberation of Italy was something which had never ceased to interest him personally. In fact, Queen Victoria seems to have been under the impression that the Emperor was still under oath to this secret society. On this point Napoleon's life-long friend Lord Malmesbury was able to put her mind at rest: as young men they had both been 'under the influence of those romantic feelings which the former history and the present degradation of Italy may naturally inspire even at a more advanced time of life', wrote Malmesbury, but he denied that Napoleon had associated with any oath-taking assassins.

By now, of course, Napoleon III's interest in Italy was as much political as romantic. A successful campaign against the Austrians in northern Italy would be very much part of the Bonaparte legend. Had it not been in Italy that Napoleon I had won his first laurels? It would fit in, too, with the Emperor's self-appointed role as champion of aspiring nationalists. 'Tell them,' he had once said to someone who asked what he intended doing for the Italians, 'that my name is Bonaparte, and that I feel the responsibility that name implies. Italy is dear to me, as dear almost as France; but my duties to France come first, and I must watch for an opportunity.'

And when Orsini, that romantic Italian patriot, threw his bombs at the Emperor's carriage that January evening, the opportunity occurred. For what the attempted assassination did was to remind Napoleon of his duty towards Italy. Although Orsini was sentenced to death, Napoleon III was committed to liberate Italy.

It was going to be a hazardous undertaking. For one thing, the Emperor would have to confine his campaign to the northern, Austrian provinces; on no account could a Catholic sovereign afford to attack the Papal States. For another, he would have to try to maintain, if not actually the approval, at least the friendship of Britain. Had Palmerston's Liberal government still been in power, it might have been easier, for Palmerston was not unsympathetic towards the Italian cause. With the Conservatives in office, Napoleon would have to tread more warily.

He began by recalling Persigny and appointing Marshal Pélissier, Duke de Malakoff, as French Ambassador to the Court of St James's. As Pélissier, for all his merry corpulence, was the Second Empire's most distinguished soldier and Britain's old ally in the Crimea, Queen Victoria considered the appointment very gratifying. 'It was *"really"* a compliment to the Army and the Alliance,' she declared.

Lord Cowley was somewhat more irreverent in his opinion. 'If Pélissier goes to London,' he wrote, 'he will make love to every woman he comes across—the Queen included. He will squeeze H.M.'s hand if she gives him the opportunity, kiss all the Royal children, and make serious havoc among the Maids of Honour. . . .'

Lest Pélissier's rotund charms prove inadequate for the maintaining of Queen Victoria's friendship, Napoleon decided to back them up with his own more subtle ones. He invited Victoria and Albert to visit him at Cherbourg, in August 1858.

2

The Cherbourg Fêtes, to which Napoleon III had invited Victoria and Albert as guests of honour, were to be a week-long celebration to mark, among other things, the inauguration of a vast new dock. The ambitious naval works at Cherbourg had been likened, by the Emperor, to 'the marvels of ancient Egypt'. It was a curious comparison, but one which afforded *Punch* the opportunity of publishing a cartoon of a sphinx, with the face of Napoleon III, rising out of the sea.

The proposed royal visit caused some grumblings in an England still resentful of recent French insults. Such grumblings King Leopold of the Belgians advised Queen Victoria to ignore. She should remain on good terms with the Emperor and, instead of worrying about increased French naval activity, concentrate on building up her own fleet.

That the Queen was concerned about French naval strength there was no question. Almost exactly a year before, in August 1857, soon after the imperial visit to Osborne, she and Albert had paid an unofficial, two-day visit to Cherbourg in the royal yacht. They had been deeply disturbed by what they had seen. The fortifications were alarming. 'Cherbourg is a gigantic works that gives one grave cause for reflection,' the unhappy Prince Albert had written to Baron Stockmar. 'The works at Alderney by way of counter-defence look childish.' The royal couple had returned to England determined to improve British defences.

Now, a day or two before this second visit to Cherbourg, Queen Victoria wrote a very strong letter to Lord Derby, impressing upon him the importance of building up Britain's sea power. What was required was 'action, and immediate action'. The plan recently put forward by the Surveyor of the Navy she dismissed as far too moderate and judicious. It was imperative that the cabinet spend more money on the building of a battle fleet. 'Time is most precious under these circumstances!' she declared.

In this troubled state of mind then, did Victoria and Albert, with the Prince of Wales, cross the Channel for a two-day visit to Cherbourg in August 1858. Though cordial enough on the surface, the meeting lacked the warmth of the previous ones. On the first evening, while the *Victoria and Albert* lay at anchor, a splendid barge, canopied in green velvet and crowned by a golden eagle, brought the Emperor and Empress on an unofficial, hour-long visit to their royal guests. The call was not a great success. Victoria found Napoleon *'boutonné* and silent', Albert was conscious of a change in his attitude, and even the sympathetic Lord Malmesbury could find nothing better to say than that the Emperor was friendly 'in his manner'. The imperial couple were upset by certain attacks made on them by the London *Times* (Eugenie had come in for some especially strong criticism) and it was with difficulty that the freedom of the British Press was explained to them. It was noticed that the Queen made a point of not kissing the young Madame Walewska, who was known to have replaced the Countess de Castiglione in the Emperor's fickle affections. In many more ways than one, it seemed, was the third Napoleon emulating the first. This latest *affaire* may have been one of the reasons why Prince Albert considered Eugenie to be looking 'out of health'.

The rather strained visit over, Victoria could hardly wait to get back to reading 'that most interesting book, *Jane Eyre*'.

Early the following morning the Queen was on deck. For over an hour she sat beneath the awning, busily sketching the animated scene before her. On landing, the royal party lunched with their hosts at the Préfecture and then toured the environs of the port. 'The nice caps of the *paysannes* were very numerous, transcendently white and they looked very pretty and picturesque,' noted the Queen. It was not, however, the quaintness of the national dress that most deeply impressed her. It was the all too apparent evidence of French naval might. 'Cannons, cannons, cannons, wherever you turned,' wrote the correspondent of *The Times*. 'They poured upon you from every corner, they commanded every turning . . . one could not help wondering what in the name of wonder they were meant to attack or defend.' On this score, Prince Albert, at least, had very little doubt. The theory put forward by one British journal, that Napoleon III would never have shown Queen Victoria these warlike preparations had he intended to use them against her country, afforded cold comfort. These massive fortifications, the enormous dock yards, this vast French fleet riding at anchor in the bay, disturbed the royal visitors considerably. 'It will be the first time in her [Britain's] history that she will find herself in an absolute minority of ships on the sea!' wailed the Queen.

When Victoria and Albert returned to their yacht later that afternoon, it was they who were *boutonné* and silent.

That evening the royal couple dined as the Emperor's guests aboard *La Bretagne*. The ship, reports one of the Queen's ladies, was 'magnificently furnished with crimson silk and filled with flowers, and dinner was laid on the second deck *à soixante couverts'*. But even here there seems to have been a disturbing emphasis on the arts of war. All the decorations, noted one of the English guests, were made of firearms: 'chandeliers of pistols etc—most capitally done'.

After dinner Napoleon, rising to propose the Queen's health, made a reassuring little speech about the Anglo-French alliance. 'I am happy to show the sentiments we entertain towards them. Indeed, facts speak for themselves, and they prove that hostile passions, aided by a few unfortunate incidents, did not succeed in altering either the friendship which exists between the two Crowns, or the desire of the two nations to remain at peace.'

It was encouraging, but defensive.

To this speech, Albert was obliged to answer. The Queen, knowing how much the Prince loathed public speaking, afterwards wrote of 'the dreadful moment for my dear husband, which was terrible to me, and which I should never wish to go through again. . . . I sat shaking, with my eyes *cloués sur la table.*'

She need not have felt so anguished. The Prince acquitted himself very well. Afterwards the entire party went on deck to watch a display of fireworks. The effect was said to have been breathtaking. Not only was the night sky ablaze with cascades of colour, but all the ships in the bay were brilliantly illuminated with the *Victoria and Albert* picked out in red, white and blue. The *pièce de résistance* was supplied by the British. When the Emperor's canopied barge, in which he had delivered the Queen to her yacht at the conclusion of the display, returned to the shore, an electric light from the royal yacht was trained on to it. This light, known as the Honourable Major Fitzmaurice's Life Light, followed Napoleon's barge all the way back, 'the light shining only on the barge, whilst all around remained in darkness'.

Lord Malmesbury pronounced the effect 'beautiful', but the Emperor's reaction to having to sit in a merciless blaze of electric light for the entire slow progress back to the shore is not known.

The following morning Napoleon boarded the *Victoria and Albert* to take his leave. The two sovereigns parted on friendly, if slightly preoccupied, terms. Napoleon returned to partake in various ceremonies connected with the Fêtes, while Victoria sailed back to England to urge her sluggish cabinet to spend more money on defence.

'The war preparations in the French Marine are immense! Ours despicable!' reported Prince Albert to the Duchess of Kent. 'Our Ministers use fine phrases, but they do nothing. My blood boils within me.'

3

Some four months later, on 10 December 1858, Lord Malmesbury wrote to assure Queen Victoria that, contrary to persistent rumours, Napoleon III was not contemplating a war in Italy. The Emperor, he told her, had just contradicted such a report officially. 'Besides this,' added his Lordship, 'Your Majesty may be assured that no warlike preparations are making in France, such as must precede such a plan as an Italian war.'

The Emperor had completely hoodwinked his old friend. On the very day that Malmesbury was writing to the Queen, Napoleon was coming to a secret arrangement with King Victor Emmanuel of Sardinia. The French and Sardinian monarchs agreed that their combined armies would drive the Austrians out of northern Italy. The campaign would be followed by the conversion of Italy into a confederation. This would be made up of a Kingdom of Northern Italy, a Kingdom of Central Italy and the Kingdom of Naples—all presided over by the Pope in Rome. Sardinia would cede Savoy and Nice to France and, as though to set the seal on the arrangement, the Emperor's cousin Plon-Plon would marry King Victor Emmanuel's daughter, Clotilde. That Plon-Plon was a fat, dissolute, thirty-six-year-old agnostic and Clotilde a naïve and deeply religious sixteen-year-old seems not to have especially bothered either Napoleon III or Victor Emmanuel. The ill-assorted pair were duly married in January 1859. The ceremony seemed to confirm suspicions of some secret Franco-Sardinian pact against Austria.

By now Queen Victoria was feeling extremely apprehensive about Napoleon's plans. 'I really *hope* that there is no *real* desire for war in the Emperor's mind,' she wrote to King Leopold; 'we have also explained to him strongly how *entirely* he would *alienate* us from him if there was any *attempt* to *disturb standing and binding treaties.*'

It was a vain hope. As the year 1859 unfolded and Napoleon—despite all protestations to the contrary—prepared for war, so did Victoria become more and more agitated. Encouraged by Prince Albert, she saw the rumoured campaign in northern Italy as the start of a general European conflagration; it was going to be like the wars of the first Napoleon all over again. Napoleon III would never rest until he had resettled the map of Europe to his satisfaction. Her Journal developed into a tirade against French iniquity; her letters became increasingly emphatic. With a wealth of underlinings she wrote off to Brussels declaring that 'the feeling against the *Emperor here* is *very strong*. I think *yet* that if *Austria* is *strong* and well *prepared* and *Germany strong* and *well inclined* towards *us* (as *Prussia certainly* is) France will *not* be so eager to attempt what I *firmly* believe would *end* in the *Emperor's downfall.*'

King Leopold lost no time in backing up his niece's views. 'Heaven knows what dance our Emperor *Napoléon Troisieme de nom* will lead us. . . . I fear he is determined on that Italian War.'

Victoria wrote to Napoleon himself, reminding him that rarely had any man such an opportunity of keeping the peace of Europe as did he, and begging him to do his best to calm international anxieties.

It was all to no purpose. In the spring of 1859 Napoleon marched his armies into northern Italy, leaving Eugenie behind as Regent. She, only too conscious of British hostility (Lord Cowley reported her as being very unhappy about the war), wrote Queen Victoria an anxious letter. The Emperor, she assured the Queen, was doing his best to localize the campaign so as to avoid a general war; would Victoria, and still more Prince Albert, do their utmost to ensure that Prussia did not come to the assistance of Austria and so spread the conflict?

Victoria's reply was concise. She, as a constitutional sovereign, could not do very much; Napoleon, as an autocratic one, was free to do whatever he liked. It was therefore up to him to confine the war to within Sardinian territory; any invasion of Austrian possessions would quite naturally lead to Prussia's wishing to help her fellow Germans.

This was no idle threat on Victoria's part. The Prussians were indeed beginning to think in terms of coming to the aid of Austria. After Napoleon's victory over the Austrians at Magenta on 4 June, Prussia mobilized. After his triumph at Solferino, three weeks later, she began concentrating troops on the Rhine. Even Vicky, now Princess Frederick Wilhelm of Prussia, and so recently the Empress Eugenie's ardent admirer, could hardly contain her anger. She wished she were a man, she exclaimed in her highly emotional fashion, so that she might take up arms against the wicked French. With this bellicose attitude her father, Prince Albert, was in complete accord. He was itching, he claimed, to strike a blow at France. Even Queen Victoria informed her Prime Minister that she resented the impression given, in a speech written for her to deliver at the opening of Parliament, that Britain would remain neutral 'at any price'.

It was as well that Britain's attitude towards the war depended more on Lord Derby and his government than it did on Queen Victoria and her relations.

To a considerable extent, it was the fear of a Prussian attack that prompted Napoleon III to surprise the world by opening peace negotiations with Austria a mere two months after the start of the campaign. Things, not only on the Rhine, but in Italy itself, could so easily get out of hand. Already various ebullient Italian states were beginning to rise against the Pope. Thus on 11 July 1859, at Villafranca, the Emperors of France and Austria agreed to end the war.

In spite of the fact that Napoleon had not, as promised, liberated all northern Italy, and that his Sardinian allies had lost faith in him, he returned to Paris a hero. 'The Emperor Napoleon,' wrote Victoria sourly two days after the armistice, 'by his military successes, and great apparent moderation or prudence immediately after them, has created for himself a most formidable position of strength in Europe.' She had no doubt that Prussia would be his next victim. The time would come, she warned her cabinet, 'for us either to obey or to fight him with terrible odds against us'.

On 15 August 1859—the anniversary of the birthday of Napoleon I—Napoleon III reviewed the troops lately returned from Italy. With the little Prince Imperial on his saddle-bow before him, the statue of his illustrious uncle crowning the Vendôme column behind and the shouts of '*Vive l'Empereur!*' ringing in his ears, he watched line after line of his superbly uniformed soldiers swing by. The ceremony marked, in many ways, the zenith of his career.

Victoria's customary end-of-the-year letter to the Emperor was distinctly cool.

'The year which has just passed has been stormy and painful and has made many hearts suffer. I pray God that the one upon which we are entering will permit us to see accomplished the work of peace-making with all its benefits for the tranquillity and progress of the world. It still remains to reconcile many divergent opinions and apparently opposed interests; but with the aid of Heaven and a firm resolve to wish only the good of those whose destiny we have to rule, we need not despair. . . .'

4

The end of the Italian war brought little improvement in the relations between England and France. Indeed, now that British suspicions against Napoleon III had been aroused, they remained almost pathological. His annexation of Savoy and Nice as a reward for his campaign of liberation was strongly resented. King Leopold, in a characteristically ponderous *bon mot*, referred to the Emperor as '*Annex*ander', and the annexation was hotly debated in the House of Commons. Napoleon, proving no less resentful of British interference than did Britain of Napoleon's conduct, tackled Lord Cowley on the subject. Forsaking his habitual calm, the Emperor claimed that he found the British attitude inexplicable. 'I have done all in my power to keep on the best terms with her; but I am at my wit's end,' he grumbled. 'What has England to do with Savoy?'

The fall of Lord Derby's Conservative administration in mid-1859 had brought the irrepressible Lord Palmerston, with his anti-Austrian and pro-Italian sympathies, to the helm once more, and the Court greatly feared the attitude that he and his Foreign Secretary, Lord John Russell (Albert referred to the two of them as 'the old Italian masters'), were likely to take towards Napoleon III. But by now even Palmerston was disenchanted. 'Till lately, I had strong confidence in the fair intentions of Napoleon towards England,' he wrote, 'but of late I have begun to feel great distrust and to suspect that his formerly expressed intention of avenging Waterloo has only lain dormant, and not died away.'

Prince Albert, who needed no convincing on this score, was in a state of acute anxiety. He was worrying, and working, himself to death. 'At the Court of Napoleon,' he complained, 'they play, they make love, enjoy themselves, dream, and between sleeping and waking make decisions on matters of the greatest importance, *et la question ne s'examine qu'après* when things have happened.'

The Prince would not rest until he had goaded the government into overhauling Britain's somewhat ramshackle defence system. He had once covered twenty manuscript sheets in his immaculate handwriting on this very subject; now he had the long-delayed satisfaction of seeing his schemes materialize. In a frenzy of anti-French sentiment the Volunteer movement sprang suddenly into life. By the summer of 1860, over 130,000 men had been enrolled. In August over twenty thousand volunteers paraded before the Queen in Hyde Park. The gratified Victoria hoped that this show of public enthusiasm would check the 'sinister designs of our neighbour'.

Her concern seemed justified when, on the outbreak of some trouble in Syria, Napoleon III proposed landing French troops there to restore order. The Levant being one of Britain's happy hunting grounds, and an international commission having agreed to the landing of French troops, Britain insisted that they remain for a limited period only. To this Napoleon, rather belatedly, acquiesced. Conscious of British ill-will over his annexations of Savoy and Nice and eager to avoid the accusation of colonial designs, he thought it best to play safe.

But the damage, as far as Queen Victoria was concerned, had already been done. 'Really it is too bad,' she exploded in exasperation at this further piece of Napoleonic meddling. 'No country, no human being would ever dream of *disturbing* or *attacking* France; everyone would be glad to see her prosperous; but *she* must needs disturb every quarter of the globe and try to make mischief and set everyone by the ears; and of course, it will end some day in a *regular crusade* against the *universal disturber* of the world. It is really monstrous!'

The disenchantment was complete.

CHAPTER EIGHT

'Grief and anxiety'

1

In spite of all these troubles, there were still moments when the dying embers of the *entente* flared into life.

Throughout the second half of the decade, the British and French had been allies in a somewhat casual war in the Far East. In 1859 their combined fleet was attacked by the Chinese at Taku and forced to retire. Such insolence on the part of China called for a show of force and during the following year an Anglo-French expedition landed and advanced on Peking. Here, with cheerful philistinism, they sacked the magnificent Summer Palace, looting and destroying property to the value of over two million pounds. In a final display of barbarism, they razed this symbol of centuries-old civilization to the ground. Some of the porcelain salvaged by the French troops was sent home, where it was rapturously accepted by the Empress and arranged in a suite of rooms at Fontainebleau.

Queen Victoria, writing to Napoleon on this *'glorieux succès'* of their combined armies, hoped that the victory would benefit both the allies and *'ce peuple bizarre'*, who had now been forced into opening relations with the rest of the world. Neither sovereign seemed to have remembered Napoleon I's advice about letting China sleep; the world, he had warned, would be sorry when she woke.

Another, less reprehensible link between the two countries was forged by the signing, on 23 January 1860, of a commercial treaty. For many years there had been talk of an Anglo-French tariff agreement; now, largely due to the efforts of Richard Cobden, the scheme was realized. This move towards a system of Free Trade was welcomed by many on both sides of the Channel, for reasons as much political as economic. Cobden considered Free Trade to be 'God's own method of producing an *entente cordiale*' and he always felt that Napoleon's reasons for giving it his whole-hearted support were 'nine-tenths political rather than politico-economical'.

Victoria and Albert were not quite so enthusiastic about the treaty. The Queen feared that it might hold up defence preparations and the Prince that it would damp down the militancy of the British towards the French. However, when Lord Palmerston urged the Queen to bestow some sort of honour on Cobden as a reward for his efforts, she proved quite amenable. She offered to make him either a Privy Councillor or a baronet. Cobden declined both honours.

The two countries were militarily allied once more during this period. This was in the early days of the ill-starred Mexican adventure.

By the 1860s the Republic of Mexico was in a sorry state. As this was a commonplace enough situation for a Latin American country, it might, in the ordinary way, have been ignored by European Powers had Mexico not owed some of them a considerable sum of money. When Benito Juarez, the new liberal and anti-clerical President of the Republic, froze the interest due to his country's creditors—Spain, France and England—those Powers took immediate action. The Treaty of London was signed wherein the three countries resolved to protect their national interests. Ships carrying Spanish, French and British troops sailed for Mexico. Dropping anchor off Vera Cruz, they made ready to teach the wayward Mexicans a lesson.

It soon became apparent, however, that France had more than this in mind. She was obviously not going to be content with a mere bullying of the Mexican government into paying its debts. Whereas neither Britain nor Spain was anxious to meddle in the political affairs of Mexico, it seemed that France was prepared not only to meddle, but to refashion the entire Mexican state. Napoleon III had long dreamed of a European sphere of influence in Central America and, egged on by Eugenie, with her more tangible scheme of a Catholic Empire in Mexico, he decided to oust Juarez and establish a monarchy. While Napoleon's motives for this undertaking were mainly practical,

Eugenie's were more romantic: *'l'accomplissement d'une très haute pensée politique et civilisatrice'* was how she put it. At this stage Britain and Spain, realizing that this was going to develop into something more than a mere showing of the flag, withdrew from the adventure.

But France was committed to it. The superior French troops threw back the Republican forces and Napoleon coerced Maximilian, brother of the Emperor Franz Josef of Austria, to accept the Mexican crown. As the new Emperor Maximilian was married to Queen Victoria's cousin—her Uncle Leopold's only daughter, Charlotte—Napoleon no doubt felt that he was doing both Hapsburgs and Coburgs a good turn.

'The undertaking is a perilous one,' wrote the gratified King Leopold to his niece, 'but if it succeeds it will be one of the greatest and most useful of our time ... dear Charlotte is not opposed to it; she is very venturesome and would go with Max to the end of the world; she will be of the greatest use to him; and, if success there is to be, much will be owing to her. That in England they appreciate the importance of this undertaking is best shown by the great rise in Mexican funds. . . .'

But it needed more than a rise in funds to save the affair from disaster. Political troubles at home forced Napoleon to withdraw his protecting troops from Mexico, leaving Maximilian and Charlotte to face Juarez alone. Charlotte returned to Europe to beg support from Napoleon and while she was away Maximilian was captured by the rebels and executed. Poor Charlotte went out of her mind. 'Too horrid!' exclaimed Victoria on hearing the news. 'Poor dear unhappy Charlotte bereft of her reason, and her husband killed. What a shocking end to a luckless undertaking, which I did all I could to prevent, and which dearest Albert was so much against. . . .'

2

On 16 November 1860, with Queen Victoria in residence at Windsor, she was astonished to hear that the Empress Eugenie had arrived in England two days before. The Empress was about to pay a visit, *incognita*, to Scotland. The reasons for this sudden expedition were obscure. Everyone had a different explanation. Some said that the recent death of Eugenie's adored sister Paca, Duchess of Alba, had left her desolate and in need of a change. Others that she had quarrelled with the Emperor about his latest love affair, or the Pope, or the arrangements for Paca's funeral. King Leopold reported that Eugenie was coughing badly and added, with characteristic malice, that he had 'never heard Scotland recommended for Winter excursions'. The Queen herself had heard that Eugenie was being hounded by 'the Priests', who were warning her that the Prince Imperial would die if the Emperor continued to champion the Italian nationalists against the Pope.

The truth was that the Empress badly needed a change of scene. Her sister's death, and the manner in which she heard of it, had been a heartbreaking experience. The Emperor and Empress had been on a State Visit to Algeria when Paca died; Napoleon, appreciating the impetuosity of Eugenie's nature, had thought it best to withold the news until the visit was over. The Empress had felt this double blow—her sister's death and what she looked upon as her husband's duplicity—very keenly. 'She seems to have been a good deal *choquée* that she had been dancing in Africa when that poor sister was dying,' wrote King Leopold. She consequently decided that she must get away from Paris for a few weeks.

She arrived in London on 14 November and took a cab to Claridge's Hotel, where she stayed for four days. On the day before she left for Scotland, she wrote a note to Queen Victoria, telling her of her plans and hoping that she would be able to see her on her return to London. She remained in Scotland for a couple of weeks, during which time she consulted a doctor (he pronounced her to be in excellent condition and advised her to avoid French doctors), made some reassuring statements about the Anglo-French alliance and ignored a jibe, on the part of the London *Times*, to the effect that newly annexed Nice might have proved more appropriate than Scotland. The Empress arrived back at Claridge's on 2 December.

Two days later she visited the Queen at Windsor. The slightly bemused Victoria had been anxious to know whether the Empress expected to be received in state or in private. She was assured that Eugenie would prefer the visit to be as informal as possible. It was a sad meeting. In pouring rain the Empress drove with Prince Albert from Windsor station to the castle. She was dressed in deep mourning and looked, according to the Queen, 'thin and pale and unusually melancholy'. When she spoke of her return from Algeria, her lovely eyes filled with tears, but she claimed that the visit to Scotland had done her good and that only since arriving in Britain had she been able to eat and sleep again. Politics were not discussed. She mentioned the Emperor once only, and that was to offer his compliments to the Queen. 'She gave me such a melancholy impression,' noted Victoria, 'as if some deep grief and anxiety weighed upon her.'

'What a contrast to her visit in '55! *Then* all a state of excitement, thousands and thousands out, and the brightest sunshine. *Now*, all private and a dreadful, foggy, wet December day!'

Lord Clarendon's version of the imperial visit to Windsor was more revealing. The Empress seems to have found Victoria's manner a little too formal. 'I am sure the Queen *intended* to be civil,' wrote Clarendon, 'but she doesn't understand scrambles and larks and hack cabs which give a vague impression of impropriety and curdle the blood in the Consort's veins.'

Eugenie remained in England for another week and, 'lest hereafter the French might say that she had not been treated with due respect', Victoria and Albert paid her a visit at Claridge's. This further week's stay seems to have done her good, for Victoria found her looking very pretty and in good spirits. It was Eugenie's personal liberty, reported the Queen, which she seemed to enjoy above all things. On the Empress's return to Paris she talked, confirmed Lord Clarendon, 'with unbounded pleasure of her visit to England where she felt she could breathe and be free which in France are forbidden luxuries'. And although Eugenie chatted a great deal to Victoria about all she was doing and seeing in London, she again carefully avoided any mention of the Emperor. It was, wrote Queen Victoria to the ever-attentive King Leopold, 'altogether very strange'.

There was talk, at that time, that the Emperor would make his wife's visit to London an excuse to visit Britain himself.

It was said that he was anxious for a 'little personal conversation' with Victoria's ministers. So strong was the rumour that crowds gathered at London Bridge and Waterloo stations to see him arrive. 'Popular feeling was most in favour of Waterloo station,' wrote Sir William Hardman, 'as that was the most roundabout and unlikely way from Dover, and it was therefore thought to be the one which he would be most likely to adopt. It was a splendid sell.'

The end of the year brought the usual polite exchange of letters between the sovereigns of England and France. Napoleon wrote of his hopes for continued friendship between the two countries; he congratulated the Queen on the success of the Anglo-French expedition to China; he told her how envious he had been of the Empress's visit to Victoria and her charming family. 'She has been very happy this summer,' he added.

Victoria's reply was every bit as polite but a trifle firmer. 'It is hoped,' commented Lord Palmerston on being shown the Queen's letter, 'that he will profit by the sound advice which that answer contains.'

3

No matter how frequently nor how firmly the Emperor Napoleon III might profess honourable intentions towards England, nothing would convince Prince Albert of his sincerity. 'Papa,' Queen Victoria wrote to her daughter Vicky, Crown Princess of Prussia, in later years, 'had the worst opinion of him, which was never removed.' And Lord Cowley always complained that on the question of Napoleon's trustworthiness the Queen had 'inherited the unreasonableness of the poor Prince Consort'.

By the autumn of 1861 the Prince—and with him, of course, the Queen—was certain that the Emperor was planning some diabolical new strategy by which he would soon have all Europe at his mercy. He would then be, claimed Victoria in a feverish letter to Lord Palmerston, 'exactly in the all-powerful position which his Uncle held, and at which he himself aims, with that one difference: that unlike his Uncle, who had to fight England all the time . . . he tries to effect his purposes in alliance with

England, and uses for this end our own *free* Press and in our own free country!'

A visit by the new Prussian monarch, Vicky's father-in-law King Wilhelm I, to the Emperor that year caused acute anxiety at Windsor. It was rumoured that Napoleon had suggested an alliance between France and Prussia or at least a promise that, in the event of a war between France and England, Prussia would remain neutral. Lord Clarendon, primed by Prince Albert, was dispatched to Berlin to warn King Wilhelm against Napoleon's machinations. There should be, on the part of the Prussian monarch, 'a careful avoidance of the traps which cajolery and flattery were setting for Prussia, because at any moment the Emperor might think it necessary for his own purpose in France to seize the left bank of the Rhine'. It was essential that Prussia evoke, as Britain had done, a national spirit against French aggression.

When Lord Clarendon, having spoken his piece in the dull Prussian capital, suggested that he return by way of the more amusing French one, the Queen would not hear of it.

By November 1861, the imagined schemes of Napoleon III were merely one of the many problems besetting the overworked Prince Consort. He was worried about so many things: about the Queen's almost irrational grief after the loss of her mother earlier that year; about the sudden spate of deaths, from typhoid, amongst members of the Portuguese royal family, to whom he was closely related; about a sexual escapade of Bertie's at the military camp at Curragh; about an international crisis concerning two British envoys and the American Civil War. By the beginning of December the Prince himself was suffering from typhoid. Two weeks later he was dead.

Queen Victoria was inconsolable. 'My *life* as a *happy* one *ended*! The world is gone for *me* . . .' she cried out in anguish. 'If I *must live* on . . . it is henceforth for our poor, fatherless children—for my unhappy country, which had lost *all* in losing him—and in *only* doing what I know and *feel* he would wish, for he *is* near me—his spirit will guide and inspire me! But oh! to be cut off in the prime of life—to see our pure, happy, quiet, domestic life, which *alone* enabled me to bear my *much* disliked position, CUT OFF at forty-two—when I *had* hoped with instinctive certainty that God would *never* part us, and would let us grow old together . . . it is too *awful*, too cruel! . . .'

Somewhere, within the flood of heartrending letters which poured from Victoria at this time, is a revealing phrase concerning the Empress Eugenie. 'The Empress Eugenie is very sympathetic,' wrote Victoria to the Queen of Prussia, 'and I know that she feels and *understands* my grief. . . .'

This was true. On the death of her sister Paca (the only person, it is said, other than her son Louis, the Prince Imperial, whom Eugenie really loved) the Empress had experienced a very deep loss. She thus had a more than conventional sympathy with the Queen in her bereavement. And, with her intense nature, Eugenie had something of Victoria's tendency to submerge herself in sorrow. In the Empress's letters of condolence, Victoria probably sensed this; she could single out Eugenie as being best able to comprehend her grief. 'She had a great admiration for my Angel,' declared Victoria, 'and the dear, good Albert liked her also.'

Albert's death was the first link in the chain of sorrows which would one day bind the two women.

CHAPTER NINE

Separate Ways

1

'How one loves to cling to one's grief,' Queen Victoria had once written. Now, clinging to it with all the intensity of her nature, she plunged her Court into its long period of mourning. Had this unrelieved sorrow lasted several months, a year, or even a couple of years, it might have been appreciated and forgiven; but year succeeded year and there seemed to be no light bright enough to pierce the cloud of the Queen's unhappiness. 'The things of this world are of no interest to the Queen . . .' wrote Victoria dolefully to one of her ministers, 'for her thoughts are fixed above.'

If Queen Victoria's thoughts were fixed, as she sighed, 'above', the thoughts of the Emperor Napoleon were fixed, very firmly, below. For as Britain settled down into the long twilight of its Queen's grief, so did France bask in the dazzling sunshine of its Emperor's glory. This decade of Victoria's mourning coincided almost exactly with the most brilliant days of the Second Empire. Rarely, if ever, had the contrast between the Courts of England and France been more pronounced. While Victoria withdrew, almost completely, from her subjects' sight, shunning all public appearances and confining herself to her more remote homes for the greater part of each year, so did Napoleon III spend more and more time in the spotlight. The British monarchy had seldom been more dowdy nor the French more dashing. London, a city without its Sovereign, was like an empty shell; Paris, on the other hand, was *la ville lumière*, the Queen of Cities, the undisputed centre of the civilized world. Outside Buckingham Palace, pranksters put up posters declaring these 'commanding premises to be let or sold, in consequence of the late occupant's declining business'. Napoleon

III's Paris was known as *l'auberge de l'Europe*, and the Emperor and Empress, in their lavish, theatrical way, played host to a seemingly endless stream of guests.

If Victoria spent one week a year in London, the capital was considered fortunate. Four months was the most she ever spent at Windsor. The rest of her time she divided between Osborne, which could be reached only by sea, and Balmoral, set in the remote Highlands of Scotland. Very occasionally, when she could be induced to open Parliament or preside at a Drawing Room, she might spend the night at Buckingham Palace. More often, when the trying ceremony was over, she would hurry back to the fortress-like seclusion of Windsor Castle. It was not until three years after Albert's death that she showed herself in London, and then for the length of a carriage drive from Buckingham Palace to Paddington Station only. She found the experience 'very painful'.

Windsor was like a morgue in those years. Victoria, swathed in crêpe, dragged her skirts through the cold, silent rooms, her only consolation being her daily visit to the Mausoleum where Albert lay buried. The Blue Room, in which he had died, was kept undisturbed; his bust dominated the two wreath-strewn beds; his clothes, fresh towels and hot water were laid out each evening. For days on end no one, other than her dressers or a single lady-in-waiting, would set eyes on her. She would communicate—even with the members of her Household—by letter. All her letters, to the end of her life, carried a half-inch wide mourning border. Her ladies were compelled to dress always in black; her maids of honour were allowed to wear white, grey, mauve or purple but never any other colour.

The Queen's sole interest lay in the continuation of her late husband's work. She was determined to fulfil all his plans—both public and private—but only in so far as they did not intrude upon her seclusion. In private she worked almost as tirelessly as ever; in her public life—perhaps the more important part of her monarchical duties—she would make no effort at all.

The winter (part of December and January) and the summer (July and August) the Queen spent at Osborne. Here, in the house designed by her husband, Victoria would endeavour to escape from her cabinet. As the journey from London to the Isle of Wight, especially in the depths of winter, was never a convenient one, Victoria's ageing ministers did their best to avoid it. If they were compelled to brave the crossing, things were not much fun when they reached Osborne. The Queen's dinner parties were deadly dull: no one spoke above a whisper and the rooms were always ice cold. Her secretary, Henry Ponsonby, describing one such dinner, claims that 'there were prolonged silences, broken by the Queen's, Leopold's and C's respectable coughs, Cowley's deep cough, S's gouty cough and all the servants dropping plates and making a clatteration of noise'. Smoking was strictly forbidden throughout the house. A burst of smothered laughter from the equerries' room was guaranteed to bring a strongly worded rebuke from Her Majesty.

Balmoral Victoria liked best of all; or rather, it was here that she was least unhappy. Amidst the desolate moors and rugged hillsides, she could get right away from the public contact which she hated so much. For even greater seclusion, she would make for the Glassalt, a lodge hidden away among the pines. In spite of the fact that the weeks which she spent at Balmoral in May and June were during the parliamentary session, she was always adamant about not changing her dates of arrival and departure. Only a crisis of the most serious nature would induce her to alter her plans by perhaps a day or two. Here she could live that simple life she so much enjoyed. With her favourite gillie, John Brown, striding by her side, she would ride along the mountain paths or go out driving at a brisk pace along the lonely, rain-swept roads. Sometimes her carriage would stop beside some stone cottage and she would lean out to talk to a little knot of people gathered outside the door. Occasionally, bearing some little gift, she might alight and enter the cottage for a cup of tea. For the members of her Court or her government, life at Balmoral was a form of torture. 'Stagnation,' complained Ponsonby, 'dulled everyone's wits.' It was like a convent, claimed one of her prime ministers. 'We meet at meals and when we are finished, each is off to his cell.'

It was all so different across the Channel. In France, Napoleon's Court was *en fête* from morning to night. The Second Empire might not have been quite as magnificent as it appeared on the surface, but there was no denying that the surface was magnificent indeed. 'One of the first duties of a sovereign,' Napoleon III used to say, 'is to amuse his subjects of all ranks in the social scale. He has no more right to have a dull Court than he has to have a weak army or a poor Navy.' In this respect, the Emperor was as good as his word.

As Victoria moved in solemn rotation from house to house throughout the year, so did the Court of the Second Empire divide its time between its various palaces. For the greater part of the year Napoleon lived at the Tuileries in the heart of his capital. A few weeks of the summer would be spent at Fontainebleau, a few weeks of the spring and autumn at Saint Cloud, August at Biarritz and November at Compiègne. And everywhere, with the exception of Biarritz, he moved in a dazzle of imperial splendour.

Life at the Tuileries was an almost ceaseless round of entertainments. There were parties, receptions and balls without number. Night after night the Place du Carrousel would be jammed with carriages, the windows of the palace blazing with light and the gardens festooned with coloured lanterns. Helmeted *Cent Gardes* would line the grand staircase, lavishly dressed guests would throng the salons. Of all the entertainments, the *bal masqué* was the most popular, providing opportunities for the most *outré* costumes and the most indiscreet behaviour. The Empress herself might appear 'literally *cuirassée* in diamonds' while the masked Emperor, in the unfounded hope that his squat figure would prove unrecognizable, would wander about in search of what he called '*petits divertissements*'.

When the imperial couple were not playing host to the *beau monde*, they would be showing themselves to their subjects. Each afternoon at four o'clock, escorted by a troop of *Cent Gardes*, their open carriage would whisk along the Champs Elysées, headed for the Bois de Boulogne. There, in full view of the brilliant assembly which made up the society of the Second Empire—the courtesans, the financiers, the foreign adventurers, the *nouveaux riches*—the imperial carriage would drive slowly around the Lac Inférieur, the Emperor tipping his hat to every pretty face, the Empress nodding in response to the cheers.

111

At Saint Cloud—the country palace within sight of Paris—things were hardly less stylish. The levees and receptions continued but, in general, the entertainments took on a more rustic flavour. The *bal masqué* would give way to the *fête champêtre*. Each day the char-à-bancs would go bowling off into the woods and there, under the trees, the imperial circle would play at *la vie simple*. Eugenie, surrounded by a bevy of beautiful women (for she, no less than the Emperor, delighted in pretty faces), would recline in the leaf-filtered sunlight while country dancers cavorted on the grass and the liveried footmen unpacked the picnic hampers.

Fontainebleau, with its elegant façade mirrored in the great lake, was the scene of some of the most impressive of the imperial *fêtes*. Particularly memorable was the reception of the Siamese Embassy, when the envoys of the King of Siam, dressed in jewel-bright silken robes, crawled the length of the Henri II gallery to present their gifts to the enthroned Emperor and Empress. Less exotic, but hardly less colourful, were the imperial hunts which were held both at Fontainebleau and Compiègne. The pageantry of these occasions was unforgettable; a recreation of the splendours of the *ancien régime*, with the presence of a few white-robed Algerian chieftains to lend the scene a touch of the bizarre.

At Fontainebleau, even the afternoon drives were spectacular. The imperial wagonettes would draw up in the Fountain Court and the postillions, resplendent in polished boots, yellow breeches, green and gold jackets, powdered wigs and glazed hats, would stand, whips in hand, while the guests took their seats. 'These drives in the woods, to the tuneful jingling of the bells answering rhythmically to the rapid trots of the horses, were an exhilarating experience,' wrote one of the company.

There were less formal outings as well. The Prince Imperial's tutor tells of one occasion when several members of the party decided to go for a scramble among the rocks after tea. 'About fifteen of us,' he says, 'hand in hand, rushed headlong down a very steep slope. We slipped, we fell, and finally we lost our footing and came down like a hurricane, the girls screaming in mingled terror and enjoyment. When we finally arrived at the bottom of the hill it was evident that several pieces of the ladies' skirts and many of their high heels had been torn off in their downward course. . . .'

It was all so different from Queen Victoria's excursions on the Deeside.

At Biarritz, that seaside resort close to Eugenie's native Spain, the imperial family was able to relax for a few weeks. During the day they would go walking or sailing or swimming and at night they would play those artless parlour games which were such a feature of mid-nineteenth-century social life. The peaceful atmosphere might be shattered by some *demoiselle d'honneur* rushing into the room to report that there was a strange man in her bed. The courtiers responsible for the dummy under the sheets would be convulsed with laughter and the evening would break up in hilarious confusion.

But it was the season at Compiègne which best captured the flavour of the Court of the Second Empire. Here the brilliance, and the gaiety, were exceptional. An invitation to spend a week at Compiègne was the height of social ambition. Its entertainments, which now strike one as *naive*, were then considered the last word in sophistication. There would be raucous games of blind-man's-buff, with a flock of shrieking matrons fleeing from the groping, blindfolded Emperor; there would be spirited dancing to the music of a mechanical piano with the handle being turned, on occasion, by no less exalted a person than the host himself; there would be elaborate *tableaux vivants*, when the Empress and her ladies would spend days preparing costumes for their brief appearances. And, of course, there would be amateur theatricals. As the *bal masqué* meant the Tuileries and the *fête champêtre* Fontainebleau and Saint Cloud, so did amateur theatricals come to symbolize Compiègne. Princess Metternich, the vivacious wife of the Austrian Ambassador, would swagger on to the stage disguised as a Parisian cabby; the son-in-law of the Duke de Bassano, dressed as the famous, husky-voiced *chanteuse* Thérésa, would give a saucy rendering of the celebrated 'Rien n'est Sacré pour un Sapeur'.

Nor was it merely for its glamour and its light-heartedness that the Court of the Second Empire became renowned; it was as well known for its licentiousness. Although the Empress herself was chaste, she was no prude, and the Emperor, of course, was notoriously sensual. By the 1860s, Napoleon III's Court was known to be the most dissolute in Europe.

It did not take long for whispers of these free-and-easy goings-on to reach even Queen Victoria's inaccessible ears. As early as 1862 she was referring to Paris quite simply as 'that Sodom and Gomorrah'. When Bertie, the twenty-year-old Prince of Wales, was due to pass through France on his way back home after a tour of the Holy Land, his mother insisted that he spend one day only in Paris; he was *not* to stay overnight. The incident at the Curragh camp was still fresh in the Queen's mind. She did not want the weak-willed young man exposed to the well-known temptations of Napoleon's Court.

The Prince appears to have emerged from the brief visit with reputation not only intact but enhanced. His morning call on the Emperor and Empress seems to have been a great success. Lord Cowley admitted himself agreeably surprised at the manner in which, in conversation with his imperial hosts, the Prince 'held his own unaffectedly and without shyness'. Yet when Sir Charles Phipps, who was in charge of Bertie, begged for the young man to be allowed to spend another day in Paris, the request was 'inexorably refused from Windsor'. He did not dare press it.

Some two years later, when the Prince was planning another visit to Paris (by now he was married to Princess Alexandra and should not have been quite so dependent on his mother's sanctioning of his every move), the Queen was no less firm in her instructions. The visit to Paris had to be '*on the complete understanding* that it is in *real incognito* which your other visits have not been. That you stop at an hotel and do not lodge with the Emperor and Empress and do not accept an invitation to Compiègne or Fontainebleau, the style of going on there being quite unfit for a young and respectable Prince and Princess like yourselves.'

Of course, continued the Queen, they could accept a day's shooting at Compiègne or even an invitation to dinner—'*but nothing more!*'

The Queen was blowing against a hurricane. The Prince of Wales was drawn towards this glittering Court as a pin to a magnet. It was made up of exactly the sort of society he adored:

rich, elegant, amusing, amoral. His first, boyhood impressions
of Napoleon III's Empire seemed to have been admirably borne
out. During the 1860s he developed the habit of spending the
month of March, *en garçon*, on the French Riviera, staying in
Paris for a few days before and again after his holiday. This
way he came to know the more diverting aspects of life during
the Second Empire very well indeed.

When Princess Alexandra accompanied him, she found herself responding, no less happily, to the warmth and gaiety of
the French Court. King Leopold might grumble that Napoleon's
Court was 'not calculated for Alix', but she declared herself
delighted with it. With Paris, and with the Parisian shops, she
was equally enraptured. 'I hope dear Alix will not spend much
on dress at Paris,' wrote Queen Victoria to Bertie during one of
their visits to France. 'There is, besides, a *very* strong feeling
against the luxuriousness, extravagance and frivolity of Society;
and everyone points to *my* simplicity.'

Her advice fell on deaf ears. To the pleasure-loving Bertie,
the Court of St James's, after the Court of the Tuileries, seemed
very, very dull.

2

The Prince of Wales was not the only one of the Queen's
children to sample the delights of Napoleon III's Paris. But
not all of them were quite so enamoured of it.

The Queen's eldest daughter Vicky, now Crown Princess of
Prussia, was distinctly more sparing of her praise. During the
1860s Prussia, under the guidance of King Wilhelm I's Prime
Minister, Otto von Bismarck, was being fashioned into the most
powerful state in Central Europe. By two successful wars, one
against Denmark in 1864 and the other against Austria in
1866, Bismarck aggrandized Prussia and, in the case of the
victory over Austria, inflicted a severe diplomatic defeat on
France. Napoleon had failed to press home the advantage
which a Prussia, actively engaged elsewhere, should have given
him. Bismarck's success had flung Vicky into a quandary. As a
passionate liberal, she might not approve of Bismarck's 'blood

and iron' methods but, on the other hand, she could not help rejoicing in the fact that he was achieving a great liberal ideal—the unification of Germany. German unification under Prussia had always been the late Prince Consort's ambition. As such, and even though it was not being realized in anything like the progressive spirit envisaged by the late Prince, the ideal was sacred to both Vicky and her mother. No less sacred was Prince Albert's conviction that Napoleon III had designs on Germany. It was 'very satisfactory, and also very useful', the Queen told Vicky, for Napoleon to see this evidence of Prussia's growing strength.

Distinctly less satisfactory was the fact that this rivalry between Prussia and France was splitting the Queen's own family into two bickering factions. Prussia's war against Denmark had infuriated the Prince of Wales and his Danish wife, Princess Alexandra. During both the Danish and Austrian wars Bertie had championed Prussia's enemies; there was no doubt where his sympathies would lie in any future Franco-Prussian conflict. About Bertie's open admiration for France and the French, Vicky was always particularly scathing.

It was thus with the eyes of a potential rival that the Crown Princess of Prussia judged Napoleon's regime. For the earnest Vicky, it was all too decadent by half. She complained to her mother of the mischief which the imperial Court 'and still more, that very attractive Paris, has done to English society, to the stage and to literature! *What harm* to the young and brilliant aristocracy of London!' Although she had to admit, on visiting Paris, that it was much more 'advanced' than Berlin, she added, with the dual patriotism which was so characteristic, that it did not bear comparison with England.

By now Vicky had outgrown her girlhood passion for the Empress Eugenie. She criticized the Empress for her bearing on public occasions; she showed 'a shade diffidence more than her station permits', considered Vicky. Yet she was forced to give Eugenie credit for her beauty, grace and charm.

When the fourteen-year-old Prince Arthur, the Queen's third son, visited Paris in 1865, and paid his call on the Tuileries, he was received by Louis, the Prince Imperial, then nine years old. Prince Arthur's governor, Sir Howard Elphinstone, de-

A watercolour sketch of Queen Victoria, aged thirty-five, at the time of her first meeting with the Emperor and Empress of the French

Louis Napoleon, sketched in 1852, the year in which he assumed the title of Napoleon III, Emperor of the French

The Empress Eugenie, at the time of her first meeting with Queen Victoria

Queen Victoria welcomes Napoleon III and the Empress Eugenie to Windsor Castle on 16 April 1855

Napoleon III, Queen Victoria, the Empress Eugenie and Prince Albert in the royal box at Covent Garden

Queen Victoria and Prince Albert photographed in 1855

Queen Victoria invests Napoleon III with the Order of the Garter at Windsor Castle

The statuesque Princess Mathilde Bonaparte, whom Queen Victoria found 'very
civil'

Prince Napoleon, the irascible Plon-P'
whom Queen Victoria described as 'not a
civil'

The royal party drive through a triumphal arch on the Boulevard des
Italiens during the State Visit to Paris in August 1855

Queen Victoria in widowhood

The Empress Eugenie at the zenith of her career, photographed in Circassian costume for a fancy-dress ball

The exiled Emperor Napoleon III in his study at Camden Place

The twenty-eight-year-old Bertie, Prince of Wales, photographed in 1870, the year of the fall of the Second Empire

Louis, the Prince Imperial, at the age of twenty-two

A sketch, from details given by Captain Carey, of the scouting party a few minutes before the Zulu attack. Louis is seated in the foreground with Carey standing beside him

A recent photograph of the cross, erected by command of Queen Victoria, to mark the spot where the Prince Imperial was killed

Queen Victoria and Princess Beatrice standing in front of the Prince Imperial's coffin

Dethroned, widowed and childless, the Empress Eugenie in later years

scribed the Prince Imperial to the Queen as being intelligent and sweet, but pale, shy and 'evidently too much by himself'. Those who knew Louis better did not find him really shy. To a courtliness inherited from his father, he brought a good deal of his mother's dashing spirit. Indeed, Sir Howard admitted that the boy showed a flash of annoyance when the officer in attendance, assuming the Prince to be ignorant on the subject, explained where Japan was. Sir Howard noted that the Emperor and Empress were most 'affable and *gratified*' on meeting young Prince Arthur.

Two years later Prince Arthur again visited Paris. In his simple Woolwich uniform 'with that exquisitely fresh Garter ribbon across it', the Queen's son rode out beside the Emperor to a review of the *Garde Impériale*. Afterwards he was conducted over Saint Cloud by the Prince Imperial. Sir Howard reported Louis as not having grown much since 1865 but as being 'very nice and with perfect manners'.

From Paris Prince Arthur went to the military camp at Châlons, where he was put up in the Emperor's pavilion. Sir Howard was greatly impressed by what he saw of Napoleon III's troops. They manœuvred, he told the Queen, with such verve, such quickness and *élan*. The ground around their tents was so prettily ornamented and behind each tent was a vegetable garden. With the soil so poor, a great deal of time and labour must have gone into their cultivation. 'At Aldershot, Your Majesty will recollect,' wrote Sir Howard, 'the troops cannot be got to do this, unless they get paid.' There was a very different spirit, he sighed, between the French and British soldiers.

'Nothing could be more satisfactory and agreeable,' concluded Sir Howard, 'than the attention the officers and men showed to the Prince and apparently the good feeling there existed towards England generally.'

The Queen's second son, Prince Alfred—'Affie'—who had already shown signs of following in Bertie's footsteps (he, also, had been involved in some youthful sexual scandal) shared his elder brother's regrettable taste for Second Empire Paris. The worldly Lord Cowley suspected that 'it would not do to enquire too closely into their proceedings when not in society'. There was a rumour that the royal brothers had once deserted their guests at a dinner party in a restaurant in order to go off with some *demi-mondaine.*

Princess Alice, the Grand Duchess of Hesse and Victoria's second daughter, visited Paris for Napoleon's greatest show-piece, the *Exposition Universelle* of 1867. That summer he was at home to almost all the crowned heads of Europe. Never had his Empire appeared more magnificent. 'I really am half killed from sight-seeing and fêtes,' complained Princess Alice to her mother, 'but all has interested me so much and the Emperor and Empress have been most kind.' Every morning they visited the Exhibition; every night there was a dinner or a ball. The ball at the Hôtel de Ville ('quite the same as it had been for you and dear Papa') was the most brilliant sight that the Princess had ever seen.

'Tomorrow morning we leave,' wrote the exhausted Alice, 'and had really great trouble to get away, for the Emperor and Empress and others begged us so much to remain for the ball at the Tuileries tomorrow night. . . .'

3

The contrast between the French and English Courts was brought home, very vividly, during that summer of 1867. Abdul Aziz, the Sultan of Turkey, was paying official visits to first France and then England, that year. His reception in Paris by Napoleon III was superb. The Emperor spared nothing in the fêting of his guest. Consequently Lord Derby, once again Prime Minister, mustered all his tact and courage and hurriedly wrote off to the Queen to beg her to make some small effort to give the Sultan a decent welcome. Apologizing for introducing a subject which he realized must be distasteful to the Queen, he humbly suggested that the Queen's plan for receiving the Sultan *five* days after his arrival in the country was really not good enough. The Sultan, he assured her, attached the greatest importance to an audience at the earliest possible time.

'The reception given to His Imperial Majesty by the Emperor of the French has been of the most magnificent description,' continued the anguished Lord Derby. 'His Majesty met him at the Railway Station, and had been unremitting in his attentions; and Lord Derby cannot but feel very strongly that a most unfortunate impression would be produced not only on the Sultan, but on the public mind of this country, if a very marked contrast could be drawn between the cordiality of his reception in Paris, and an absence of any similar indication here.'

If only, begged Lord Derby, the Queen could postpone her journey to Osborne for three days and give the Sultan a mere *ten minutes* at Buckingham Palace on his arrival, he would be satisfied. The denial of this gesture, especially when set against the lavishness of the Sultan's reception in Paris, might well antagonize and alienate him; it could well 'throw him into the arms of France'.

Again and again the Prime Minister apologized for the inconvenience which these arrangements would cause the Queen. He assured her that only the strongest sense of duty would lead him to press this 'unpalatable' advice on her.

Unpalatable, as far as Victoria was concerned, was hardly strong enough. She lost no time in letting Lord Derby know that his suggested scheme would not only be extremely inconvenient but positively 'disadvantageous for the Queen's health'. Why could not the Sultan be induced to arrive a day earlier and thus save her the bother of having to postpone her departure to Osborne for three days? She was being driven to a state of desperation, she declared, 'by the want of consideration shown by the *public* for her health and strength'. She could see, before long, 'a *complete breakdown* of her nervous system'.

'It is very wrong *not* to say that the Queen IS *incapable* of those fatigues and of this excitement, working and drudging as she does from morning till *night*, and weighed down by the responsibility and cares of her most unenviable position, and with the anxieties consequent upon being the widowed mother of so large a family. . . .'

And in case Lord Derby had not been entirely convinced by this letter, Victoria dispatched Dr Jenner to tell him of the real state of her health and nerves.

But, grumble as she might, Queen Victoria was not one to shirk a duty which she considered absolutely necessary. She postponed her journey and received the Sultan. And, a few days later, when she was at Osborne, they attended the Naval Review together. The Sultan, violently seasick, spent a great deal of time below, but the stout little Queen remained on the heaving deck to watch her ships steam by. The review over, luncheon was served in the deck saloon for sixteen 'royal persons only'. The guest of honour was not amongst their number.

Queen and Sultan took leave of each other after luncheon. They parted, declared Victoria, 'with many mutual expressions of goodwill, and of gratitude on his part'.

CHAPTER TEN

Decline and Fall

1

Although, throughout these first years of the Queen's widow-hood, Victoria exchanged occasional letters with the Emperor and Empress, the three of them never met. The Queen had last seen Napoleon during that disturbing visit to Cherbourg in 1858 and Eugenie on her sudden flight to Scotland a couple of years later. Not until the summer of 1867 was there any personal contact between them: in July that year the Empress Eugenie spent three days with the Queen at Osborne. She had been invited to attend the Naval Review at Spithead, but as the imperial Court was in a month's mourning for the death of Napoleon III's puppet Emperor—Maximilian of Mexico—the visit was changed to a private one.

Since their last meeting, the rôles of Victoria and Eugenie had been dramatically reversed. In the winter of 1860, the Empress had been the tragic figure; now it was a widowed, retiring Queen who welcomed an Empress in the full tide of her beauty and assurance. The contrast between the two women was now more noticeable than ever. The forty-eight-year-old Queen had grown stouter during her long period of mourning; her face, turning yearly more florid, had settled into a perma-nently disgruntled expression; she was always dressed in black, with her greying hair hidden by a widow's cap. Eugenie, on the other hand, Victoria considered 'but little altered'. If anything, the forty-one-year-old Empress was better looking than she had ever been; to her beauty had been added an almost theatrical aura of majesty. Her figure was well-proportioned, her bearing superb, her clothes magnificent. Her enormous skirts had their fullness drawn to the back in the fashion of the late 1860s; on her elaborately coiffured head would be perched a small, sharply tilted hat. 'But it was the way she wore her clothes, and not the silks themselves, that impressed the beholder . . .' wrote a young Englishman who saw her at this time, 'the Empress was a commanding figure'.

Of course, in Queen Victoria's company, the Empress tended to temper her self-assurance a little. Of the pride, the arrogance and the impetuosity for which Eugenie was—somewhat unfairly—criticized, there was very little evidence to be found in her manner towards Queen Victoria. The Empress had never really mastered her awe of this imperious little sovereign and she remained grateful for the friendship which had meant so much to the imperial regime in its early days. Moreover, Eugenie was obliged to tread rather carefully during this visit: not only was she conscious of the Queen's disenchantment with the Emperor, but there were several subjects on which the two women could not hope to agree. Victoria was thus able to refer, albeit with a little less rapture than before, to Eugenie's kindness, amiability and discretion.

One of the questions on which they did not see eye-to-eye was the Empress's scheme for the rebuilding of the Church of the Holy Sepulchre at Jerusalem. About two years before, the Empress had suggested that all the queens and princesses in Christendom donate money for the erection of a multi-denominational place of worship on the site of the decaying Church of the Holy Sepulchre. The imaginative project never materialized. The Pope would not hear of it; the Queen of Holland dismissed it as a plan, on Eugenie's part, for saving her soul; Lord Clarendon reported that Queen Victoria 'won't have the Holy Sepulchre at any price. . . .' The Queen complained that whereas she could not afford to give as generous a donation as the Empress, neither as Queen of England, could she afford to give a less generous one. In refusing to take part in the scheme Victoria was none the less careful to speak of her 'great esteem and liking for the Empress whose genuine sympathy with her she had heard from many quarters'.

It is unlikely that this still-born project was mentioned at Osborne during that summer of 1867. There were many more immediate topics to be discussed. One was the Mexican expedition which had just ended so disastrously with the execution of the Emperor Maximilian and the madness of the Empress Charlotte. It could not have been without some sense of guilt that Eugenie, who had championed the scheme with such fervour, now spoke to the Queen of 'poor Max's murder' and Charlotte's 'state of health'.

More delicate still was the question of the growing hostility between France and Prussia. The Queen's sympathies were all with Prussia, or rather with the recently created Prussian-controlled North German Confederation. General Grey, Victoria's secretary, writing to Disraeli sometime before Eugenie's visit, impressed upon him that the Queen favoured a 'thorough understanding for mutual support, in the interest of peace, with North Germany'. This had been the firmly held opinion of the Prince Consort and, as such, was more than good enough for the Queen. She wished, of course, to be on the friendliest terms with France, but wanted it made quite clear that in the event of open hostility between the two countries, Britain would favour Germany.

It is rather ironic that Victoria, in clinging to her late husband's progressive concepts, found herself championing Bismarck's autocratic and militaristic Prussia against a France to which the once-authoritarian Napoleon III was gradually granting liberal reforms.

To Eugenie, Victoria expressed herself with more subtlety. She urged the Empress to do all she could to maintain peace between the two countries. Taking care to lay the blame on Prussia, Victoria advised against any further arming on the part of France. The build-up of arms could not continue, declared the Queen, 'without imminent danger of some, possibly trifling, incident bringing about a collision which would involve all Europe in war'.

Earlier that year Victoria had written to King Wilhelm of Prussia, urging him to be as conciliatory as possible towards France; now Eugenie assured her that it was due almost entirely to her letter that peace had thus far been preserved.

The Empress sailed back to France on 24 July. On the last day of her stay the two women breakfasted together on the lawn and then, accompanied by several of Victoria's children, drove down to the pier. Two of the princes escorted Eugenie to

La Reine Hortense, lying at anchor in the bay, and then the royal party returned home.

'Greatly relieved the visit was over,' noted Victoria, 'as I am feeling far from well, and everything tires me so.'

2

Just over a year later, in August 1868, the Queen and the Empress met again. Victoria passed through Paris on her way to Switzerland for a holiday. The meeting, for all its brevity, led to a further deterioration in the relationship between the two Courts.

Queen Victoria arrived in the French capital on the morning of 5 August 1868. She was *en route* to the Pension Wallace in Lucerne, where she planned to spend a few weeks. The Queen was travelling *incognita,* under the somewhat improbable name of the Countess of Kent. The alias deceived no one but it did emphasize the private nature of her journey and allowed her new Prime Minister, Disraeli, to refer to her as 'our dear Peeress'. In the Queen's party travelled John Brown. Parisians were thus able to catch a glimpse of this handsome, kilted and by now highly controversial figure.

The Queen, having travelled from Cherbourg in the luxuriously appointed imperial train, spent one day at the British Embassy in Paris. She was to leave again, for Switzerland, that evening. After what Lord Lyons, who had replaced Lord Cowley as Ambassador, described as 'prodigious correspondence', the question of the Queen's reception had been settled. There was to be as little fuss as possible. With the imperial Court in residence at Fontainebleau and the Emperor at Plombiers, formalities would be restricted to the Empress coming up to Paris to pay a short courtesy call on the Queen.

Eugenie duly travelled up from Fontainebleau, established herself in the Elysée Palace, which stands beside the British Embassy, and visited the Embassy for three-quarters of an hour in the afternoon. Of this three-quarter-hour period, Eugenie spent only ten minutes in the company of the Queen. Victoria left for the station at seven that evening.

'Took an interesting drive through the beautiful town, less noisy than London, and yet with everybody living in the streets, sitting there reading and taking their meals outside the cafés. Not a soul knew us,' wrote the Queen. 'The shops, of every kind and description, are beautiful and so well arranged. The absence of smoke makes all look bright and clean, but I regret the endless new formal building destroying all the picturesque old streets. We started at half past seven and it was very hot in the train.'

No sooner had the Queen left Paris than there was an outcry in the French Press. By neglecting to return the Empress's call, the Queen had insulted France. She should have waited until Eugenie had gone back to the adjoining Elysée and then have visited her there. The Empress's explanation that she had begged the Queen not to fatigue herself by returning the call convinced very few. The Parisian papers complained about the Queen's 'aloofness' and maintained that the slight had proved that she favoured the exiled House of Orleans above the reigning Bonapartes.

Nor was this reaction confined to the Press. The Queen of Holland claimed that Victoria's behaviour had raised the 'ire of the French Court'. And Lord Cowley, paying a friendly visit to Fontainebleau a few days later, noted that the Empress was 'sore at heart about the visit'.

But, of course, the Queen had intended no slight. For one thing, she had been, as she put it, 'overpowered' by the heat: the minute the Empress had left, the Queen had had to return to the bed on which she had been resting for most of the day. The incident served as an example, too, of Victoria's refusal to make any special effort, of her horror of appearing in public. Yet she dismissed any criticism of her secluded way of life as '*ill natured* gossip . . . caused by dissatisfaction at not forcing the Queen *out*'.

'It is very wrong of the world to say that it is merely her *distaste* to go out and about as she could when she had her dear husband to support and *protect* her,' she cried out, 'when the *fact is* that her shattered nerves and health *prevent* her doing so.'

Why, asked the Empress of the Queen of Holland, if the Queen found public life so unbearable, did she not abdicate?

Napoleon, throughout this flurry, held his tongue. Not once, noticed Lord Cowley during his stay at Fontainebleau, did the Emperor mention the Queen's visit. Indeed, Napoleon did not have much to say for himself at all during this period. One reason for this was that he was very ill. Never really strong, the Emperor had been suffering increasingly from pains in the bladder during the last few years. Although his doctors had once diagnosed a stone, no treatment had been carried out, and the discomfort experienced by the Emperor during subsequent ministrations had made him even more loath to be examined. As a result, his pain became worse. This, in turn, was sapping his energy, clouding his brain and weakening his resolve. His tendency to evade, to procrastinate, to drift with the tide, was becoming more and more pronounced. Eugenie, in conversation with the Queen of Holland, complained of his langour and depression; he was no longer capable of making a decision, she declared.

Nor was the Emperor's condition improved by the host of problems by which he was finding himself beset: the fiasco in Mexico, the menace of Prussia, the loss of prestige, the lack of allies, the resurgence of republicanism.

And it is not unlikely that this affair of the Queen's visit, trivial in itself, but symptomatic of the coolness between Windsor and the Tuileries, depressed him still further. How different from her last visit to Paris in 1855. Then he had all but made love to her; now he had not even set eyes on her. It served as yet another straw on that overburdened back. 'It is even asserted that he is weary of the whole thing,' reported Lord Lyons, 'disappointed at the contrast between the brilliancy at the beginning of his reign and the present gloom. . . .'

To avoid any repetition of the *fracas* on the Queen's return through Paris at the end of her holiday, it was decided that the imperial couple would leave for Biarritz before her arrival. But, in fact, when Victoria reached the capital on 10 September 1868, the Empress was still at Fontainebleau and the Emperor, much recovered, was reviewing his army at the great military camp at Châlons. While the London *Times* thundered against this display of Napoleonic militarism at Châlons, Queen Victoria again spent the day at the British Embassy. The

Empress did not stir from Fontainebleau. She telegraphed, 'most kindly'; that was all.

Late that afternoon the Queen drove out to the Palace of Saint Cloud. It proved a poignant visit, very different from her last, in the summer of 1855. 'We went through the Champs Elysées,' she wrote later that evening, 'past the Arc de Triomphe, which I recognised well, through the Bois de Boulogne, which looked dull and dreary at this time of year, through the small town of Boulogne, over the bridge to St Cloud, which I much wished to look at again, in remembrance of the happy days spent there with my dearest Albert in 55.'

Her carriage turned into the quadrangle and stopped for a moment at the main entrance. As she was tired and did not have much time, the Queen did not alight. She merely looked through the open door and up the Great Staircase. On the landing, as a heart-catching reminder of the change in circumstances since the palmy days of the Anglo-French *entente*, hung a vast painting of her ceremonial arrival at the palace thirteen years before. 'In all this blaze of light from lamps, torches, amidst the roar of cannon, and bands, and drums, and cheers, we reached the Palace . . . it was like a fairytale and everything so beautiful', she had written on that occasion. Now she merely noted that she recognized all and that 'the fine avenues and silent house made a very dreary and sad impression upon me. It was dull, heavy and oppressive'.

When she returned to the Embassy her head, she said, 'was very bad, the heat in the house very great, and a Café Chantant, at the end of the garden outside, made such a noise that I could get no rest'. She left for home at ten that evening.

Not until the following morning did her one-time 'faithful ally and *friend*' pass through Paris on his way to join the Empress at Fontainebleau. The French Court left for Biarritz two days later.

3

Towards mid-March 1870, Queen Victoria received a confidential letter from her son-in-law, Fritz, Crown Prince of Prussia. He wanted to know what her reaction would be to the acceptance of the crown of Spain by one of his relations—Prince Leopold of Hohenzollern-Sigmaringen. The Spanish throne had been vacant since the expulsion, some eighteen months before, of the fat, oversexed and incompetent Queen Isabel II. Queen Victoria's reply was non-committal. She assured the Crown Prince that after discussing the question, *quite* confidentially, with her Foreign Secretary, she could express no opinion. It was a matter for the Hohenzollern Prince himself to decide; she would not like to exercise the least influence.

Victoria's letter was duly passed on by the Crown Prince to his father, King Wilhelm, and by Wilhelm to his Chancellor, Count Bismarck. Into the Queen's circumspect phrases, the Prussian Chancellor read a promise that, in this matter of placing a Hohenzollern Prince on the Spanish throne, Britain would not interfere.

Reassured, Bismarck continued his secret negotiations. The Prussian Chancellor was playing a shrewd game; there was far more to this business of filling the Spanish throne than Queen Victoria imagined. In order to bring the independent South German states scurrying into the Prussian fold, and so complete German unification, Bismarck needed an altercation with France. As the French would never tolerate a German king in Madrid, Bismarck felt certain that the proposed candidature of Prince Leopold would provide him with the necessary 'red rag to the Gallic bull'. Provoked, France would threaten Prussia, and the kingdoms of South Germany, bound by treaty to Prussia, would join her in resisting the French threat.

In this, Bismarck was proved correct. When, on 3 July 1870, the news broke of Prince Leopold's acceptance of the Spanish crown, the French were furious. They immediately recognized the manœuvre for what it was—a calculated slap in the face for France by Prussia.

With public opinion at fever pitch, the French government insisted that King Wilhelm of Prussia command Prince Leopold of Hohenzollern to withdraw his candidature. The King refused to do any such thing. But if, conceded the King, Prince Leopold were to withdraw on his own accord, he would do nothing to dissuade him. This, in fact, is what happened. Prince Leopold, overwhelmed by the entreaties of half the crowned heads of Europe (including, indirectly, the desperately worried Napoleon III) withdrew his candidature. Bismarck had been thwarted.

But not for long. France, its passions thoroughly aroused, was in no mood for peace. Although the Emperor would have been content with Prince Leopold's withdrawal, his less level-headed advisers, including the Empress Eugenie, wanted something more. The cry now went up that a mere withdrawal of the candidature was not enough: Prussia, who had tried to humiliate France, must herself be humiliated. She must give a guarantee that the candidature of Prince Leopold would never again be raised. This, politely but firmly, King Wilhelm refused to give. Bismarck, grabbing at this second chance, published a shortened and therefore more abrupt-sounding version of the King's refusal, and France, insulted before all the world, declared war. By 19 July 1870 France and Prussia were at war.

Throughout this sixteen-day-long crisis, Queen Victoria had been in a state of acute anxiety. Although never doubting that vainglorious France was at fault, she did everything in her power to 'avert the frightful storm which threatens the Continent'. Letters and telegrams flew between Queen, ministers, ambassadors and foreign royalties. 'The Queen,' she admitted to her Foreign Secretary, Lord Granville, 'is overwhelmed with letter-writing, telegrams and the terrible anxiety and sorrow which this horrible war will bring with it. The Queen hardly knows how she will bear it! Her children's home threatened, their husbands' lives in danger, and the country she loves best next to her own—as it is her second home, being her beloved husband's, and one to which she and all her family are bound by the closest ties—in peril of the gravest kind, insulted and attacked, and *she* unable to help them or to come to their assistance. . . .'

Her whole heart and fervent prayers, she assured her daughter Vicky, the Crown Princess of Prussia, were with her 'beloved Germany'. Like all the world, with the possible exception of Napoleon III, Bismarck and the Prussian General Staff, the Queen believed that France would be victorious. She was in full agreement with the London *Times* when it claimed that the French attack on Prussia was 'the greatest national crime that we have had the pain of recording in these columns since the days of the First Empire'. It was an 'unjust, but premeditated war' said *The Times*, and the act of one man alone—Napoleon III. There could be no doubt 'as to the side on which the world's sympathies will be enlisted'.

That British sympathies were enlisted, for the most part, on Prussia's side, was largely due to yet another of Bismarck's astute moves. Four years before, in 1866, when Napoleon III had been casting about to obtain some sort of compensation from Bismarck for French neutrality during Prussia's war with Austria, the Emperor had proposed a secret treaty between Bismarck and himself. By the terms of this treaty, Prussia might—at some future date—help France annex Belgium. The French Ambassador had made a copy of the draft treaty in his own handwriting and had handed it to Bismarck. The Prussian Chancellor, while taking care not to commit himself to the proposal, had led the Emperor to believe that he approved of it and had put the copy safely away in a drawer. It lay there for four years.

As soon as France declared war on Prussia, Bismarck instructed the Prussian Ambassador in London to show the explosive document to Gladstone, the British Prime Minister. A few days later the text of the treaty was released to *The Times*. This timely publication of Napoleon's designs on Belgium— Britain's godchild—appalled public opinion. 'Your Majesty will, in common with the world, be shocked and startled,' wrote Gladstone to Queen Victoria. She was. Thoroughly alarmed, the Queen asked her Prime Minister for an immediate assurance that Great Britain's defences were on a satisfactory footing; the country might be exposed to a sudden and unexpected attack at any moment, she declared.

'Words are too weak to say *all* I feel for you or what I think of my neighbours!' she wrote to Vicky. 'We must be neutral *as long as* we can, but no one here conceals their opinion as to the extreme *iniquity* of the war, and the unjustifiable conduct of the French! Still, *more publicly*, we cannot say; but the feeling of the people and the country is *all* with you. . . .'

Not quite all. Within the Queen's own family there were sharply conflicting loyalties. The Prussian Crown Princess and her sister Alice, Grand Duchess of Hesse, might be heart and soul for Germany, but the Prince and Princess of Wales were no less ardently Francophile. For Napoleon and Eugenie, Bertie had the highest regard. At a dinner party at the French Embassy on the evening before the declaration of war, the Prince of Wales is claimed to have expressed to the Austrian Ambassador the hope that Austria might join France in defeating Prussia. The Prince's partisan remarks were repeated to the Prussian Ambassador in London, who promptly forwarded them to Berlin. The Crown Princess was furious and lost no time in dashing off a letter to her mother about it. 'The King and everyone are horrified at Bertie's speech which is quoted everywhere,' she declared.

Despite these heatedly expressed royal preferences, Britain remained firmly uncommitted. She was determined to hold aloof from any Continental entanglements. British sympathy might be with worthy Prussia rather than with frivolous France but she was not prepared to go to war on what her Foreign Secretary called 'a point limited to a matter of etiquette'.

On the morning of 28 July 1870, the Emperor, accompanied by the fourteen-year-old Prince Imperial, left Saint Cloud for the front. Although hopelessly ill, he was to take personal command of the army. The Empress remained behind as Regent. Two days later King Wilhelm of Prussia, accompanied by the gratified Count Bismarck, left Berlin for Mainz, near the French frontier. 'What suffering may be in store for us we do not know,' wrote Vicky to her mother; 'but one thing we all know that, as our honour and the safety of the country is at stake, no sacrifice must be shunned. Our feelings are best expressed in Lord Nelson's words, saying Germany (instead of England) expects every man to do his duty. . . .'

4

The Crown Princess's passionate concern for her country's safety proved quite unnecessary. The campaign went against France from the very start. Defeat followed defeat; 'the poor French,' noted the Queen, 'always to be driven away'. Lord

Granville, the Foreign Secretary, blamed the rapid French disintegration on 'a loose, unprincipled Government, and to everything having become so corrupt', whereas, in fact, the French defeats were due more to bad organization and uninspired leadership. Her generals were incompetent and the Emperor ill and apathetic. And, as imperialism reeled back from the front, so did republicanism gather strength in the capital. Lord Lyons, the British Ambassador in Paris, reported that the dynasty was falling lower and lower and that the Empress, as Regent, showed 'much pluck but little hope'. By the end of August, Gladstone was already preparing for the fall of the Second Empire. It might be the best thing for Europe, he assured the Queen. Although the Prime Minister was 'always fond of the French', noted Victoria in her Journal, 'he thought a Bonaparte on the throne had always an element of uncertainty and danger'.

As the Prussian victories mounted, so did the previously outraged tone of Vicky's letters to her mother become more patronizing. 'I am very glad that I am not in the Empress's position,' she wrote, 'the Emperor's too, must be a dreadful one. . . . Ever since the Emperor's health has been failing, the prestige of his genius has been waning and he has made one blunder after another. It is a melancholy history.'

Nor, in her exultation, could the Crown Princess resist having a dig at her brother, the Prince of Wales, by comparing his inactivity with the achievements of her husband, Crown Prince Frederick. 'I am sure dear Bertie must envy Fritz who has such a trying, but such a useful life. I had rather see him serve his country than sit by my side. . . .'

On 3 September 1870, just six weeks after the outbreak of hostilities, the Queen, who was in residence at Balmoral, was handed a telegram. Its contents almost took her breath away. One of the two French armies had capitulated at Sedan, and the Emperor Napoleon had surrendered himself to the King of Prussia.

'What astounding news!' wrote the ecstatic Crown Princess to her mother. 'Really I could hardly believe my ears when I heard it! Here the excitement and delight of the people knows no bounds. Poor Emperor! his career has ended, and he brought his fall upon himself. . . .'

Napoleon III was imprisoned, in some style, at Wilhelmshöhe near Cassel. Two days after his surrender a threatening mob forced the Empress Eugenie to flee the Tuileries. By that evening France was once more a Republic.

The fall of the Second Empire brought forth a triumphant flood from the Crown Princess. 'What will Bertie and Alex say to all these marvellous events?' she asked maliciously. 'When I think of the Emperor and Empress in the zenith of their glory, in '55 and at the time of the Exhibition when all the Sovereigns in Europe paid them their court, and they were so amiable and courteous to all, it seems a *curious* contrast! . . . It would be well if they would pause and think that immoderate frivolity and luxury depraves and ruins and ultimately leads to national misfortune. Our poverty, our dull towns, our plodding, hard-working *serious life,* has made us strong and determined; is wholesome for us. I should grieve were we to imitate Paris and be so taken up with pleasure that no time was left for self-examination and serious thought! Ancient history teaches us the same lesson as modern history—a hard and stern one for those who have to learn it by sad experience; the poor Emperor has leisure now to study it!'

The Queen showed more compassion. The entry in her Journal for 5 September noted that in Paris a mob had rushed into the Chambers to vote for the downfall of the Bonaparte dynasty and that a Republic had been proclaimed from the Hôtel de Ville. 'Not one vote was raised in favour of the unfortunate Emperor! How ungrateful!'

For the Empress, a message was drafted to the effect that the Queen was 'not insensible to the heavy blow which had fallen on her, nor forgetful of former days'.

'No one knows where she is!' concluded the Queen.

Part Three
'This time of terrible trial'

CHAPTER ELEVEN

Camden Place

1

Not until five days after the fall of the Second Empire did the Queen learn of the whereabouts of the Empress Eugenie. On 9 September 1870 she received a telegram to say that the Empress had landed at Hastings, in Kent, the day before. There she had been reunited with the Prince Imperial. Having separated from the Emperor before the capitulation at Sedan, the Prince had fled to England by another route.

A day or two later Victoria heard a fuller and more graphic account of the Empress's escape. The Queen's Private Secretary, Henry Ponsonby, received a letter from a certain Sir John Burgoyne; in it, the writer gave details of his own, purely fortuitous, involvement in the imperial drama.

On the afternoon of 6 September, Sir John Burgoyne, aboard his yacht in Deauville harbour, had been visited by two unknown men. They asked to be shown over the vessel. After a while one of the men (it was an American dentist, by the name of Evans, who practised in Paris) drew him to one side and revealed that the Empress Eugenie was in hiding in Deauville. It had been in Dr Evans's house that Eugenie and a single lady-in-waiting had sought refuge on her escape from the Tuileries two days before. As the Empress was anxious to escape from France, Evans had driven her, in secret, to Deauville. 'The Empress had no luggage of any sort or kind . . .' wrote Burgoyne, adding, darkly, that 'what she had to undergo in her journey from Paris to Deauville had far better never be known.'

Dr Evans then asked Burgoyne whether he would take the Empress to England that very evening. At first the Englishman demurred. The night was going to be stormy and he may well have been anxious to avoid any involvement in so political an escapade. However, after consultation with his wife, Burgoyne agreed. A little after midnight, Dr Evans brought the Empress and her companion, Madame Lebreton, on board. Eugenie seemed very upset but, on being assured by Burgoyne that she had nothing to fear, replied, in English, that she would be safe in the care of an English gentleman.

She was indeed. Despite mountainous seas which kept poor Madame Lebreton on her knees in prayer for most of the voyage, Burgoyne landed the Empress safely at Ryde, in the Isle of Wight, the following morning. From there she hurried to Hastings to join her son.

'I am especially anxious,' wrote Sir John Burgoyne to Henry Ponsonby, 'that it should be known, that all that occurred was by the most pure accident, as I fear an impression has got abroad that I was in Deauville harbour waiting events.'

The Queen lost no time in writing to the Empress to commiserate with her. 'Without appearing importunate,' she wrote, 'may Your Majesty permit me to repeat, myself, that which I have already made known to you—that is, that I think often of you during this time of terrible trial for you and for all that is dear to you. The memory of past times when Your Majesty and the Emperor received us under your hospitable roof, the visits which you have paid to us, and the kindness with which you have welcomed our children cannot leave me insensible to your great sorrow.'

The Prince of Wales showed even more compassion, if less circumspection. Extremely upset by the misfortunes of the imperial family, he wrote a letter to the Empress, offering her Chiswick House, near London, as a home. His impulsive gesture caused an uproar. Lord Granville, while expressing admiration for the Prince's generous sentiments, considered the offer indiscreet: after all, the Empress was still technically Regent of France. The Lord Chancellor thought that the gesture would be misunderstood: Britain, he argued, was about to recognize the new Republican government in France. The Queen regarded the offer as a 'presumptuous indiscretion'.

The Empress saved the day by declining the Prince's offer. She assured him that Camden Place, the house in Chislehurst,

Kent, in which she had recently established herself, would admirably provide her with the 'tranquillity and calm' which she so much desired.

Eugenie, with the Prince Imperial and a small suite, had moved into Camden Place towards the end of September 1870. Camden Place was no more than a modest country house but as it was inexpensive, secluded, close to a Catholic church and a mere half-hour's train journey from London, it suited the Empress very well. The exiles looked upon it as a temporary home only. With the war still raging in France (the new Republican government was continuing the fight), the Emperor a prisoner at Wilhelmshöhe, and the Prussians tending to treat Eugenie as Regent, the Empress imagined that her return to France would not be long delayed. She might protest that she was steering clear of all political action but she was certainly not regarding her exile as permanent. The situation in France was still far too fluid.

But by the end of November the Empress was still at Camden. And it was here, on a raw, dull and bitterly cold day, that Queen Victoria came from Windsor to see her. With the Queen was her youngest daughter, the thirteen-year-old Princess Beatrice.

The Empress and the Prince Imperial were at the door of the three-storeyed, red-brick mansion to meet the Queen. Behind them, in the hallway, stood the members of Eugenie's suite. The Empress was dressed entirely in black. 'She looks very thin and pale, but still very handsome,' noted Victoria. 'There is an expression of deep sadness in her face, and she frequently had tears in her eyes. She was dressed in the plainest possible way, without jewels or ornaments, and her hair simply done, in a net, at the back.'

The Prince Imperial the Queen pronounced to be 'a nice little boy but rather short and stumpy'. His eyes were down-slanting, like his mother's, but on the whole he looked more like the Emperor.

Princess Beatrice presented a posy to the Empress and then Eugenie led the Queen and her little party into a small drawing-room overlooking the park. The Queen, strangely enough, thought the house 'very French' and claimed, with her uncertain taste, that there were 'many pretty things about'. In fact, Camden Place had been rented, fully and tastelessly furnished, by the Empress; as yet she had added very little of her own. The Queen and the Empress sat side by side on a sofa. Taking care to avoid any topic which might prove embarrassing, Eugenie gave her visitor a full account of her last, nightmarish days in France. She had remained in the Tuileries as long as she could on 4 September, but after the mob had invaded the Chambers, a threatening crowd had seethed about the palace gardens, shouting for her dethronement. With few troops at her command and anxious to avoid bloodshed, the Empress had decided to leave. She had escaped by way of the Louvre. With only Madame Lebreton beside her, she had flung herself into a passing *fiacre* and had driven to the home of an imperial *conseilleur d'état*. He had not been at home; nor had the second person on whom they had called. They had then driven to the home of the Empress's dentist, Dr Evans. It was he who had taken them to Deauville. Never, declared the Empress, would she forget that flight from Paris.

With consummate tact, the Empress asked whether the Queen had had news of her two daughters in Germany, Vicky and Alice. *Oh! si seulement l'on pouvait avoir la paix!'* she cried out.

After half an hour, the Queen took her leave. Again the Empress came to the door. 'It was a sad visit,' wrote the Queen, 'and seemed like a strange dream.'

2

Six days later, on 5 December 1870, the Empress and her son returned the Queen's visit.

Victoria, accompanied by Prince Arthur, Prince Leopold and Princess Beatrice, met them at the door. The Empress was obviously upset; on mounting the stairs, she burst into tears, crying, *'Cela m'a fait une telle émotion.'* The Queen took her hand and led her into the Audience Room. Until the Empress was calmer, they spoke generally—of the room, of Windsor and of various mutual acquaintances. Then the Queen packed the children off on a tour of the Castle and the two women settled down to an intimate talk.

Victoria asked Eugenie about the sudden visit which she had paid to the Emperor at Wilhelmshöhe a few weeks before. This short, dramatic visit had helped reconcile husband and wife after many years of coolness. It was probable that Eugenie, feeling some prick of remorse for her often high-handed treatment of her husband, had been eager to make amends. Napoleon, the most forbearing of men, had appreciated her gesture and she had returned to England somewhat easier in her mind. It had taken the 'day of storm' she later admitted in one of her letters to Wilhelmshöhe, to prove that the ties between the two of them had not broken. She had intended staying at Wilhelmshöhe for two days, Eugenie told the Queen, but the imminent arrival of three important French prisoners, Napoleon's marshals, had sent her hurrying home. She had not wanted to face them.

Inevitably, the talk between the two women turned to the prospects of peace. She prayed for it unceasingly, claimed the Empress, but how could there be any hope of making peace when *'il n'y a pas de Gouvernement'*? With this Victoria was in complete agreement. The Republic certainly had no proper government; the revolution had been a 'misfortune'. Had it not been for the revolution, argued Eugenie, peace would have been concluded much sooner.

The Empress could not be allowed to take her leave without a visit to the mausoleum where Prince Albert lay buried. As it was pouring with rain, the two women drove from the Castle in a closed carriage. With due reverence the Empress entered the brightly lit, Byzantine-style temple and fell to her knees before the tomb. That done, she mounted the steps of the sarcophagus for a closer look at the 'dear reclining statue'. Victoria made careful note of Eugenie's comments. *'C'est bien beau,'* breathed the Empress, *'c'est chaud et clair, et cependant sérieux.'* The Queen could not have wanted better than that. The pilgrimage over, they returned to the Castle. Eugenie and the Prince Imperial left for Chislehurst at four.

'What a fearful contrast to her visit here in '55,' exclaimed Victoria when it was all over. 'Then all was state and pomp, wild excitement and enthusiasm—and now? How strange that I should have seen these two Revolutions, in '48 and '70! The poor Empress looked so lovely in her simple black, and so touching in her gentleness and submission.'

Victoria's use of the words 'gentleness and submission' to describe the Empress's demeanour is another example of that false light in which the Queen tended to see her guest. To those who were obliged to share Camden with Eugenie, it was a very different story. Away from Victoria's awe-inspiring presence, the Empress's behaviour was anything but gentle and submissive. Exile was proving extremely difficult for Eugenie. Just over three months before, as Regent, she had been in the thick of things; now, quite suddenly, she had nothing to do. She was like some powerful bird which had had its wings clipped: the will to fly was there, the ability to do so was gone. Restless, highly strung and impulsive, Eugenie was having trouble in adjusting herself to life at Camden. She fretted, she stormed, she railed on and on against those who had deserted the imperial cause.

'She seemed unable to overcome her resentments or to free her mind of its burden of rancour and revolt . . .' wrote Marie de Larminat, her favourite *demoiselle d'honneur* at Camden. 'She found it difficult to forgive; a caustic article in a newspaper, an odious insinuation; or a mere nothing would wound her to the quick, and sometimes put her completely out of humour, and we would pass some unpleasant hours. Her impetuous, passionate nature must have made her suffer more intensely than others.'

But to Victoria, the impression of Eugenie as a gentle, almost diffident creature had remained constant, and the fact that she had seen so little of her during her most triumphant years and was to see so much of her during the tragic ones, would confirm her first impressions. There was one slight difference: in the pages of the Queen's Journal, the 'dear Empress' now gave way to the 'poor Empress'.

It was during these first months of Eugenie's exile that Victoria's liking for her began to develop into something stronger. The Queen had always admired the Empress for her beauty, her sparkle and her good sense; now that Eugenie—like

Victoria herself—had been struck by tragedy, the Queen's heart went out to her. She saw her as a sister in sorrow. Gradually, Victoria became Eugenie's protector, champion and friend. The Prince Imperial's tutor, young Augustin Filon, who had joined his pupil at Camden, once analysed the friendship between the two women. 'They were very different in character and habits, and time rendered the contrast more striking,' he wrote. 'The Queen was hardworking and methodical, desirous of housing facts in her brain and marshalling them in good order; the Empress was impulsive like all her race, but incapable of continuing any regular routine, quick to perceive a truth which might have escaped better-trained eyes, yet losing sight of it again after much reflection and discussion: the one woman was very reserved, the other very imprudent, but both were incapable of deceit; they had reached the age when one esteems sincerity above everything.'

In addition, they were both women of sterling character, blessed with extraordinary powers of endurance.

3

Early in January 1871, with the Franco-Prussian war in its sixth month and Paris in a state of siege, the Crown Princess dashed off a characteristically tactless letter to her mother, telling her that she had sent her a large parcel. The parcel contained a screen.

'This screen,' she went on to explain, 'stood in the Empress's Boudoir at St Cloud. When the French shells set fire to the house, the Prussian soldiers, as you know, tried to extinguish the fire and save the valuable things. A Prussian soldier made his way through smoke and flames at great risk to his own life, and carried off this screen, which he delivered up to General Kirchbach (a few minutes later it would have been burnt). General Kirchbach asked the King's leave to send me this screen, and obtained it. Although St Cloud is *not* the private property of the Emperor and Empress, and the *mobilier* belongs to the State—consequently is no longer theirs, yet *I* consider this, and everything else saved, *not* a trophy of war, and do *not* see *what right* I have to keep it. Moreover, I would not wish to have anything in my possession which had belonged to the Empress, who has always been *so kind* to me, and on different occasions made me such handsome presents. I have said nothing to anyone at Versailles, neither to the King nor Fritz, as I can do what I like with a thing that has been sent to me, but I would ask you, dearest Mama, to restore this screen to the poor Empress when you think fit; you can tell her its history and how I came by it. Of course, *I cannot offer* it as *a present* whilst we are at war, that would not do; besides, I consider it simply restoring a piece of property to its rightful owner, which must be YOUR doing. I trust in this way no one will blame me, whilst I am doing simply what I consider my duty.

'I do *not* approve of war trophies, at least of *ladies* possessing them; for soldiers they are lawful of course, and every Army in the world considers them so. Perhaps you will kindly tell me *when* the parcel arrives and when it has through your kindness reached its destination. . . .'

Lord Granville, on being consulted about the screen, imagined that its presentation to the Empress would do no harm. However, after further thought on the matter, he sent a second letter to the Queen, this time advising her against the handing over of the gift. Taking care to refer to the Crown Princess's 'elevated sentiments', he went on to explain that whereas war trophies might mean something else to other nations, to the British they meant things like flags and guns. The taking of objects from palaces and country houses, such as was being practised by the victorious Germans, would, in England, be called 'acts of plunder, or looting'. It might have been better, thought Lord Granville, if the Crown Princess had abstained from anything that might be regarded as such. Moreover, there was something not quite right about restoring, to the Empress in England, an object which belonged to the State in France. And then what if the Empress, regarding the screen as proof of plunder, refused to accept it? No, it was all too risky by half. The best thing, thought Granville, would be for the screen to remain unpacked until the war was over. Let the Crown Princess then decide what to do with it.

144

Victoria, appreciating the sense of Granville's reasoning, thanked him for his advice and let the matter drop. It was as well. The story of the stolen screen would have done nothing to endear British public opinion towards Germany. Already British sympathies were swinging away from the arrogant victors towards the desperate defenders. Even *The Times*, which had consistently championed the Prussians against the French, was beginning to wonder whether the conquerors would show proper magnanimity towards the enemy. What finally disenchanted the majority of Englishmen was the German bombardment of besieged Paris; not even the militant Crown Princess could entirely stifle her feelings of guilt. 'The bombardment is too dreadful to be thought of, and yet I know it cannot be helped,' she wrote. 'The French should have thought of all the risks they were running in case theirs should not be the winning side when they forced the war!'

A fortnight after the commencement of the bombardment, on 18 January 1871, the German Empire was proclaimed at Versailles. In the same Galerie des Glaces where, as the guest of Napoleon and Eugenie, he had been presented to Victoria and Albert in 1855, Bismarck now read out the proclamation which made King Wilhelm of Prussia Emperor of a united Germany. Peace was signed a few weeks later.

'Now [that] we have *peace at last*,' wrote the Crown Princess petulantly to her mother, 'the news of *our* doings will no longer exasperate the English by working up their pity for the unfortunate but guilty French.' Count Bismarck, she added defensively, was not immortal; 'he will be as quickly forgotten as the poor Emperor Napoleon, who is now scarcely remembered. . . .'

CHAPTER TWELVE

'That same pleasing, gentle and gracious manner'

1

The end of the Franco-Prussian war meant the release of Napoleon III from Wilhelmshöhe. On 20 March 1871 he arrived in England to join the Empress at Camden.

There had been some correspondence, between Napoleon and Eugenie, on the question of whether or not they should live in England once he was free. The Emperor had toyed with the idea of living in Switzerland; the Empress had suggested Trieste. On one point Napoleon had been adamant: it was essential that they live in a 'free' country, such as England or Switzerland. In less stable states, they were likely to prove an embarrassment to both government and individuals. 'So when I am free,' he had written rather whimsically, 'I should like to go to England, and live with you and Louis in a little cottage with bow-windows and creeper.'

That Napoleon III was in favour of living in England was one thing; would England itself be quite so enthusiastic about the idea? After all, Napoleon I had cherished fond hopes of being allowed to settle down in an English country house; would his nephew, for all his less frightening reputation, prove any more welcome? Any doubts which the Emperor might have had on this score were dispelled as soon as he landed at Dover. He was given a vociferous welcome. He was cheered, applauded and pelted with flowers. If the British public had been somewhat wary of him during the last few years, they were ready to take him once more to their hearts. The warmth of this reception alarmed Napoleon's unrelenting critic, *The Times*, considerably. 'What,' it asked the following day, 'are we to think and what will the German people think and what will the French people think, of all this effusive and unqualified admiration?' *The Times* simply could not understand Napoleon III's popularity in England. The truth was that the majority of Englishmen never shared the late Prince Consort's antipathy towards Napoleon III. Queen Victoria was correct in assuring the Empress that 'the dear Emperor was much loved here'.

The Queen herself, now that the Emperor had been stripped of power, found herself falling under the old spell of his personality. A week after his arrival at Camden, she invited him to Windsor. For Victoria, the meeting was fraught with emotion. She could not help drawing a parallel between this doleful occasion and their first, enchanting meeting in 1855. Then he had come 'in perfect triumph, dearest Albert bringing him from Dover, the whole country mad to receive him. . . .' Now, as she stood at the door, it was a very different Napoleon whom she watched alight, rather painfully, from the carriage. Gone were the dashing uniform, the cat's-whisker moustaches, the dyed chestnut hair: 'he had grown very stout and grey and his moustaches are no longer curled and waxed as formerly,' she noted. The Queen must have been conscious of the change in her own appearance as well. No longer was she the alert, brightly dressed young woman who had responded so readily to his flattering attentions; who had once laughingly threatened to arrive in Paris by train, bag in hand, to beg dinner and a night's lodging at the Tuileries.

For the Emperor, the occasion was no less poignant. He looked depressed and his eyes were wet with tears. Victoria embraced him '*comme de rigueur*' and he, pulling himself together, remarked quietly, 'It's been a very long time since I have seen Your Majesty.'

Together, they mounted the stairs to the Audience Room.

As the two of them sat talking, so did the Queen find herself responding, as of old, to 'that same pleasing, gentle and gracious manner'. Not quite all the magic had worn off since the halcyon days of the Anglo-French *entente*. They spoke about the Emperor's captivity (he had no word of complaint against his German captors), about the present regrettable state of France and about Napoleon's 'renewed' admiration for England.

147

Unfortunately, their discussion on the origins of the war was interrupted; Victoria considered this 'most provoking'.

The Queen's Household had been assembled in the corridor, and before he left the Emperor passed along the line, pausing to say a few kind words to each of them. Again, it was a heart-rending echo of the triumphant imperial visit sixteen years before. Napoleon left for Chislehurst at half past three.

Queen Victoria returned the Emperor's visit a few days later.

Since the arrival of Napoleon at Camden Place, things had taken on a more formal flavour. Even Chislehurst had become conscious of being, in a way, an imperial seat. It was thus through a great crowd of cheering people that the Queen drove in an open carriage from Chislehurst station to the house. She was met, at the door, by the Prince Imperial ('looking very much better') and, inside the house, by the Emperor and Empress and their suite. Victoria presented Eugenie with a posy of violets and primroses and they all settled down in the small and over-furnished drawing-room. They spoke about the situation in Paris, where yet another battle was raging—this time between the Communards, who had seized control of Paris, and the Republican government troops, stationed at Versailles. It was proving an extremely bloody insurrection. It lasted for two months and was crushed by the Republican government with the utmost ruthlessness. Over twenty thousand people were killed during 'Bloody Week' alone, and half Paris, including the Hôtel de Ville and the Tuileries, was gutted by fire.

The Empress, declared Queen Victoria, was greatly excited by the revolution but the Emperor was more restrained. His sole comment was, *'Je ne vois pas comment ils peuvent payer.'*

The Queen took her leave at a quarter to five feeling, she admitted, very tired and sad.

Victoria's feeling of tiredness was not due entirely to emotional strain. There had been an important contributory factor. Throughout the visit she had been obliged to sit in a room in which all the windows had been tightly closed. Victoria's horror of stuffy rooms was matched only by Napoleon's horror of fresh air. Whereas in the Queen's apartments, even on the coldest day, the windows were always flung wide open,

Napoleon's rooms, even in the height of summer, were kept
almost airtight. His suite of rooms at the Tuileries had resembled
nothing so much as a succession of hot, golden boxes, and now,
at Camden, he was never comfortable unless the windows were
shut tight and a fire blazing in the grate. 'The heat in the room
overpowering,' noted the Queen in her Journal that evening.

Quite clearly, something would have to be done about the
matter before the Queen again visited Camden. The delicate
task fell to Lady Jane Ely, one of Victoria's ladies. Lady Ely
wrote about it to Lady Sydney, wife of the Lord Lieutenant
of Kent, who lived near Camden Place. Lady Sydney, in turn,
dropped a hint to the Duke de Bassano, head of the imperial
Household. Bassano mentioned it to the Empress. Before long
Lady Ely was able to assure the Queen that when next she
visited Camden Place, the rooms would be 'fresher'.

There was one feature of the Emperor's attitude which the
Queen found especially striking during this exchange of visits.
That was his stoicism. It was a characteristic which also amazed
his fellow exiles. Whereas Eugenie railed almost continuously
against those whom she considered had betrayed the Empire,
Napoleon said nothing. He never complained. There was never
a murmur against those who had misled him, deserted him, or
who were now covering him with abuse. Nor did he complain
about the little things: the food or the weather or the same,
sad faces. On that bored, irritable and often despairing company
at Camden Place, his presence had a soothing and inspiring
effect. His self-control was an example to them all. 'He bore
his terrible misfortunes,' wrote the admiring Victoria, 'with
meekness, dignity and patience.'

Lord Malmesbury, who had been in attendance on the Queen
during that unfortunate visit to the Cherbourg Fêtes in 1858,
was one of the first people to visit the Emperor at Camden; he
too, was impressed by Napoleon's resignation. 'His quiet and
calm dignity and absence of all nervousness and irritability
were the grandest examples of human moral courage that the
severest stoic could have imagined,' he wrote.

And years later, when Eugenie was a very old lady, she would
speak of her husband's great qualities of forgiveness which she,
no matter how hard she might try, could never emulate. 'I

want to tell you how fine he was,' she once said, 'how unselfish, how generous. In our happy times I always found him simple and good, kindly and compassionate: he would put up with opposition and misrepresentation with wonderful complaisance . . . when we were overwhelmed with misfortune, his stoicism and gentleness were sublime. You should have seen him during those last years at Chislehurst: never a word of complaint, or blame, or abuse. I often used to beg him to defend himself, to repulse some imprudent attack or the vile execrations hurled at him, to check once and for all the flood of insults that were endlessly pouring over us. But he would reply gently: "No, I shall not defend myself . . . sometimes a disaster falls upon a nation of such a kind that it is justified in blaming it all, even unfairly, upon its ruler. . . . A sovereign can offer no excuses, he can plead no extenuating circumstances. It is his highest prerogative to shoulder all the responsibilities incurred by those who have served him . . . or those who have betrayed him."'

2

Not only was Queen Victoria once more warming to Napoleon III's relaxed and gentlemanly manner; she was reverting to her former political opinion of him as well. That he was not as much to blame for the Franco-Prussian war as she had previously assumed was gradually becoming clear to her. Her son-in-law, Crown Prince Frederick, visited Victoria soon after the war and from him she learnt something of its origins. Fritz, whose patriotism towards his own country was never quite as blind as his wife's towards her adopted country, revealed that Bismarck's part in the promoting of the conflict had been considerable. The German Chancellor might be clever and energetic but he was also 'bad, unprincipled and all-powerful'. The Crown Prince declared that he would not be at all surprised if Bismarck were one day to make war on England. The Franco-Prussian war had certainly been as much his as Napoleon III's doing. 'This corroborates and justifies what many people have said,' wrote Victoria.

And after Napoleon's death, the Queen assured her sceptical

secretary, Henry Ponsonby, that the Emperor was 'a most faithful ally to this country, much attached to it and most hospitable to the English and, to those who trusted him, most lovable, charming and amiable'.

Once the Emperor had settled permanently in England, the Queen went out of her way to make him feel welcome. No one would ever believe, said the Empress in old age, how many 'delicate attentions' the Queen lavished on them during the first years of exile. She always treated them as sovereigns. If the Emperor and Empress happened to be visiting some member of the royal family near Windsor Castle, the Queen would drive over to see them. On the occasion of her State drive to St Paul's Cathedral to give thanks for the Prince of Wales's recovery from a serious illness, the Queen invited the imperial couple to view the procession from the privacy of Buckingham Palace. Once when she visited Camden, she delighted her hosts by assuring them that she had no wish to visit Paris now that they were no longer there.

She was no less attentive to Louis, the Prince Imperial. First reports of the Prince, since his arrival in England, had not been altogether favourable. The Queen had been told that his spell with the French army had spoiled him, that he was conceited and assertive. Someone had reported that he looked undistinguished; Victoria herself had described him as 'short and stumpy'. But she was beginning to revise her opinion. Each time she saw him, she had something more complimentary to say about him. Indeed, there were few who could resist his particular blend of high spirits and good manners. Even the stiff-backed Mr Gladstone found himself succumbing to the boy's charm. At a military review at Bushey Park, to which the sixteen-year-old Prince had been invited, Victoria noted that he came in for a good deal of cheering. What the newspapers called his 'somewhat melancholy grace', plus the expertise with which he handled his horse, made a considerable impression on the public. The Queen had him called over and for a while he sat his horse beside the royal carriage, chatting to her with an ease of manner which amazed her attendants. The Queen, with her *penchant* for dashing, dark-haired men, thought that he looked 'very nice'.

Towards the end of 1872, Louis entered the Royal Military College at Woolwich as a cadet. If he were one day to be Emperor of the French (on this, the Household at Camden were determined) he must, as a Napoleon, prove himself a soldier first. His move to Woolwich had Queen Victoria's full approval.

In the meantime, the Emperor had fully regained his old popularity with the British public. On the rare occasions that he left the grounds of Camden Place to walk across Chislehurst Common, the villagers were always impressed by his unaffected manner. His presence at local cricket matches won delighted approval, despite the fact that he once asked, in all innocence, whether the game was played for money. 'No, Sire', answered a shocked fellow spectator, 'for honour.' One day the blaring of a band brought the Emperor and Empress to the gates of Camden to investigate the noise. They found themselves amongst the employees of the Greenwich District Board of Works on their annual outing. Napoleon was obliged to listen to a flowery speech in his honour and when, in reply, he claimed that he had always been a good friend to England, the crowd was ecstatic. 'We know you have! You have!' they cried.

In September 1871 the Emperor and the Prince Imperial spent a few weeks at Torquay. The train journey from Chislehurst to the coast was a triumphant progress; in Torquay itself Napoleon drove through an enthusiastic crowd, all shouting '*Vive l'Empereur!*' His visit to Bath, on the way home, was no less successful. 'The Emperor,' wrote the excited Prince Imperial to his mother, 'was given an extraordinary ovation; he was escorted by a crowd from the station to his hotel, and from the hotel to the station, with a great accompaniment of cheers and handshakes. . . .'

Although Napoleon had been made to feel so thoroughly at home in England, he had no intention of remaining there indefinitely. He had certainly not given up hope of regaining his throne. Hardly had he arrived at Camden before he began thinking in terms of a return to France. About this particular aspect of his life at Chislehurst, Queen Victoria knew nothing; Napoleon, as always, was working underground. His agents were crossing the Channel on secret missions; France was being flooded with Bonapartist literature; money was being borrowed from here and there; party members were closeted, for hours on end, in the Emperor's study.

By the end of 1872, a plan had been worked out. It was to be another 'Return from Elba', another triumphant and bloodless march to Paris. Napoleon III would leave England in secret, join his cousin Plon-Plon in Switzerland and make for Lyons, where the commander of the garrison was known to be loyal to the Bonapartist cause. From here they would set out for Paris. A date was fixed for March 1873.

It was a bold plan and one which depended, almost entirely, on the Emperor. Would he be able to withstand its rigours? By the end of the year 1872, it seemed very doubtful that he would.

3

Late in December 1872, Sir William Gull, the Queen's physician, and Sir Henry Thompson, the renowned urologist who had once performed a successful operation on Victoria's Uncle Leopold, were summoned to Camden to examine the Emperor Napoleon III. During the past few months, the Emperor's physical condition had deteriorated badly. By now he was in almost continuous pain. The doctors diagnosed a stone in the bladder, 'the size of a large date', and an immediate operation was decided upon. Sir Henry Thompson was installed in the house and the first operation performed on 2 January 1873. The stone was found, crushed and as many fragments as possible removed. A second operation was performed on 6 January. After careful manipulation, a further fragment was removed. The presence of yet another obstructing fragment was suspected and a third operation decided upon.

Queen Victoria, in residence at Osborne, was kept fully informed on what was happening at Camden. At luncheon on 7 January—the day after the Emperor's second operation—she was handed a letter from the Prince of Wales. In it were enclosed two bulletins from Sir Henry Thompson. Sir Henry reported having performed the operations but admitted that he still considered the case very serious. He was not sure that he would be able to pull the Emperor through.

The bulletins alarmed the Queen considerably. For the following two days the thought of the Emperor's suffering was almost continuously on her mind. On the morning of 9 January—the day on which the third operation was to be performed—she asked if any news had come through from Chislehurst. She was told that there was none. Not until she returned from her afternoon drive did she hear anything more. Lady Jane Ely came into her room, carrying a telegram and saying, 'It is all over.' The telegram was from Napoleon III's secretary, Franceschini Pietri, asking Lady Ely to tell the Queen that '*L'Empereur a cessé de souffrir à II heures moins 14. L'Impératrice est dans les larmes.*'

There and then the Queen sat down to write to the Empress. Her letter was much more than a conventional expression of sympathy; the sincerity of Victoria's feelings is apparent in every line. She assured Eugenie that she would never forget the Emperor's kindness to her; the memory of the days they had spent together in France and England would never fade from her heart. She signed her message, as in the great days of the Second Empire, 'Your Imperial Majesty's affectionate sister, Victoria R.'

The letter was sent off with an equerry and the Queen spent the rest of the afternoon dispatching and receiving telegrams. The German royalties seem to have been especially concerned about the death of their recently vanquished enemy. Their 'particularly kind' messages to the Empress, the Queen addressed to the Prince Imperial—the sixteen-year-old boy who had suddenly been elevated to Head of the House.

'Had a great regard for the Emperor, who was so amiable and kind . . .' wrote the Queen in her Journal that evening. 'He had been such a faithful ally to England and I could but think of the wonderful position he had, after being a poor, insignificant exile, of the magnificent reception given to him in England in 1855, and his agreeable visit here in '57, and ours to Paris in '55! And now to die like this from the results of an operation, though it may have been inevitable, seems too tragic and sad.'

Her letter to the German Empress Augusta struck a less lyrical note. 'I am furious at the horrid indelicate details which the newspapers have published and are still publishing, day after day,' she exclaimed. 'Doctors and especially surgeons, are like butchers, nearly all of them without feeling!'

The Emperor's funeral posed a problem for the Queen. Should she risk offending the French Republic by attending the funeral of the enemy of the new regime? She decided that she could not. It was as well; had the news of the restoration plot being hatched at Camden at the time of Napoleon's death leaked out, the Queen—although unaware of it—would have been in a compromising position.

For the Prince of Wales, as heir to the throne, the situation was less well defined. He, of course, was very anxious to attend the funeral. At first, Victoria was inclined to let him go. But on second thoughts, and after consultation with Lord Granville and others, she decided against it. As the Bonapartists were flocking to Camden in their thousands to pay homage to the late Emperor, Victoria feared some sort of imperialist demonstration. It would be better if the Prince were in no way involved. She suggested that one of her other sons, perhaps Prince Alfred, or her son-in-law Prince Christian, might be a more appropriate representative. But Bertie insisted. He claimed that if he were not present, no lesser royal representative should be. 'One cannot be wrong in showing respect to fallen greatness,' he wrote stubbornly. For once, Victoria gave way. It was not really much of a *volte-face* on her part: she had been in sympathy with her son's wish all along.

Mr Gladstone was not anything like so resigned on the matter. In a letter to Lord Granville, he contrasted the Prince's 'real good nature and sympathy' with his 'total want of political judgement, either inherited or acquired'.

None the less, on 14 January 1873, the Prince of Wales attended the lying-in-state. He was accompanied by Prince Alfred and Prince Christian. The three of them were met at the door of Camden Place by the Prince Imperial and led into the hall in which the Emperor's body was displayed. Napoleon III lay, in uniform, in a satin-lined coffin. His moustache was jauntily waxed as of old and his hair combed flatteringly forward. The embalming had turned his face a somewhat unfortunate shade of yellow. The atmosphere was heavy with the scent of violets and the heat of candles. The sons of Queen Victoria bowed low to the late Emperor of the French and then went upstairs to pay their respects to the Empress. Eugenie, wrapped in mourning veils and sitting in a shuttered room, received them briefly. She was conserving her strength for the hordes of Bonapartists who would have to be faced the following day.

On 15 January 1873, the Emperor was buried in the little church of St Mary on Chislehurst Common. The great crowds, the hundreds of carriages, the beautiful weather, gave the proceedings something of the atmosphere of a fashionable race meeting. The Prince of Wales was able to see all his old Parisian friends; the only awkward moment was when a deputation of artisans, assuming him to be sympathetic to the Bonapartist cause, offered to present him with an address. Very wisely, the Prince declined to receive it. This was the extent of his involvement in what the Queen had feared would be an imperialist demonstration; when that demonstration took place, the Prince had already left Chislehurst. The deputation of workmen, frustrated in their efforts to present an address to the royal heir, turned their attention to the imperial heir instead. Waving a huge tricolour, they bounded across the lawns of Camden Place, shouting '*Vive l'Empereur!*' The slight, bareheaded figure, with the red cordon of the *Légion d'honneur* gleaming under his mourning cloak, betrayed, says one of the Household, 'a movement of disapproval, almost of distress', and hurried into the house.

Ten days later the Empress wrote to the Queen to thank her for her expressions of sympathy. 'If anything in the world could mitigate my sorrow, Your Majesty's kind words would have done so, but my heart is broken with sorrow.'

Victoria had asked Eugenie for some souvenir of the late Emperor and the Empress decided to give her his travelling-clock. With it came this message. 'It has marked the happy times of other days and the long hours of moral and physical suffering, both the years of joy and those of grief; but how great a part of them were the latter!'

4

Less than a month later, the Queen herself visited Chislehurst. With her, as always, was her youngest daughter Princess Beatrice. They drove first to St Mary's, where the Emperor lay buried. Each carrying a wreath, the Queen and her daughter entered what Victoria described as 'a pretty, rural little place, quite the village church'. The interior was distinctly less appealing. It was cramped and dark, and only when her eyes had grown accustomed to the gloom did the Queen see the Emperor's coffin. To the right of the altar, behind a railing, in 'the smallest space possible' rested Napoleon III's remains. The coffin was covered with a black velvet pall, embroidered with golden bees. On it were heaped innumerable wreaths. The Queen and Princess Beatrice duly added theirs to the pile.

The scene in St Mary's made a poignant contrast to the grandiose resting place of Napoleon I which the Queen had visited, eighteen years before, in the company of Napoleon III. Then, on the arm of an attentive Emperor in the full flood of his popularity and power, she had stood in the midst of a distinguished company—the torches flaring, the organ thundering, the uniforms glittering, the storm crashing—paying homage at the tomb of Britain's greatest enemy. Now, in the company of her daughter and a few members of her Household, she stood in this dim, draughty little church to pay a last tribute to the memory of a dear friend.

From St Mary's they drove to Camden Place. At the door, looking pale and sad, stood the Prince Imperial. Behind him, 'in the deepest mourning, looking very ill, very handsome, and the picture of sorrow, was the poor dear Empress'. In silence, the two women embraced and then, taking the Queen's arm, Eugenie led her upstairs to her little boudoir. 'She cried a good deal,' noted Victoria, 'but quietly and gently, and that sweet face, always a sad one, looked inexpressibly pathetic.'

Pulling herself together, Eugenie told the Queen all about the Emperor's last days. He had been suffering for months, she said; even a carriage drive had been agony for him. On the morning of his death, Eugenie had been preparing to drive over to Woolwich to see the Prince Imperial when the doctors stopped her. The Emperor, they said, was having '*une petite crise*'. She took off her hat and hurried to the sickroom. As she did so, one of the doctors dashed past her, calling for the priest. Realizing the worst, she crossed to the bedside and kissed her husband's hand. Someone whispered '*Voila l'Impératrice, Sire*', but he was no longer able to see her. He merely moved his lips as though to kiss her. A few minutes later he was dead.

The preparations for the funeral—the hammering and knocking in that small house—had been a painful ordeal. But far worse had been the behaviour of the late Emperor's cousin, the irascible Plon-Plon.

The full story was this. As soon as he heard of the Emperor's death, Plon-Plon came bustling over to Camden Place. This, surely, was the moment for him to take charge of the destinies of the imperial House. With the Prince Imperial still a minor and the Empress, whom Plon-Plon detested, a mere woman, it would be up to him to manage affairs from now on. With hopes running high, Plon-Plon rummaged about for, discovered and opened the Emperor's will. Its contents astounded him. The will had been drawn up during the Empire and never revised: Eugenie was left in control of everything. Plon-Plon was furious. He accused the Empress of having destroyed a second will and slammed out of the house.

A day or two later he sent her a message. It outlined the conditions on which the two of them could be friends. The first was that he be given absolute control of the Imperial Party. The second was that he should assume sole guardianship of the Prince Imperial.

It was Eugenie's turn to lose her temper. Did Plon-Plon imagine that she—three times Regent of France—was unfit, not only to direct the policies of the Party, but to bring up her own child? So strong was her upsurge of anger against Plon-Plon that it all but eclipsed her grief for her husband. Indeed, there was nothing like a good row for shaking Eugenie out of herself. Grief, she admitted, might have crushed her, but Plon-Plon had roused her numbed sensibilities.

The Queen was now treated to an account of Plon-Plon's infamous behaviour. However, in the telling, Eugenie would have been careful to play down her own fiery reaction and to stress Plon-Plon's inhumanity. He had wished, she sobbed, to take Louis ('all that I have') away from Woolwich and away from her. He had told her that the Prince of Wales disapproved of Louis being at Woolwich (this Victoria denied hotly) and that he was therefore getting him out of England. But Eugenie had remained firm. She was not going to allow Plon-Plon 'faire l'aventure' with her son. Nor was Louis prepared to yield to his cousin's wishes. All in all, noted the Queen, Plon-Plon had 'behaved very badly'.

Having got this off her chest, Eugenie showed the Queen the Emperor's apartments. They consisted of two small rooms—a study and a bedroom—at the back of the house. They were exactly as he had left them. 'All his things on the table, so sad to see,' wrote the Queen, adding, in her own, ever-fresh grief, 'as I know but too well.'

Victoria took her leave, but the sight of the Empress, dressed from head to toe in unrelieved black, haunted her for days afterwards. 'It was a melancholy visit,' she sighed, 'and I see the Empress's sad face constantly before me.'

These mournful events had had one remarkable effect on Queen Victoria: they had converted her to Bonapartism. 'The Queen does *not* [think] the Bonapartist cause will lose by the poor Emperor's death,' she wrote to Prince Albert's biographer, Theodore Martin, 'on the contrary *she* thinks the reverse. *For* the peace of Europe, she thinks (though the Orleans Princes are her dear friends and connections and—some—relations, and she would not for the world have it *said* as coming from her) that it would be best if the Prince Imperial was *ultimately* to succeed.'

That France might just possibly manage to drag itself along without some form of monarchy was unthinkable to the Queen of England.

CHAPTER THIRTEEN

The Prince Imperial

1

Exactly how the Prince Imperial was going to succeed to the throne of France was an open question. It was going to need rather more than the Queen of England's conviction to turn him into an Emperor of the French.

For the moment the Empress Eugenie was quite content to let things remain as they were. Louis was at Woolwich ('which the boy likes very much, and is only half an hour's drive from Chislehurst', wrote the Queen) and, all things considered, he was doing remarkably well there. Although his English was not quite perfect and his unselfconsciousness smacked of showing-off, he was a hard worker. He was also—and this counted for more among his Anglo-Saxon colleagues—an extremely good sport. So the imperial succession would have to wait for a year or two until the imperial heir was ready to do something about claiming it.

The Imperialists themselves did not show the same commend-able patience. Making the Prince's eighteenth birthday an excuse for one of those imperialist demonstrations which Victoria feared so much, they braved the Channel crossing and packed the grounds of Camden Place to acclaim their leader. Louis made a very creditable speech, both he and the Empress were loudly cheered, and the Bonapartists trooped back to France, delighted in the knowledge that the heir was shaping well. The festivities over, Louis returned to Woolwich.

He passed out at the end of 1874. Victoria, who had kept a friendly eye on his career, wrote to the Duke of Cambridge, Commander-in-Chief of the army, expressing her gratification at the success of the dear young Prince Imperial. 'Who knows,' she continued, 'what his future may be, and the Academy will,

I am sure, always feel proud that he distinguished himself in their school, and that he should have acquitted himself so honourably, and, above all, *behaved* so well!'

Louis's behaviour, in fact, was beginning to please her more and more. He was developing into exactly the sort of young man she liked. Like his father, whom Victoria had once found so attractive, he was short, sallow-skinned and dark; he had, too, something of the late Emperor's romantic aura. He, also, was an exotic. 'In features,' wrote a contemporary, 'with his long oval face and black hair . . . and lean shapely head, he was a Spaniard of the Spaniards. One recognized in him no single characteristic of the Frenchman, he was a veritable hidalgo. . . .' For, if Louis had inherited his father's seductive charm, he had inherited much of Eugenie's particularly Spanish beauty: he had the same down-slanting eyes, the same straight nose, the same firm jaw. In personality, too, he was very much his mother's son. All the Empress's more commendable characteristics were there—her enthusiasm, her vivacity, her vitality and her honesty. He was extraordinarily self-confident. Nothing unnerved him.

Henry Ponsonby always claimed that he knew of only two people who were quite unafraid of Queen Victoria: the one was John Brown and the other the Prince Imperial. Louis's unselfconsciousness, which had tended to embarrass his colleagues at Woolwich, remained unshaken in the face of this imperious little lady whose level stare once reduced even the redoubtable Bismarck to a cold sweat. And she, in turn, found his naturalness thoroughly disarming.

Once, when the Prince and his mother were guests of the Queen at Osborne, Louis was seated beside her at dinner. To most people, the Queen's dinners were a form of torture: the rooms were ice cold and no one spoke above a nervous whisper. This chilly atmosphere affected the young Prince not at all. He chatted happily to his hostess throughout the meal. When, after dinner, a fellow guest asked if the Queen did not terrify him, Louis looked at his questioner in amazement.

'Good heavens, no!' he answered, 'Why should she? We like each other.'

And so they did. The Queen certainly gave many proofs of

her growing fondness for him. Pride of place among the books on his shelves were two from the Queen. One was an edition of Shakespeare, the other a copy of Victoria's own book, *Leaves from the Journal of Our Life in the Highlands*. Both sported the inscription: 'To my cousin the Prince Imperial, from his affectionate Cousin Victoria R.' In 1875, when Theodore Martin finally completed the first volume of his monumental *Life of the Prince Consort*, the Prince Imperial was among those who received autographed copies from the Queen. In a letter worthy of his late father, Louis wrote to thank the Queen for her gift. '*Rien ne pouvait avoir plus de prix à mes yeux,*' he wrote gallantly.

In 1875 Louis took part in the manœuvres at Aldershot, and Queen Victoria made a point of writing to Sir Howard Elphinstone, who was there with Prince Arthur, to ask after him. She felt a really affectionate interest in the Prince, she wrote, and would be most grateful if Sir Howard could tell her how he was getting on. Was he *in good hands* and in a good set? What made her especially anxious was the fact that the Prince was there quite alone, with not even a confidential valet to keep an eye on him. The Queen's heart sank at the thought of this unattended young Prince—or indeed, any young man— being 'exposed to the contact' of a certain colonel.

Sir Howard hastened to reassure her. The Prince was in safe hands. The captain of his battery was an excellent man— quite different, one assumes, from the notorious colonel.

In order to find the Prince, Sir Howard had been obliged to trudge across soggy fields in streaming rain. He had discovered Louis encamped in a dismal, rain-lashed field called 'Colony Bog'. While his brother officers were busily digging trenches to drain the water away from the tents, the Prince Imperial was attending to the cooking. As a Frenchman, he smilingly told Sir Howard, it was his *métier* to look after the cuisine. He was extremely gratified by the Queen's interest in his welfare; would Sir Howard assure her that he was 'as happy as it is possible to be'?

Louis was no less of a favourite with the Prince of Wales. Although too young to be a member of the Marlborough House set (Louis was some fourteen years younger than Bertie), the Prince Imperial often met with the Prince and Princess of Wales in the course of his excursions into English society. The occasions were not always notable for their decorum. Both princes shared the contemporary passion for practical jokes, with Louis proving particularly resourceful. Lillie Langtry, then in the first flush of her social success, tells the story of a seance, attended by both princes, at which Louis was discovered emptying bags of flour over Bertie's head. On another occasion the two men, having hoisted a live donkey through a bedroom window, dressed it in nightclothes and tucked it up in a guest's bed. It was all faintly reminiscent of Biarritz during the Empire.

But although Louis was renowned for his charm, his frankness and his high spirits, there was a great deal more to him than that. He had a more serious, almost solemn side to his nature of which only his most intimate associates were aware. That he would one day be qualified to fill the French throne, the Household at Camden never doubted. Even Eugenie, who had been loath to abdicate her leadership of the Bonapartist party when Louis came of age, did so because of his abilities rather than because it was expected of her. The Prince had about him an air of authority of which even his assertive mother stood in awe.

The Prince of Wales always claimed to have recognized these qualities of leadership. 'If it had been the will of Providence,' he said in later years, 'that he should have been called to succeed his father as the sovereign of that great country our neighbour, I believe he would have proved an admirable sovereign and that he, like his father, would have been a true and great ally to this country.'

2

Throughout the 1870s it was rumoured that the Prince Imperial would one day be tied to the British royal family by a bond closer than friendship.

It had all started in the year 1872. On the occasion of that military review in Bushey Park, when the Queen had noted that the Prince had been loudly cheered and that he looked 'very nice', the fifteen-year-old Princess Beatrice had been sitting beside her mother in the carriage. After spending a few minutes in conversation with the Queen, the Prince had ridden round to the other side of the carriage to talk to Princess Beatrice. The watching public, seeing the dark, self-confident French Prince and the fair, reserved English Princess chatting so happily, had put two and two together. The *World*, that indefatigable purveyor of society gossip, had been the first to get the rumour of a match between Louis and Beatrice into print; from then on, speculation on the subject had been rife.

The possibility of a marriage between the Prince Imperial and Princess Beatrice was by no means remote. Indeed, there was a great deal to recommend it. By the year 1878, the Prince was twenty-two and the Princess a year younger. Queen Victoria was known to be devoted, not only to Louis himself, but to his mother the Empress. The Prince would be able to provide the British royal family with some of that 'fresh, dark blood' for which the Queen was always hankering. And then, to have one daughter as German Empress and another as French Empress would be a masterstroke indeed. What wonders might it not do for the peace of Europe!

On the other hand, the snags were considerable. Louis was a Roman Catholic who might one day be Emperor of the French, while Victoria was the Defender of the Protestant Faith on the lookout for a son-in-law who would make his home with her. Of the two obstacles, the religious one was the lesser. The Coburgs had never hesitated to embrace Catholicism if it meant gaining a throne; Victoria herself, although no lover of the Roman Catholic faith, was not bigoted in religious matters. She had once had something very sharp to say in answer to the criticism levelled at a Coburg relation who had bartered faith for a crown.

When the Queen and her daughter visited Baveno, on Lake Maggiore, the newspapers were quick to report that Princess Beatrice had attended a Roman Catholic service, 'apparently for the first time'. Here was a straw in the wind indeed! In fact, it was not the first time that the Princess had been to a Roman Catholic church. During their visit to Lucerne in 1868, the Queen and the Princess had listened to a Mass. The chanting had interested Victoria but on the whole she had not been favourably impressed; there was no danger of the Queen 'forsaking the Protestant faith', reported Ponsonby.

The need for a stay-at-home son-in-law was a more serious

164

matter. Having distributed most of her daughters well away from home, Victoria was determined that her youngest should stay by her to comfort her in her approaching old age. It was therefore essential that Beatrice marry some tame, uncommitted young man, willing to make his home in the Queen's Household.

This, of course, the Prince Imperial would never consent to do. Whatever else he might be, Louis was neither tame nor uncommitted. Adventurous and independent, he was dedicated to two principal causes: the one was to redeem his father's name, the other to regain his father's throne. Neither of these ambitions could be achieved by sitting tight. Marie de Larminat, the Empress's *demoiselle d'honneur*, always claimed that Louis never forgot the accusations of cowardice that had been levelled at the Emperor Napoleon III after the Franco-Prussian war. 'He never spoke about it,' she says, 'but his intimate friends knew only too well that he would never have either respite or repose until he had, even at the cost of his own blood, attested to his courage, and shown the whole world that a Napoleon knew how to fight. . . .' Such proof of his military prowess would have another effect as well: it would draw French attention to himself. For how else, other than on the field of battle, could the Prince prove himself worthy of his destiny? He had no wish to emulate his late father's youthful and unsuccessful attempts at restoring the Empire by leading an armed expedition against the existing French regime. He was thus constantly on the lookout for some suitable war from which he could return covered in glory; only after that could he hope to become the Emperor Napoleon IV.

Fired with such ambitions, the Prince was not really much of a candidate for the domesticated son-in-law of Queen Victoria's imaginings.

To the Empress Eugenie, the idea of a marriage between Louis and Princess Beatrice must have seemed very attractive. If he did not achieve his ambition to restore the Empire, then life as the son-in-law of the Queen of England would be a very good second best. Might it not, after all, make for a happier existence? She knew, only too well, that the lot of a sovereign was an unenviable one; that of an idle, ageing pretender could be even worse. Might it not be far better for Louis to be leading an active, respected life as Queen Victoria's son-in-law than to be forever crying for the moon?

What Princess Beatrice's views were on the subject one does not know. She was an extremely shy young woman and one who kept her own counsel. She hated any mention, not only of her own matrimonial prospects, but of marriage in general. Once, when Henry Ponsonby, who was sitting beside her at dinner, announced that a mutual acquaintance had recently become engaged, his cheerful words were greeted by an unnerving silence. After dinner, he received a curt message to say that the subject of marriage was never to be mentioned in the Princess's presence.

The story, long current, that the Princess, in later life, hinted to her son, the Marquess of Carisbrooke, that she had once been in love with the Prince Imperial, has been denied by the Marquess himself. However, it is said that a photograph of the Prince stood on her desk until the day she died. And in 1920, immediately after the Empress Eugenie's death, Princess Beatrice wrote a hurried note to one of the late Empress's companions, suggesting that certain of her letters be destroyed at once. What information, one wonders, was Princess Beatrice so anxious to obliterate? Could it have concerned the possibility of her engagement to the long-dead Prince Imperial?

Some time after Louis's death, the Empress Eugenie presented Queen Victoria with a little package. The Queen was to promise that she would not open it until after Eugenie's death. Victoria promised, but curiosity getting the better of her and emotion the better of the Empress, they decided to open it together after all. It contained a magnificent emerald cross—the gift of the King of Spain to Eugenie on her marriage to Napoleon III. The Empress had intended it, she told the Queen, for Louis's bride.

Today, on Louis's coffin in the crypt of St Michael's Abbey, Farnborough, lies only one wreath: it is a cluster of white and purple porcelain flowers from Princess Beatrice.

3

'Directly after breakfast,' wrote the Queen in her Journal on 11 February 1879, 'there came a telegram from Colonel Stanley to General Ponsonby, telling of a great and most unfortunate disaster at the Cape, or rather more Natal, the Zulus having defeated our troops with great loss, and Lord Chelmsford obliged to retire. How this could happen one cannot yet imagine. . . .'

How this had happened was that Lord Chelmsford, leading a punitive expedition into Zululand, in South Africa, had gone out on a reconnaissance-in-force, leaving the bulk of his army behind in an undefended position. With Chelmsford away, the Zulus had attacked his camp and all but annihilated the British force.

When the news of this disaster of Isandhlwana reached England, it caused an uproar. An emergency cabinet meeting was called and the decision taken to send out strong reinforcements. British honour must, immediately and at all costs, be avenged.

Few were more eager to avenge it than the Prince Imperial. It was not that the loss of a few hundred British troops in some obscure corner of the British Empire upset him so terribly; it was simply that in this campaign he saw at last the opportunity of winning for himself some sort of distinction. He had been itching to see active service for years ('He anxiously scanned the face of the earth, his sword burning in his hands,' wrote Marie de Larminat poetically), but somehow or other the right sort of war had never come his way. Fighting for Britain against some European nation would have been too complicated : one never knew when one might need their friendship in the future. Indeed, any war in which rival European interests were involved had to be left severely alone. But here was an ideal campaign; a war with which only England was concerned; a war against savages. Might not he, like the first Napoleon, return from Africa haloed in glory? Might this not be the first step on the road to the throne?

An additional incentive was the fact that all Louis's old army friends were going out to Natal. So spirited himself, he could hardly bear the thought of the members of his battery setting off without him.

So, without a word to his mother, the Prince wrote to the Duke of Cambridge, Commander-in-Chief of the British Army, asking permission to embark with his battery for South Africa. When Eugenie heard what he had done (in his boyish way, he could not keep the news from her for long) she was appalled. But try as she might, she could not dissuade him; he had an answer for every one of her anguished arguments. He had made up his mind. She could only hope that his request would be refused.

It was. A couple of days after he had sent off his letter, the Empress met him in the corridor at Camden. He was looking like death. She asked him what was wrong.

'*On m'a refusé*,' he blurted.

'Tears came rushing from his eyes,' the Empress said later to the Queen, 'he, who never cried.'

Realizing the depths of his disappointment, the Empress's heart went out to him. She understood his feelings so well; she would have felt exactly the same in his position. From now on she gave him, not only her sympathy, but her active support. For, of course, he did not intend to let the matter rest with a refusal. He wrote to the Governor of his old Military Academy at Woolwich, begging him to plead his cause with the Duke of Cambridge; then he wrote a second letter to the Duke himself.

'Though I am not so conceited as to think that my services can be useful to the cause which I wished to serve,' he wrote, 'I nevertheless looked upon this war as an opportunity of showing my gratitude towards the Queen and the nation in a way that would be very much to my mind. When at Woolwich, and later, at Aldershot, I had the honour of wearing the English uniform, I had hoped that it would be in the ranks of our allies that I should first take up arms. Losing this hope, I lose one of the consolations of my exile. . . .'

The Prince had struck exactly the right note: there was no mention here of his political ambitions. The Duke of Cambridge was touched. He forwarded the letter to the Queen. She, inevitably, was charmed. His expressions were so kind, so gratifying. What could be more natural than that the dear young Prince should be eager to repay her hospitality by fighting with her troops? 'But I am glad,' she added in her reply to the Duke, '[that] I am not his mother at the moment. Still,

I understand how easily in his position he must wish for active employment.'

His mother, in fact, had actually been pleading on his behalf. She had driven to the War Office to put his case before the Commander-in-Chief. In this she was successful. Thus it was that between the two of them—the sympathetic Queen and the partisan Empress—Louis got his way. The cabinet (for it had been they, and not the army, who had been proving difficult) finally consented to his going.

'Well,' Disraeli was afterwards to say, 'my conscience is clear. I did all that I could to stop his going. But what can you do when you have two obstinate women to deal with?'

The Prince was being allowed to go, but it was in the capacity of a spectator only; he was not to be a combatant. The cabinet had insisted on this. In his letters to the Governor of the Cape and to Lord Chelmsford, the Duke of Cambridge made the position abundantly clear. 'He expressed the wish to be enrolled in our Army, but the Government thought it impossible to grant this,' wrote the Duke. His only fear, he admitted to Lord Chelmsford, was that the Prince might prove too courageous.

The Queen echoed this fear. The Prince 'must be careful not unnecessarily to expose himself, for we know he is *very venturesome*,' she wrote.

On the afternoon of Wednesday, 26 February 1879, Louis travelled from Camden to Windsor to take leave of the Queen. Victoria received him with 'touching kindness' and is reported to have taken a ring from her finger for him to wear as a token of her regard. On arriving back home that evening the Prince settled down to write his will. 'I shall die,' he wrote in the sixth and final clause, 'with a sentiment of profound gratitude for Her Majesty the Queen of England and all the Royal Family and for the country where I have received for eight years such cordial hospitality.'

Napoleon III's hopes that his son might inherit his 'feelings of sincere friendship for the Royal Family of England and of affectionate esteem for the great English nation' had been realized.

On the following day, accompanied by the Empress, Louis travelled down to Southampton. The train journey was a triumphant progress, proving how popular the imperial family had become during the eight years of their exile. Eugenie had the bitter-sweet consolation of seeing her son fêted all the way. At Southampton itself, proceedings were no less enthusiastic. The crowd roared their approval of Louis's gesture, and at a banquet for the imperial party various civic and military dignitaries echoed their sentiments. The banquet over, Eugenie accompanied her son to his ship, the S.S. *Danube*. There, clutching a posy of violets and sobbing bitterly, she kissed him good-bye. She did not leave Southampton until the ship had disappeared from sight.

Before the Empress returned to Chislehurst, she was handed a telegram. It was from the Queen. 'I ask you, dear Sister, to accept the expression of all my good wishes for your beloved son, who is departing accompanied by good wishes of the entire nation. May God bless and keep him.'

CHAPTER FOURTEEN

Sorrow's Crown of Sorrow

1

Some four months later, on the evening of 19 June 1879, Queen Victoria was sitting writing in the lamplit quiet of one of her rooms in Balmoral Castle. There was a knock at the door. John Brown entered. He told her, in his bluff, protective way, that he had bad news for her. In rising alarm, she asked him what it was. 'The young French Prince is killed,' he said. At first, the Queen could simply not take it in. Several times she asked Brown what he meant. Suddenly Princess Beatrice, holding a telegram in her hand and sobbing bitterly, burst into the room. 'Oh! The Prince Imperial is killed!' she cried out.

Understanding at last, Victoria clutched her head in both hands and shouted 'No, no!' It could not possibly be true, she protested. Mutely Beatrice handed her the telegram. The Queen read the terrible message herself. The Prince Imperial had ridden out with a small scouting party on the morning of 1 June and, while bivouacking, the party had been attacked by a band of Zulus and the Prince killed.

'Oh, it is too, too awful!' cried the Queen in her anguish. 'The more one thinks of it the worse it is.'

Once the first, numbing shock had worn off, Victoria's thoughts turned to Eugenie. As yet, the Empress would be unaware of the news. 'Poor dear Empress,' she cried distractedly, 'her only child, her *all* gone! I am really in despair.' The Queen's great fear was that the Empress might learn of her son's death from the following morning's newspapers. On no account was this to happen. She telegraphed instructions for the news to be broken to the Empress by Lord Sydney, the Lord Lieutenant of Kent.

'Got to bed very late; it was dawning, and little sleep did I

171

get . . .' wrote the Queen. 'Had a bad, restless night, haunted by this awful event, seeing those horrid Zulus constantly before me and thinking of the poor Empress who did not yet know it. . . . My accession day, 42 years ago; but no thought of it in the presence of this frightful event.'

At seven the following morning Lord Sydney sent a message to the Duke de Bassano, head of the Household at Camden. He told him the news and asked him to keep it—and the morning papers—from the Empress until he himself arrived at half past nine to break it. While the Household waited, the Empress was upstairs in her room reading that morning's mail. Among her letters was one from a comrade of Louis's in Natal, saying that her son was in excellent health and that she was to rest assured that he was being kept out of harm's way. Then, by mistake, the Empress opened a letter addressed to her secretary; it was full of the 'shocking news' which the writer had just heard. In sudden terror, the Empress cried out and the Household doctor, Baron Corvisart, came dashing into the room. She demanded to know what news this was. Corvisart, who knew the truth, told her that the Prince had been dangerously wounded and that Lord Sydney was coming to give her full details.

In a state of acute anxiety, Eugenie dressed herself and waited for Lord Sydney. As soon as he arrived he hurried up to her room; with him were Bassano and Corvisart. At the sight of the three of them, the Empress seemed to guess the truth. When she was told (she could not afterwards remember which of the men had broken the news) she sat quite still, pale and mute. It was several hours before she broke down and cried.

Cutting short her stay at Balmoral, Victoria hurried south to be near Eugenie. She was at Chislehurst within three days of hearing the news.

Camden Place was rapidly filling up with friends and party supporters. The Empress received very few of them. When she did consent to see any of them, it was for a few minutes only. Even Marie de Larminat was not admitted until several days had passed. For most of the time the Empress sat alone in her darkened room, unable to eat, unable to sleep.

But for Victoria, Eugenie made an exception. She had always been grateful to the Queen for her unswerving friendship and she was immensely touched by the way the Queen had hurried south to comfort her. As for Victoria, her sympathy for the Empress was immeasurable. The Queen understood only too well what it meant to lose the one person one really loved. When the Emperor had died, Eugenie had been sad but not prostrate; their marriage had not been a very happy one. Moreover, she had had Louis to support her. Since then, the boy had been her whole life. His death was to her what Albert's death had been to the Queen, and Victoria realized this.

The Queen was led into the dark little boudoir in which the Empress was sitting. She could hardly distinguish Eugenie's grief-smudged features. As the two black-clad, heartbroken women sat talking, Victoria's admiration for Eugenie increased with every passing moment. 'The dear Empress Eugenie's conduct is *beyond* all praise,' she afterwards told Disraeli. 'Her resignation, her unmurmuring, patient submission to God's will, her conviction that it could not be otherwise, and the total absence of all blame of others are admirable. But her heart is broken and her poor health seems sadly shaken. . . .'

A thought which had been haunting Eugenie was that Louis might have suffered horribly before he died. She confided this fear to the Queen, but Victoria assured her that it must all have been over very quickly. Indeed, one of Louis's friends had given Eugenie the same assurance: 'he was so much excited that he would have felt nothing'.

'Poor child,' sobbed Eugenie, 'only twenty-three years old.'

It appeared that a nervous contraction in Eugenie's throat prevented her from swallowing. She could manage only fluids, and was living on milk and rum. This alarmed Victoria. She insisted that the Empress try to eat something; she would arrange for her own doctor to come and see the Empress.

The doctor, arriving to attend to Eugenie the following day, found her ready to comply with his instructions. 'Your visit has comforted her,' he reported back to the Queen, 'and after you left she ate something because she said you had told her she ought, and she knew you would tell her only what was right, and Her Majesty added, "I will always try to do what the Queen wishes and tells me." '

A week or two later the Empress received yet another token

of the Queen's sympathy. It was in the form of a jewelled frame, especially designed to enclose the last photograph of the Prince Imperial. A garland of violets was surmounted by an imperial eagle, from whose claws flowed a scroll bearing, in gold lettering, the comforting message, 'Not lost, but gone before.'

2

Queen Victoria's reference to the Empress Eugenie's 'total absence of all blame of others' was significant. In the days following the first news of Louis's death, more facts concerning it had come to light. They were by no means reassuring. It appeared that the scouting party had been under the command of an officer by the name of Carey and that, when the little troop had been attacked, Captain Carey, instead of making a stand, had been among the first to mount his horse and ride off. Without giving a thought to his important charge, he, followed by such others as could get mounted, had galloped away, leaving the Prince quite alone to face between thirty and forty of the enemy. Louis's own horse had bolted and, after vainly trying to catch it, he had turned to face his attackers. His right hand, having been trampled on by his horse when he tried to mount, was useless, and with his left hand he fired his revolver at the slowly advancing Zulus. The shots went wide. With assegais poised, they closed in on him. When he caught his foot in a hole, they struck. He fought, they were afterwards to say, 'like a lion'. When they had finally finished with him, his body bore seventeen wounds—all in front. They stripped him of everything bar a chain of medallions about his neck (they had a strong suspicion of anything which might be 'magic') and left him lying in a little hollow.

Not until the following morning did a search party of enormous strength, commanded by Lord Chelmsford himself, arrive to retrieve the little naked body. The corpse was embalmed, sealed in a hastily knocked-together coffin and sent down to the coast. At Cape Town it was put aboard H.M.S. *Orontes* and was now on its way home to England.

Meanwhile, in Zululand, Captain Carey faced a Court Martial.

His behaviour throughout his trial was remarkably cool. He shifted the entire blame on Louis, denying that he himself had been in command of the scouting party. As for the accusation that he had deserted the Prince, he had, he claimed, done his best to rally the men.

'I did everything I could to save the Prince,' he maintained unblinkingly.

'You did absolutely nothing,' countered the prosecutor.

Carey was cashiered, but the final verdict lay with the Duke of Cambridge. Carey was sent home to England.

However, there was more to it than this. It was quite likely that Carey was being made a scapegoat for the sins of his superior officers. It was carelessness on the part of others, as much as cowardice on the part of Carey, that killed the Prince Imperial. Lord Chelmsford, whose prestige had never quite recovered from the disaster of Isandhlwana, could not afford to have his name associated with yet another misfortune, and there is no doubt that Colonel Harrison, to whom the—admittedly headstrong—Prince had been assigned, had erred in allowing him to venture out with this small troop. But by playing up Carey's undeniably cowardly behaviour, attention was diverted from the negligence of his superiors.

As one by one these facts came to light, so did Queen Victoria become more and more appalled. The Duke of Cambridge forwarded her all the evidence produced at the Court Martial in Zululand, and reading it shocked her profoundly. 'This evidence is terrible!' she exclaimed. 'Indeed, every word seems to me most unfavourable in every way towards all who deserted the poor young Prince. All seem to have been so indifferent to his fate.'

That no one should have remained, or have returned, to help him, when the annals of the army abounded in instances of such courage and self-sacrifice, seemed incredible to Queen Victoria. Nor did she blame only the members of the scouting party. The whole business, she exclaimed, was 'terrible evidence of want of right feeling and decency and of lamentable want of firmness or even of comprehension of their duty on the part of Lord Chelmsford and others!' The reputation of the British Army had been sullied in no uncertain fashion.

However, there was one way in which she could try to make amends for her army's deficiencies: Louis would be given a magnificent funeral. On this she was determined. Although he was to be buried beside his father in the modest little church of St Mary on Chislehurst Common, Victoria was resolved that he should go to his grave with all possible honour. To this end she now directed her abundant energies.

From the outset, she came up against a wall of opposition. Her cabinet was having none of it. The Prime Minister, Disraeli, who had never shared his mistress's enthusiasm for the Prince Imperial, proved unusually unco-operative. Fearing an insult to republican France, the cabinet wanted the whole affair played down as much as possible. Louis had gone out to Africa in search of fame; he had been warned not to take part in any actual fighting; his subsequent death was certainly no fault of the British government. They saw no reason why they should be associated with this manifestation of what the Foreign Secretary, Lord Salisbury, called 'national self-reproach'. When Queen Victoria announced her intention of placing the Order of the Bath on the Prince's coffin with her own hands, they advised her against it. To this advice she submitted. But when they decided against attending the funeral at all, she flew into a towering rage. So outspoken was her indignation that the cabinet was forced to relent. They agreed that two ministers—the War and Colonial—should go in full dress. Even then Lord Salisbury hastened to assure the French Ambassador that all this ceremonial would not give the funeral an 'official' status.

Poor Disraeli, whom the Queen had been bombarding with telegrams for days, was finally obliged to journey down to Windsor in person. He went in considerable trepidation, expecting, as he put it, 'a distressing scene'. His apprehensions were justified. The Queen kept him for an hour and a half and talked, he confided to a friend, 'only on one subject'.

If, in Victoria's opinion, the British cabinet was behaving badly, the French was behaving even worse. Four of the late Emperor's marshals had applied to the French government for permission to attend the funeral; their request had been refused. 'This is disgraceful!' thundered the Queen.

By wrangling, chivying and demanding, Victoria managed to get her way in most particulars. Louis would be given the next best thing to a State funeral. When H.M.S. *Orontes* reached England on 11 July, a galaxy of princes, headed by the Prince of Wales, would be at Woolwich to see the coffin carried ashore. The funeral itself would be attended by the Queen.

'Nothing could be more injudicious than the whole affair,' grumbled Disraeli to Lady Chesterfield.

3

The Prince Imperial was buried on 12 July 1879. Although it would be an exaggeration to say that the Queen—despite her *penchant* for funerals—actually enjoyed the occasion, there is no doubt that she found the ceremony beautiful, moving and 'not at all gloomy'.

The weather was perfect. When the Queen, accompanied by the Princess of Wales, Princess Beatrice and a large suite, drove to Camden Place just before eleven that morning, Chislehurst Common was already seething with people. With the pedlars doing a brisk trade in imperial souvenirs, it seemed more like a country fair than a funeral. Within the grounds of the house things were no less animated. The driveway was alive with brilliant uniforms, restive horses and jingling accoutrements. To Victoria, it was all very gratifying.

The royal party was met at the front door by a collection of Bonaparte princes and princesses. From here they were led into the main hall, which had been converted into a *chapelle ardente*. As a tribute to the Prince's blameless youth, the room had been hung entirely in white. The coffin lay on a catafalque in the centre of the room. It was covered with a violet velvet pall embroidered with golden bees. On it rested the Order of the *Légion d'honneur* and countless wreaths. To these Victoria added her own tribute: two white peonies and a wreath of laurel. The wreath bore the inscription: 'To him who lived the purest of lives, and died the death of a soldier, fighting for our country in Zululand'. The royal ladies knelt for a moment in prayer and then withdrew.

In a room which had once been Louis's study, they were introduced to the various members of the Bonaparte clan. Always observant, the Queen had telling comments to make on each member of the family. Plon-Plon, as Head of the House, effected the presentations. Victoria found him looking older, balder and more like the first Napoleon than ever. His manner was 'very civil, and very subdued and embarrassed'. When she spoke to him of the tragedy of the Prince Imperial's death, he answered, *'C'est bien triste. Votre Majesté a été si bonne.'* For Plon-Plon, this was civil indeed.

His sister, Princess Mathilde, the Queen thought hardly altered at all. She was as handsome and as statuesque as ever. She was also no less forthright. Even on this melancholy occasion, Mathilde could not quite conceal the lack of affinity between her branch of the Bonapartes and the branch to which Eugenie belonged. She had never understood how the Empress could allow a Napoleon to fight for the British. When Victoria offered her condolences, Mathilde answered: *'Il s'est précipité'* and that he must have had *'l'esprit malade'*. The Queen countered this by saying that she thought it only natural that Louis should wish to distinguish himself and 'to do something'.

Plon-Plon's eldest son Victor was 'tall and nice and intelligent-looking, very like the Italian family, but with the fine Bonaparte brow and complexion'. His second son was shorter and darker but looked no less of a Bonaparte.

Unbeknown to Queen Victoria, or to any of the assembled Bonapartes, there was a shock in store for Plon-Plon and his sons. Louis's will, which had recently been opened by the Empress's confidential secretary, was found to contain this significant sentence: 'At my death, the task of continuing the life work of Napoleon I and Napoleon III falls on *the elder son of Prince Napoleon. . . .'* In other words, Plon-Plon had been cut out. The eagerly anticipated succession had been passed on to his eldest son Victor—he of the 'fine Bonaparte brow and complexion'.

When Plon-Plon came to hear of this after the funeral, he was furious. It had been bad enough at the time of the Emperor's death, when his expectations of taking control of the imperial destinies had been foiled by Napoleon III's out-of-date

will; but now, when he had every right to the succession, the
door had once more been slammed in his face. As on the first
occasion, Plon-Plon blamed Eugenie. However, this time they
did not have a row about it. Ignoring the Empress's summons,
Plon-Plon simply ordered his carriage and drove off. For a
moment all Eugenie's old antagonism flared up. But it quickly
subsided. Her son's soul, she told herself, pleased with her for
having offered to receive the cantankerous Plon-Plon, had spared
her the sight of Plon-Plon 'by leaving him to the perversity of
his instincts'.

But now, as Queen Victoria stood talking in a hushed voice
to the members of the family in Louis's study, Plon-Plon was
still oblivious of the impending blow. He might, indeed, have
shown himself considerably less civil to the Queen had he known
about it.

'The moment was now fast approaching when what remained
of the dear young Prince had to leave his mother's roof for
ever,' wrote Victoria afterwards. Rejoining her suite in another
room, she had the blinds raised that she might see the colourful
company assembled in the driveway. A gun-carriage had been
drawn up opposite the main entrance. Presently the coffin,
carried on the shoulders of officers of the Royal Artillery, was
placed on it. The pall bearers included the Prince of Wales, the
Duke of Edinburgh, the Duke of Connaught and the Prince
Royal of Sweden. There was a roll of muffled drums and the
minute guns began their solemn thudding. 'It was a fearfully
thrilling, affecting moment!' declared the Queen.

Victoria and her party were led to an especially erected dais
in the driveway to see the procession pass by. It seemed endless.
The Queen had the satisfaction of seeing for herself that it was
every bit as impressive as she had intended it to be. With
characteristic thoroughness she noted every detail of the vast
cortège: the special escort of two hundred cadets from Woolwich;
the band of the Royal Artillery playing the 'fearfully solemn,
wailing and too well-known' Dead March from *Saul*; the Bishop
of Constantine, whose mitre had such a fine effect; the six horses
dragging the gun-carriage; the coffin draped in the flags of
Britain and France; her wreath of laurel in as conspicuous a
position as she had wished; the late Prince's horse caparisoned

in black and gold; the two servants who had been with Louis in Zululand; Plon-Plon, still the chief mourner, followed by the rest of the Bonaparte princes; foreign royalties, ambassadors, cabinet ministers, officers and numberless Frenchmen. 'This was the end of all that was once so splendid and brilliant,' sighed the Queen, 'and of one who promised to be a blessing not only to his country, but to the world.'

When the cortège had passed, Victoria returned to the house. The Empress's great friend, the Duchess de Mouchy, told the Queen that the Empress was in a terrible state. The crash of each minute gun seemed to tear right through her. She had nevertheless asked to see the Queen. Victoria, accompanied by Princess Beatrice, hurried upstairs. The room was so dark that the Queen could not at first see Eugenie, but presently they fell into each other's arms. The Empress was sobbing bitterly. When Victoria assured her that no one felt for her as she did, Eugenie replied gently, '*Je vous remercie, Madame, pour toutes vos bontés.*' She asked if Princess Beatrice were there and kissed her as well.

When Queen Victoria arrived back at Windsor that afternoon, she at once sent a telegram to Disraeli, expressing her entire satisfaction with the day's proceedings. She was 'highly pleased' with all that had taken place at Chislehurst that morning.

'I hope,' wrote Disraeli to Lady Chesterfield, 'the French Government will be as joyful.'

CHAPTER FIFTEEN

'In affectionate remembrance . . .'

1

As yet, the Queen and the Empress had not discussed Captain Carey. The two of them—Victoria from a sense of embarrassment and Eugenie from a sense of tact—had avoided the subject. However, a few days after the funeral, when the Queen was again visiting the Empress, Eugenie suddenly broached it. 'Tell me,' she asked fervently, 'they'll do nothing to that poor man? Oh no, I beg of you! He may have a mother!' For a moment Victoria hesitated. Then she promised that, although the matter was not really in her hands, she would see what could be done. To this Eugenie cried out '*Merci! Merci!*' The Queen went on to tell her about Carey's unhappiness and to allude to her own feelings of shame. But Eugenie cut short her apologies. 'I do not wish to know anything,' she exclaimed. 'I only know that he has been killed, that is all.'

But she did know more than this; a great deal more. Although Eugenie had not had access to the evidence at the Court Martial, she had devoured every scrap of news about the tragedy in the newspapers. And just recently, the most conclusive evidence yet of Carey's guilt had come to her hand. While sorting dispassionately through her neglected mail, the Empress had come across a bundle of letters addressed to Carey's wife. They had been written by Carey in Zululand during the days following the Prince Imperial's death. Exactly why Mrs Carey had passed these letters on to the Empress is uncertain. Perhaps she imagined that their unhappy, guilt-confessing tone might soften the Empress's heart towards her husband. Whatever the reason, all the letters revealed, in no uncertain terms, Carey's guilt. Every other word confirmed his cowardice.

The Empress had the letters translated into French and then

showed them to certain close friends. They begged her to publish them, but she refused. Nor would she allow any mention of them. Not until after Carey had faced the Duke of Cambridge did Eugenie forward the most damning of these letters to the Queen. She had not wanted to prejudice Carey's chances of acquittal, she told Victoria. And she went even further than this. Before the Duke of Cambridge gave the final verdict, the Empress issued this plea for clemency.

'The one earthly consolation I have is in the idea that my beloved child fell as a soldier, obeying *orders*, on a duty which was *commanded*, and that those who gave them did so because they thought him competent and useful.

'Enough of recriminations. Let the memory of his death unite in a common sorrow all those who loved him, and let no one suffer, either in his reputation or his interests. I, who desire nothing more on earth, ask it as a last prayer.

Eugénie

'Speak to all, English and French, in this way.'

These moves by Eugenie—the suppression of the letters and the intervention on behalf of Carey—must have astounded some of her companions. Not only was the Empress keeping silent on the subject of Carey's guilt but she was actually working for his acquittal. There were several reasons for this. For one thing, all the recrimination in the world was not going to bring the Prince Imperial back to life. For another, Eugenie was not anything like as impetuous and unforgiving as she had been in former days; the late Emperor had taught her something of the dignity of silence. But perhaps, most of all, it was the Empress's affection for Queen Victoria which encouraged her course of action. She had no wish to humiliate the Queen or her army. Already, in France, criticism of Britain was rife. That Anglophobia which Charles Greville, twenty years before, had claimed slumbered but never died, was once more fully awake. Frenchmen were quick to point out that the British had a very different conception of 'military honour' from their own: the French soldier, with his warm heart, would always risk his life to help a comrade; the British soldier, with his cool head, was more concerned with self-preservation. There was simply no understanding '*ce peuple froid, barbare, perfide, infâme*'.

In no time the Parisian air was thick with rumours about Louis's death: he had not merely been deserted by the cowardly British, he had been murdered by them. They had all—Carey, Harrison, Chelmsford—had a hand in the assassination of the Prince; even the Prince of Wales was somehow implicated. Precisely why the British should go to such lengths to kill the Prince Imperial was never made clear.

Such talk infuriated Eugenie. When her mother, the aged Countess de Montijo, wrote from Spain mentioning the possibility of a plot against the Prince, the Empress's reply was sharp.

'One can understand the people being taken in,' she wrote, 'but you, an intelligent woman, who should have more judgement, how can you say my dear child was assassinated? He died like a hero among the enemy, and there was no betrayal, leave that word to the ignorant who talk of nothing else. . . . There may be cowardice without adding treason as well; it's terrible enough, dramatic enough, without adding what has no existence. It's for those who were with my child to ask themselves that question. Did they act like *brave men* or did they *run away*, they can answer and have been obliged to answer. It's frightful enough like that. I beg of you, never say again that my boy was murdered; you can't conceive how you hurt me. He fell *fighting like a hero*.'

And there were stories more bizarre than the assassination one. Some Frenchmen claimed that the Prince Imperial had not been killed at all and that a strange corpse had been put into the coffin. It was true that there had been some difficulty in identifying Louis's putrefying remains on their arrival in England; this was all that was needed to start a rumour that the Prince Imperial was still alive. Like the Man in the Iron Mask, Louis lived on. The reasons for this particular subterfuge on the part of the British army were made no more clear than those for their alleged murder of the Prince.

It was in order to discourage such hysterical ravings that the Empress intervened on Carey's behalf: she must protect the British army and the British Queen from any further vilification.

Her attitude saved Carey. The Duke of Cambridge, hamstrung by her written intervention and by the Queen's plea for leniency, was obliged to let Carey off. The sentence of the Court Martial in Natal was revised and Captain Carey was restored to his rank.

In the general outcry which followed Carey's acquittal, few were more indignant than the two women who had engineered it. The fact that his acquittal would entail, *ipso facto*, his justification, had not really occurred to them. They had meant to be magnanimous, not approving. To see the cowardly scramble to get away—the *sauve qui peut*—now condoned, and to see Carey restored to his rank, was quite a different thing from his being forgiven for his misdeeds. Victoria was enraged. She considered it scandalous, she told Disraeli, that Carey should be let off so lightly. Tactfully if a little wearily, Disraeli agreed. Yet, he argued, it was probably the best thing: the Court Martial had so mismanaged the case that a verdict of guilty might easily have transformed 'this mean wretch' into a hero or a martyr.

Disraeli was right. The British public, in a perverse fashion, was tending to take Carey's side. There was a feeling—not without foundation—that he was being made to suffer for the sins of his superiors. As usual, ran the argument, the common man was being blamed while the top-brass was getting off scot free. Warming to this sympathy, Captain Carey embarked on a programme of public self-vindication. He granted interviews, he issued statements, he wrote letters to the Press. His publicity-hunting is said to have exasperated the Empress. 'Why cannot he leave my poor dead boy alone?' she is reported to have cried out on one occasion. 'He left him alone once!'

But he could not. Unsure of himself despite his acquittal, Carey tried another method of clearing his name. He wrote to Camden. Only by gaining the Empress's sympathy, possibly even her friendship or her patronage, would the stain be completely removed from his character. 'Now that I think I may say I stand freed from the charge of cowardice or misbehaviour,' he wrote blandly, was there anything that the Empress would like him to tell her about her son? His letter earned him a cool reply from Camden. Undeterred, he wrote a second time. This too, was answered with some sharpness. His defence of his behaviour was impressing no one at Camden; how could it, when his guilt-confessing letters lay locked in the drawer of Eugenie's desk? But he persisted until a short note informed him that the Empress considered the correspondence closed.

Louis's death finished Carey. No one ever forgave him for his desertion of the Prince. Despised and ignored, he drifted from regiment to regiment. He died, four years after the Prince Imperial, in India.

2

Although controversies, such as the Carey business, might momentarily distract Eugenie from her grief, nothing seemed to reawaken her interest in life. As the weeks after Louis's funeral dragged by, she seemed to sink lower and lower into the state of lethargy which so often follows great crises. Like Victoria after the death of Albert, Eugenie was concerned only with her sorrow. 'Her eyes, worn out with weeping, could see nothing on the horizon, her thoughts could imagine nothing but a hopeless void,' wrote Marie de Larminat; 'nothing seemed able to awaken her interest, and I began to fear that nothing would arouse her from this state of coma.'

Eugenie admitted this herself. Were the entire universe to disappear, she told her mother, she would be utterly indifferent. The world had become no more than an 'empty desert'.

It was now that Queen Victoria came, once more, to the Empress's aid. She had earlier invited Eugenie to stay with her at Osborne but the Empress had declined the invitation; now Victoria tried again. She would soon be returning to Balmoral; would the Empress like the use of nearby Abergeldie? The Queen assured her that she would be quite undisturbed at Abergeldie, that she need see no one other than Victoria herself. On these conditions Eugenie accepted the invitation. Towards the middle of September 1879, accompanied by a small suite, the Empress travelled north to Scotland. There, as tactfully as possible, Victoria set about trying to revive Eugenie's interest in life.

The house in which the Empress established herself was both isolated and unpretentious. As such, it suited Eugenie perfectly.

From the outset Marie de Larminat noticed that her mistress seemed to be recovering. The two of them would tramp all day across the wild, rainswept hillsides, returning at sunset—soaked to the skin and muddy to the knees—to a crackling fire and a laden tea-table. Nothing could have done Eugenie more good than these brisk, exhausting walks. However, the evenings, those long, lamplit evenings, tended to undo a great deal of the good. Poor Marie never knew what to talk about. 'What subjects could possibly interest the unhappy woman? What memories could I recall without making her suffer? Nevertheless, I had to break those terrible silences. . . .'

When the Queen came visiting, it was easier. Always accompanied by the gruff John Brown, Victoria would sit chatting quietly on one subject or another; never attempting to console the Empress but trying, rather, to interest her in everyday things. At other times she would drive the Empress to some nearby beauty spot. There, in a little pavilion adorned by the inevitable bust of the Prince Consort, the two widows would sit drinking tea. One afternoon they drove to Glen Gelder Shiel. Victoria showed Eugenie over a little cottage standing on a wild, desolate slope. Then, with the dogs yapping at their heels, they walked a mile or so. Eugenie talked, noted the gratified Queen, 'a great deal, most pleasantly, of former times'. Their walk over, the two women returned to the cottage to find that Brown had caught some trout and cooked them in oatmeal for their tea. Eugenie enjoyed them immensely and said that they would be her dinner.

It was, thought Victoria as they drove back to Abergeldie, a glorious evening: 'the hills pink and the sky so clear. . . .'

Due, very largely, to the Queen's skilful handling, Eugenie began to regain her hold on life. Marie de Larminat professed herself amazed at her mistress's day-to-day recovery. Her naturally buoyant nature was beginning to reassert itself. She was beginning to look forward again, to plan, to regain her vitality. Naturally active, Eugenie was looking about for some occupation. 'The tree which had been bent down to the ground had not been broken,' wrote Marie, 'and the powerful sap was running through it once more.'

The Queen's comment was more matter-of-fact. 'She has

benefited from the good air here and the beautiful surroundings and is sleeping much better now,' she wrote.

Eugenie's little suite was delighted to find that she was beginning to touch on subjects other than the Prince or Carey. They did everything they could to encourage and distract her. One day they arranged for her to discover, as if by accident, her French servants trying on kilts. She was considerably amused by the sight.

Although Marie often came across the Empress, in tears, kissing the portrait of her son, she realized that her mistress's strong will would eventually overcome her sorrow and that 'she whom everyone had thought buried in her affliction, would one day rise from the tomb'.

There was one aspect of Eugenie's attitude which Marie simply could not understand. This was her unaltered affection for England and the English. Naturally Anglophobe, all those surrounding the Empress had felt, after Louis's death, a blind and bitter hatred for the British people. For the British army, they had felt a particular aversion. For it was they, in their self-interested cowardice, who had robbed the exiles of their glory and their hopes. Marie herself, on the arrival of Louis's body at Camden Place, had cried out that whereas they had given the English their Prince 'in all the splendour and beauty of his youth', the English had given them back his coffin. Now the sight of a British uniform turned them pale, the sound of the English language broke their hearts. How could the Empress bear to go on living there?

It would never have occurred to Eugenie to leave. She loved England and she loved the British army. Her son had grown up amongst these people and he had served amongst these soldiers. He had loved them and they him. He would die, he had written in his will, with 'a sentiment of profound gratitude' towards, not only the Queen of England, but England herself.

There was another reason for Eugenie's remaining in England. In no other country in Europe would she have met with the same sympathy and the same respect. What other nation would have treated her dead with such reverence and herself as though she were still a sovereign? And what other ruler would have shown her as much affection as Queen Victoria?

No, Eugenie remained in England and the English took her to their hearts.

3

It was during this visit to Abergeldie that Eugenie told Victoria of a scheme which had slowly been taking shape in her mind. She was thinking of paying a pilgrimage to Zululand. For if, as Marie de Larminat claimed, the Empress was beginning to plan and look forward again, such plans were still all concerned with her son's death. The first sharp edge of Eugenie's grief might have been blunted but she was by no means ready to give it up. So great a loss must, she felt, have a corresponding measure of sorrow. Already she was complaining that people were forgetting Louis, that life was moving on despite his tragic, heroic end. But Eugenie, like Victoria after the death of Albert, was determined to cling to her grief and, by visiting the scene of her son's death, to remind others of his sacrifice.

Ever since hearing the terrible news, the Empress had been obsessed with the idea of finding out everything about Louis's death. She had read every newspaper account and had questioned a great many of the men returning from Zululand. But that had not satisfied her. She now felt that she must retrace her son's steps, re-enact his last days and, above all, see for herself the place where he had died. She must go to Africa.

Her scheme fired Victoria's imagination. The Empress's preoccupation with her son's death was something which the Queen understood very well. How *natural* that the Empress should wish to see the spot where her beloved son had fallen. Had not the Queen herself, after her husband's death, paid a pilgrimage to Coburg? Did she not sit for hours, in silent contemplation, beside the Prince's tomb? Did she not visit and revisit those places at Balmoral which she and Albert had known together? In complete sympathy with Eugenie's scheme, Victoria promised to do all she could to help.

However, a pilgrimage to Zululand was going to be quite a different proposition from Victoria's customary acts of homage. A two-month-long journey across the veld was a far cry from taking tea in little pavilions or climbing hillocks to stand beside some white-washed cairn. It was true that the Zulu War was over, but the country was still in an unsettled state and the journey would not be without its hazards. Eugenie, with her strong sense of occasion, was hoping to coincide her visit with the first anniversary of Louis's death; one could only hope that things would have settled down by then. The scheme might be difficult to carry out, thought Victoria, 'but not impossible'. And as Eugenie was determined on it, the two women put their resourceful heads together.

The first thing to do would be to assemble an expedition. Who could lead it? The Queen favoured Sir Evelyn Wood. General Wood was one of the few officers to emerge from the ill-fated Zulu War with reputation intact. Lord Chelmsford, whom Victoria always championed despite the disaster of Isandhlwana, considered him one of his best officers. When, after the war, Sir Evelyn Wood had visited the Queen, Victoria had been charmed by his manner. 'Sir E. Wood is a remarkably intelligent man,' she had written; 'not only an admirable General with plenty of *dash* as well as prudence, but a man of what is *now* called *Imperial* views, loyal and devoted to Sovereign and country. . . . He is most agreeable as well as amusing; very lively yet *very* discreet.'

A few weeks later, after the Queen and the Empress had returned south, Victoria noted that Wood had made an 'admirable' speech in the City. It had been at a public dinner and Wood had paid fulsome tribute to the qualities of the late Prince Imperial. This, quite naturally, endeared him to the Empress as well. She asked him to visit her at Camden. His breezy manner charmed her no less than it had the Queen. So, between them, Victoria and Eugenie agreed that Sir Evelyn Wood would be the most suitable person to organize the pilgrimage to Africa.

Wood was duly commanded to Windsor, where the Queen entrusted him with the delicate mission of escorting the Empress. She urged him to take the greatest possible care of her 'sister'. This he would do, promised Wood, on the condition that the Empress followed his instructions as if she were a soldier at his command. This somewhat stringent proviso meeting with the Queen's approval, Sir Evelyn took his leave and set about planning the journey.

189

He decided to take with him his wife, two aides-de-camp, a military doctor by the name of Frederick Scott and the Hon. Mrs Campbell—wife of his late Chief Staff Officer, also killed in the war. One by one the members of the party were summoned into the Royal Presence and charged with the task of looking after the Empress's safety and comfort. Mrs Campbell was instructed to write regularly to the Queen, giving details of the journey.

The sudden elevation of Sir Evelyn and Lady Wood into these royal and imperial circles caused some ripples of discontent. Lady Wolseley, whose husband was at present Commander-in-Chief of the British forces in Natal (Chelmsford had been superseded) and who was soon to play host to the Empress, was decidedly jealous of the favoured position of the Woods. The fact that the Queen made no secret of her intense dislike of Sir Garnet Wolseley did little to soothe her Ladyship's ruffled feelings.

'The Woods are basking in the sunshine!' wrote Lady Wolseley from London to her husband. 'Lady Wood went to last week's Drawing Room where all the Royalties shook hands with her, and the Queen smiled and shook hands with her after she had kissed her hand! Sir Evelyn has twice been asked to dine with the Duke [of Cambridge] and last week at Marlborough House.'

This letter must have brought cold comfort to the ambitious Sir Garnet fretting, far from royal favours, in Government House, Pietermaritzburg, Natal.

As his aides for the journey, Sir Evelyn had chosen Captain Bigge and Lieutenant Slade. Both had been good friends of the late Prince Imperial, having been with him at Aldershot and in Zululand. While Eugenie had been at Abergeldie, Arthur Bigge had visited her in order to tell her something of Louis's last days. The Empress had introduced him to the Queen. Victoria, always kindly disposed towards anyone of whom Eugenie approved, had been enchanted with him. 'He is a charming person,' she reported to her daughter the German Crown Princess, 'of the very highest character, clever, amiable and agreeable, as well as good-looking.'

In fact, the Queen was so taken with Bigge that she had him

190

appointed groom-in-waiting early in 1880. The Empress, on hearing from the Queen of Bigge's appointment, wrote back expressing her 'great pleasure and satisfaction'. She also thanked Victoria for allowing Bigge leave to accompany her on her pilgrimage which was to take place later that year.

Already, in 1880, when hardly out of his twenties, Arthur Bigge was showing evidence of the qualities which were to stand him in such good stead in later life. For when the pilgrimage was over and he resumed service with the Queen, Bigge was appointed Assistant Private Secretary to Her Majesty. In 1895 he succeeded Sir Henry Ponsonby as the Queen's Private Secretary. When she died, he became Secretary to the new Prince of Wales—the future King George V. In 1911, after George V's accession, he was created Lord Stamfordham. 'He taught me,' George V was to say in later life, 'how to be King.'

Besides helping to organize the expedition from the English end, the Queen was busily attending to the South African aspects of it. Letters were sent to Sir Bartle Frere in the Cape and Sir Garnet Wolseley in Natal, commending the Empress to their care. Orders were given for a cross to be erected on the site of the Prince's fall. This monument, known as the Queen's Cross, was lugged up to Zululand from Pietermaritzburg and set up in the little hollow where Louis had met his death. Having erected the cross, the 'Queen's Cross Expedition', with misplaced military efficiency, set about sprucing up the sight. They spread layers of cement, they set out neat lines of stones, they planted trees at regular intervals, they built a tidy stone wall. In the end the place presented, says Augustin Filon, 'the peaceful and orderly appearance of an English cemetery instead of that wild ravine which had witnessed a scene of death and carnage. The Empress thus experienced a bitter disappointment. . . .'

The Empress sailed from England on 29 March 1880 and was away for some four months. When she arrived at Government House, Cape Town, there was a telegram of welcome from the Queen waiting for her. And from then on, throughout her fatiguing and harrowing journey, she was sustained and comforted by the many proofs of Victoria's concern.

She spent the night of the first anniversary of Louis's death in prayer beside the Queen's Cross. It was a simple stone cross; on it, in small letters, was cut this inscription:

THIS CROSS IS ERECTED BY QUEEN VICTORIA
IN AFFECTIONATE REMEMBRANCE OF
NAPOLEON EUGENE LOUIS JEAN JOSEPH
PRINCE IMPERIAL
TO MARK THE SPOT WHERE
WHILE ASSISTING IN A RECONNAISSANCE WITH
THE BRITISH TROOPS
ON THE 1ST JUNE 1879
HE WAS ATTACKED BY A PARTY OF ZULUS
AND FELL WITH HIS FACE TO THE FOE

Of those long hours which Eugenie spent beside the cross that night, only the following description remains.

'More than once,' she afterwards said, 'I noticed black forms on top of the banks, which moved silently about and watched me through the tall grasses. This scrutiny was full of curiosity, but it was not hostile. I believe these savages wished rather to express their sympathy and their pity . . . and doubtless they were the very men who had killed my son on the same spot. . . .

'Towards morning a strange thing happened. Although there was not a breath of air, the flames of the candles were suddenly deflected, as if someone wished to extinguish them, and I said to him: "Is it indeed you beside me? Do you wish me to go away? . . ."'

She rose, and withdrew to her tent.

4

While the Empress was playing out her personal drama beside the Queen's Cross in Zululand, another drama, on a national scale, was being staged in England. It concerned the erection of a memorial to Louis in Westminster Abbey.

Soon after Eugenie set out for Natal, Algernon Borthwick, editor of the *Morning Post*, suggested that a fund be opened to erect a monument to the memory of the late Prince Imperial. The idea was enthusiastically received. A Memorial Committee was formed (its leading members were the Prince of Wales, the Duke of Edinburgh and Prince Leopold) and the Dean of Westminster was asked to sanction the setting up of the monument in the Abbey. With this the Dean was only too happy to comply. The sculptor Johannes Boehm, darling of the mid-Victorians, was commissioned to create the memorial. He started work immediately. The result was a white marble representation of the Prince lying stretched like some medieval knight on a tomb, in full uniform, his sword clasped in his hands, his helmet resting beneath his feet. It was, like all Boehm's work, inoffensively second-rate. But the committee was delighted with it. Queen Victoria—who had, of course, taken a lively interest in the proceedings—even went so far as to describe it as 'one of the finest productions of modern art'. Preparations were put in hand for its erection in the Abbey.

Then something quite unexpected happened. There was a violent outcry from a section of the British public. They did not want a statue of the Prince Imperial in Westminster Abbey.

The Zulu War had never been popular in England. Nor was it for the sake of England that Louis had gone out to fight in it. He had gone out to Natal solely to attract French attention to himself; the fact that he had been killed there had had nothing to do with the British. They felt that they were in no way indebted to Louis. They had no wish to make a national hero out of him. The sooner the whole wretched business was forgotten, the better. Besides, there was always republican France to be considered. Louis's grandiose funeral had been insult enough; why antagonize France further by erecting a statue to the imperial heir whom she herself had rejected?

So strong was this feeling against the proposed Abbey Memorial that over five thousand people joined in protest against it. The poor Dean of Westminster, who had so readily given permission for its erection, now found himself in the centre of a violent controversy. Rival newspapers either attacked or defended him; two of the royal patrons threatened to resign from the committee; the International Peace Association begged him to withdraw his sanction; he was inundated with abusive letters—'chiefly anonymous', he complained, 'but some have come from highly respectable persons and conservatives'. He professed himself only too willing to withdraw but, knowing that the Queen was in favour of the project, he dared not do so without her permission. This, of course, he would never get. 'The Queen is by no means willing to abandon the idea of Westminster Abbey . . .' was Henry Ponsonby's tactfully worded answer to the Dean's inquiry on the subject.

Eventually, the question was raised in the House. Here a motion by Brigg against the erection of the Abbey Memorial was enthusiastically championed by that pair of tireless protesters, Charles Dilke and Joseph Chamberlain. They feared, not only the insult to republican France but, more obscurely, the resentment of the working classes in both England and France. After a long and violent debate, a motion against the erection of the statue in the Abbey was carried by a majority of fifteen.

Queen Victoria was furious.

'The Queen,' she wrote to Gladstone (Disraeli's government had fallen in April 1880) 'has been greatly shocked and disgusted at the success of Mr Brigg's motion and at the language used to England's most faithful ally, as well as the want of feeling and chivalry shown towards the memory of a young Prince, who *fell* because of the *cowardly desertion* of a *British officer*, and whose spotless character and high sense of honour and noble qualities would have rendered a monument to him a proud and worthy addition to Westminster Abbey, which contains many of questionable merit. But where is chivalry and delicacy of feeling to be found these days amongst many of the Members of Parliament?'

The objectors she dismissed as '*bornés, ignorants et radicaux*'. If this incident did not, as has been claimed, estrange the Queen even more from her Prime Minister (Gladstone had, in fact, remained strictly neutral during the debate), it certainly did nothing to endear him to her. However, she had no intention of letting things go at that. Her blood was thoroughly up. If Parliament would not allow the statue to be erected in Westminster Abbey, then she would see that it had a place in St George's Chapel at Windsor. 'As it is,' she wrote tartly, 'St

George's will be a fitter and a safer place for this monument....'

The Empress returned from Africa (the Queen had sent Princess Beatrice to Southampton to welcome her home) knowing nothing of all these complications. She was told that a memorial was to be erected and that it had been decided to change the setting from Westminster Abbey to St George's Chapel. That was all.

But in time she came to hear of the debate in the House. The news upset her terribly. It badly shook her faith in the generosity of the British public. She even thought, for a moment, of quitting England forever. When Borthwick of the *Morning Post* called to see her, he found her in a state of acute distress. She was all for writing an open letter to the Dean of Westminster, begging the Monument Committee to give up the idea entirely. It took a great deal of talk on the part of Borthwick to soothe her. Her chief concern, he noted, was for the Queen. She seemed afraid that Victoria might be compromised by 'her own, ever-thoughtful kindness'.

'She spoke with enthusiasm about the Queen,' said Borthwick, 'and repeated several times, "I could die for her!"'

It was the adored Queen herself who finally put the Empress's mind at rest. With customary kindness and tact, Victoria wrote to Eugenie, smoothing away her suspicions and setting out to illustrate how everything had turned out for the best. There had never been a shadow of doubt as to the erection of the monument, and she herself had *always* favoured Windsor. The Chapel was, after all, the resting-place of so many of her nearest and dearest relations. The monument would certainly be safer and quite as accessible as in Westminster Abbey.

'And how could there be a better place for the monument of your beloved Son—"who wore the Lily of a blameless life" as Tennyson said of my Husband—than that beautiful Chapel where his Father's Banner floated until his death, and which contains the plaque with his Arms?'

That settled it. Louis's effigy came to rest in St George's Chapel and Eugenie's regard for Victoria increased a hundredfold.

'For the Queen's goodness her words had no limits,' reported Borthwick, 'she simply worships her.'

Part Four
'My dear Sister, the Empress'

CHAPTER SIXTEEN

Victoria and Eugenie

1

On the death of Prince Albert in 1861, Queen Victoria had cried out that her own life had ended; the Empress Eugenie, in later life, always declared that she herself had died in 1870. Both women were reckoning without their splendid constitutions. Their lives had run approximately half their courses at the time of these seemingly insurmountable tragedies. Queen Victoria, forty-two at the time of her husband's death, died almost forty years later, in 1901. The Empress Eugenie, having survived the fall of the Second Empire by fifty years, died in her ninety-fifth year, in 1920. Far from having been cut off in their prime, the two women lived on long enough to enjoy a forty-five-year-long association. During the last three decades of the nineteenth century, the friendship between Victoria and Eugenie developed until it became a permanent feature of the English scene; it became difficult to remember a time when the Empress Eugenie had not been treated like an additional member of the British royal family.

Having decided to settle permanently in England, the Empress set about planning a mausoleum in which to house her dead. She hoped, at first, to acquire a site near St Mary's in Chislehurst but, when this proved impossible, she moved from Camden Place to a mansion at Farnborough in Hampshire. Here, on a hilltop opposite her new home, work began on the erection of a fitting tomb for the bodies of her husband and her son. The result was a graceful, honey-coloured, distinctly un-English-looking church, its dome a modest echo of the Dôme des Invalides in Paris. Into the vast, shadowy crypt were transferred the bodies of Napoleon III and the Prince Imperial.

By few was the building of the Memorial Church followed

more sympathetically than by Queen Victoria. Indeed, the two enormous sarcophagi, hewn from red Aberdeen granite, were presented to the Empress by the Queen. At great expense and with still greater trouble, these two weighty royal gifts were installed in the transepts to the right and left of the altar in the crypt. A third sarcophagus, of the same rust-coloured granite, was to be positioned above an archway behind the altar; there it would lie in readiness for the body of the Empress herself.

It remained empty for a very long time. Eugenie's spirit might have been battered but there was nothing wrong with her health. She was as active, as alert and as restless during the second half of her life as she had been during the first. Whatever else she may have lost, the Empress had lost nothing of her zest.

Eugenie, who had always adored travel, was now able to indulge this passion to the full. She built herself a villa at Cap Martin, near Monaco, in the South of France. There, away from the mists and drizzles of Farnborough Hill, she spent the winters. She bought herself a yacht (all the palaces in the world were not worth a ship's deck, she would exclaim) and explored the coasts of England, Scotland, Ireland and Scandinavia. She cruised the Mediterranean, visiting Spain, Italy, Greece and Asia Minor. She went to Egypt and, at the age of eighty, rode out sight-seeing on a donkey in the blazing desert sun. She travelled to Austria and sat reminiscing with the aged Emperor Franz Josef. She took passage on a steamer and sailed to the East, spending six weeks in the enervating climate of Ceylon.

But Farnborough Hill meant home. In her huge, rambling house, set among the rhododendrons, the Empress kept her treasures. All her souvenirs of the Second Empire—the flotsam of one of the most glittering periods of French history—were assembled in this English country house. It was as though the Tuileries, or Compiègne, had been set down in Hampshire.

Each time the Empress arrived back home from her travels, she and Queen Victoria would take up, quite naturally, the threads of their friendship. It was a friendship which developed, as the years went by, into one of equals. The further the Second Empire receded into history, the more Victoria came to treat

Eugenie as though she were still a reigning Empress. While the Emperor and, later, the Prince Imperial had been alive and the chances of a restoration had seemed probable, the Queen had regarded the Empress simply as an esteemed guest in her country. After 1879, she encouraged her to take her place beside her as a fellow sovereign. During the first years of the exile the Empress had addressed the Queen in the third person, calling her 'Madam' and 'Your Majesty'; but by now, on Victoria's insistence, she called her *Ma Soeur*, as in the great days of the Empire. At public functions, which Eugenie rarely attended, she always stood a pace or two behind the Queen; in private they stood together as equals. No one living in England ranked closer to the Queen than the Empress, and Victoria did everything she could to emphasize this fact.

That the Queen's attitude towards the Empress should be so generous was due, not only to the fact that she was fond of her, but to Eugenie's conscious self-effacement. Ever since her arrival in England at the fall of the Second Empire, the Empress had withdrawn from public life entirely. She made no public appearances, she issued no statements, she opened no exhibitions, she laid no foundation stones. There were many charities which would have been only too delighted to benefit from her patronage, but Eugenie declined their invitations. For her to have courted public attention would have been the easiest thing in the world: she was beautiful, popular, blessed with boundless energy and an easy social manner. But to have moved about the country in a blaze of publicity, to have set herself up as some sort of rival to the Queen, would have been both foolish and ungrateful. Nor did Eugenie ever contemplate doing any such thing. Her common sense and deep feeling of gratitude towards the Queen made it impossible. Moreover, her taste for public life had long since left her. Such yearnings as she might have had for the limelight were finally stilled after her son's death in 1879. Thereafter she effaced herself completely, preferring to move about unnoticed and with quiet informality. 'When Eugenie went about with us, where the public could see her,' wrote one of her companions, 'she very much disliked being followed and stared at. . . .'

Eugenie's withdrawal from the public gaze, this renunciation of her once-acclaimed position, made Victoria all the more eager to treat her as a reigning sovereign in private. Her attitude emphasized the fact that Eugenie's retirement was voluntary and not due to any lack of proper respect on the part of England or her Queen. Nowhere, in fact, was the Empress treated with more deference than in England. On the Continent she was looked upon as an august old lady and little more; only in England was she accorded the honours fitting to her rank. This was due to the example set by the Queen. By the close of the nineteenth century, this equality between the sovereigns had been firmly established and everywhere accepted. As Eugenie herself put it, they were not mere friends, but *sisters*.

Once, when some members of the Orleans family asked permission to visit the Queen at Windsor, the Empress, who had been invited to spend a few days there at the same time, immediately wrote to the Queen, suggesting that she postpone her visit. Her presence at Windsor would be awkward, she claimed, for both the Queen and the rival French royalties. Victoria's reply was prompt and characteristic. 'No,' she instructed Princess Beatrice, 'by no means put off the visit. If anyone postpones it, it had better be *they*. The Orleanists are my relations, but the Empress is my friend and that is much more sacred to me.'

2

What was the quality of the relationship between these two women? Despite their frequent expressions of mutual regard, they were never really intimate friends. That would have been all but impossible. Royalties—even those of equal rank—do not easily form friendships with one another; their lives are too circumscribed, too artificial, too ordered to allow for the development of a close friendship. And then both Victoria and Eugenie were solitary women, too self-obsessed, perhaps, to give themselves over wholeheartedly to a platonic friendship. In many ways, their temperaments were quite different. Where Victoria was shy, unapproachable, even brusque on occasion, Eugenie was lively, talkative and socially accomplished. The Queen's air was formidable and awe-inspiring, the Empress's graceful and unselfconscious. Victoria led a well-ordered, domesticated life and was loath to deviate from her familiar routine; Eugenie was restless, prone to sudden changes of plan and indifferent to her own comfort. She adored travel. Had *she* been the ruler of such a far-flung Empire, Eugenie once claimed, she would long since have explored its furthermost corners. The Queen was conscientious, industrious and methodical, the Empress questing, impulsive and imaginative. Victoria looked upon politics as a somewhat painful duty; to Eugenie politics, and foreign affairs in particular, were a passion.

Yet the two women had much in common. For one thing, they both had somewhat deceptive public images. To the general public, Victoria was still the 'Widow of Windsor' and Eugenie 'the Tragic Empress'—two sad-eyed, black-clad women, living out their secluded and sorrow-steeped lives. The truth was rather different. The public knew little of the Queen who could dance so energetically at her gillies' ball and laugh so uproariously at some funny story. Nor would they have been prepared for the Empress's side-splitting mimicry or her flood of vivacious chatter. Neither of them were prudes. They were both practical, down-to-earth personalities, surprisingly broad-minded and well-endowed with common sense. A strongly bourgeois streak marked both their personalities. They were intelligent, without being intellectual, and religious without being bigoted. Of race and class prejudice, they were almost entirely free. Both were shrewd, observant, sharp-witted women, not easily deceived. In turn, they had no hint of deceit or duplicity in their natures: they were always sincere, honest and open. Their minds were intuitive rather than rational; both had a certain impetuousness. They tried, not always successfully, to be impartial but tended, in the main, to be rather partisan. Their kindness to those they liked could be exceptional, almost excessive; each had the capacity for inspiring deep affection among those who served them.

Through their otherwise practical natures ran a strongly romantic thread. Both responded to youthful good looks and dashing manners: Victoria never lost her *penchant* for swashbuckling young men nor Eugenie her delight in a pretty face. Both were sentimental, making much of anniversaries, especially the melancholy ones. 'Just 25 years ago we arrived in state and splendour at Paris and St Cloud, [and were] so kindly received by the Emperor and Empress,' noted Victoria in her Journal on 18 August 1880, 'and now! she, at Osborne, a widow, childless, and an exile! Terrible!' Both women were inclined to dramatize and to dwell upon their misfortunes; each spent half a lifetime in mourning for a loved one. Not for a moment would they have considered discouraging the public conception of them as two tragedy queens.

Both had a taste for harmless gossip. They could spend hours discussing the affairs of acquaintances, even of strangers. A member of Eugenie's circle names the Empress's love of scandal as her only failing, and Victoria was never averse to a little bit of gossip. Their day-to-day conversation seldom rose much above the exchange of domestic news or of memories, with an occasional scrap of homely philosophy thrown in to give a little weight.

Yet there were occasions when their conversation took a more serious turn. To the Empress, the Queen could unburden herself on topics which she was able to discuss with few others. She could talk of the tensions within her family: of her relationship with the Prince and Princess of Wales, of the lack of sympathy between the German Crown Princess and her eldest son—the future Kaiser Wilhelm II—of the marriage of her daughter, Princess Beatrice, to Prince Henry of Battenberg. In Eugenie, Victoria was always assured of an understanding listener.

But no matter how intimate their conversation, the Empress's attitude towards the Queen always remained slightly deferential. She adopted towards Victoria, noted one of Eugenie's companions, a manner which she reserved exclusively for the Queen: it was 'something of the manner of an unembarrassed but attentive child talking to its grandmother'. For if Victoria's attitude towards Eugenie tended to be one of sympathy and concern, Eugenie's remained one of admiration and appreciation.

And there were times when it was simply one of awe. Once,

when the Empress was staying as the Queen's guest at Aber-geldie, she was visited by Victoria's secretary, Henry Ponsonby. He found Eugenie in a highly nervous state. She told him that she was expecting the Queen to tea at half past five that after-noon and, knowing the Queen's aversion to heat, was anxious to know if the room was cool enough. The Queen, admitted the agitated Eugenie to Ponsonby, 'sometimes terrified her'.

On another occasion, during a dinner party at Balmoral, Victoria told Eugenie that Lord Torrington, one of her lords-in-waiting, had died. The Empress promptly asked who the new Lord Torrington would be. Victoria, imagining that Eugenie had asked who the new lord-in-waiting was to be, said, 'I cannot tell you', so tartly that the Empress supposed that there was some doubt about the successor to the title. Perhaps Lord Torrington had been illegitimate. Acutely embar-rassed, she murmured an excuse for having asked. Victoria, realizing her mistake, hastily explained away the misunder-standing and then led the party into the drawing-room.

The poor Empress was so shaken by even this mild exchange that she was reduced to a state of utter confusion. Going up to Sir Henry Byng, whom she knew very well, and mistaking him for Sir John McNeill, she asked him whether a certain Miss McNeill, who was present in the room, was his sister. Byng, extremely puzzled, assured the Empress that she was not.

'Oh,' persisted the fright-bemused Eugenie, 'your cousin?'

'No, no,' exclaimed Byng, 'no relation at all.'

Abashed, the Empress retired into a corner with an album of photographs and would speak of nothing but the weather for the remainder of the evening lest, in her nervousness, she make another gaffe.

3

One day during the first week of the year 1883, Queen Victoria was startled to hear that the Empress had suddenly gone to Paris. Victoria had been told nothing of Eugenie's decision and it was not until she read an account in that morning's news-papers that she learnt her reasons for going. Somewhat alarmed, the Queen sent Captain Bigge to Farnborough to await the Empress's return.

Eugenie had gone to Paris for two days to attend to what has been called her 'last political act'. Between the fall of the Empire in 1870 and the death of the Prince Imperial nine years later, Eugenie had not set foot in France. Since then, she had twice passed through it. The experience had been half-pleasurable, half-painful, and very fleeting; now in 1883, she returned to Paris and stayed overnight. She put up at the Hôtel du Rhin in the Place Vendôme, within walking distance of the Tuileries. What her thoughts were at the first sight of the blackened ruins which now marked the scene of her most brilliant years, one does not know; they must have been extremely poignant. However, her mind, for the most part, was on other things.

Prince Napoleon—surly, capricious, irresponsible Plon-Plon—had landed himself in trouble. On the death of Gambetta, the French Republican leader, on the last day of 1882, Plon-Plon demanded a plebiscite; he imagined that it would lead to the overthrow of the existing regime. He was promptly arrested and imprisoned in the Conciergerie for a few days. The leaders of the Bonapartist Party, anxious to dissociate themselves from Plon-Plon's rash action, wanted henceforth to exclude him entirely from the councils of the party. With this the Empress could not agree. She might detest him, but she appreciated that Plon-Plon was a figure of some stature. With the imperial succession having been passed on by the late Prince Imperial to Plon-Plon's son Victor, and not to Plon-Plon himself, the party was already in danger of splitting into two bickering factions; Eugenie was anxious to do all she could to avoid this.

At not inconsiderable risk to herself (Plon-Plon's action had been in the nature of a *coup d'état*) the Empress crossed to Paris and called together the party leaders. She begged them not to break with Plon-Plon. 'I have forgiven him, why can't you?' she pleaded. 'It's the only way to preserve our party, its unity and even its existence.' But the assembled Bonapartists could not agree. It would be Plon-Plon's continued presence in, and not his exclusion from, the party that would lead to its downfall, they argued. They could not take him back.

Unsuccessful in that direction, Eugenie appears to have been successful in another: she achieved some sort of temporary reconciliation between Plon-Plon and his sons. That accomplished, she returned to Farnborough.

There she found Captain Bigge awaiting her. He handed her a letter from the Queen. In it Victoria wrote of her great admiration for the Empress's courage and self-sacrifice. Eugenie, deeply touched by Victoria's solicitude, explained to Bigge that she had purposely not told the Queen of her plans lest Victoria be compromised by them; her move, after all, had been blatantly political. In her answer to the Queen, Eugenie admitted that one of her chief worries had been that this political act might have antagonized the British government and so have affected her friendship with the Queen.

She need have had no fear on this particular score. Victoria was never one for putting politics before personalities. Indeed, the Queen was all sympathy. Writing to Lord Lyons, her Ambassador in Paris, Victoria was full of admiration for the 'poor Empress's very courageous and unselfish and most painful act'. She claimed that '*no one* but herself *could* do what she has done, viz. effected a reconciliation with Prince Napoleon and his family'. The Empress 'had met with *nothing but* the greatest respect from *everyone* at Paris'. Two visiting-books had been quite *filled* with the names of Parisian well-wishers.

Even Plon-Plon was grateful for Eugenie's intervention. Later that year, wearing the *Grand Cordon* of the *Légion d'Honneur*, he crossed to England to attend the mass on the anniversary of the death of the Prince Imperial. Eugenie, spotting him standing in the dim interior of the church, whispered to one of her suite, 'There's Prince Napoleon; go and pay your respects to him; we must be nice to him.'

The Bonapartist Party might be having its troubles, but Queen Victoria had not lost faith in it. Her championship of the imperial cause had not died with the Prince Imperial. Some years later, in conversation with her suite on the rival claims of the Orleans and the Bonapartes, Victoria declared for the latter; 'the Bonapartes are the only dynasty with any hold on the French imagination,' she said. The reason for this partisanship, claimed one of the group after the Queen had left them, was that the Emperor Napoleon III had been the first sovereign to take Prince Albert seriously: he had always treated him as a reigning Prince.

4

Although the Empress, unlike some members of her entourage, felt no antagonism towards the British army, the sudden sight of a French uniform could still move her as no British uniform was able to do. Madame Waddington, wife of the French Ambassador to Britain during the 1880s, has a moving little story to tell of the Empress's unabated affection for her country's fighting men, particularly its sailors.

The occasion was a naval review at Spithead. In addition to the British fleet drawn up for the Queen's inspection, there were two French ships present, the *Iphigénie* and the *Élan*. Victoria, aboard the yacht *Osborne*, had announced that she would receive the captains of all the ships on review, but the captain of the *Iphigénie*, misunderstanding the invitation, assumed that he could bring his officers with him. When the large party of French officers boarded the *Osborne*, the British Admiral was extremely agitated. The Queen had made it quite clear that she intended receiving the captains only. The Admiral appealed to the Prince of Wales. Tactfully, the Prince settled everything. The Queen agreed to receive all the Frenchmen present. They joined the long row of captains waiting to be presented.

The line of uniformed men moved slowly across the deck towards the black, rotund figure of the Queen. About her, in nervous attendance, stood a distinguished group of royalties and naval personnel. Above towered the creaking superstructure of the *Osborne*. Beyond it, on the wind-tufted sea, lay the great fleet of ironclads.

One by one the officers passed before her. She had a word to say to each. As the Frenchmen reached the Queen, they noticed, standing a few paces behind her, a woman dressed in black. She was tall, handsome and silver-haired, with sad, down-slanting eyes, boldly outlined. She seemed to be in a highly emotional state and was looking at the French uniforms with particular concentration. The shuffling line of Frenchmen had no idea who she was or why she should be so upset. It was only after they had moved on that they were told that she was Eugenie, the woman who, for almost twenty years, had been Empress of the French.

CHAPTER SEVENTEEN

Osborne, Balmoral and the Côte d'Azur

1

As the years passed, so did the meetings between Victoria and Eugenie fall into a regular pattern. In the summer the Empress would spend a few weeks at Osborne. In the autumn she would stay for a month or so at Balmoral. In the spring the two sovereigns would exchange visits on the Côte d'Azur. At other times during the year, the Empress would spend a few days at Windsor Castle or the Queen would pay her a visit at Farnborough Hill.

When Eugenie stayed with the Queen at Osborne, Victoria usually placed Osborne Cottage at her disposal. This cottage, which had been built to accommodate the overflow from the main house at the time of the imperial visit of 1857, was a sizeable little building, separated from the main grounds by a private road. The separation by no means guaranteed independence; indeed, being a guest in one of the Queen's houses was not the most relaxing way of spending a holiday. It could be extremely nerve-racking.

The Empress had to impress upon her suite, and more particularly on the younger members (Eugenie adored young people and usually had two or three about her) that they would have to be extremely careful with everything in the house. The Queen, she warned them, was most particular. When the visit was over, Victoria was quite likely to come in person to inspect the recently vacated cottage. Together with a housekeeper, she would move from room to room to see that everything was in order. If anything had been damaged her keen eye would notice it immediately. The cottage having only one drawing-room, and this being the room in which the Queen was received, no personal things could be left lying about. 'The chairs must remain during our stay arranged exactly as we found them,' noted Agnes Carey, one of Eugenie's young companions, 'also the books on the central table; anything that is moved must be put back on the same spot.' They were not even allowed to carry inkstands about for fear of spilling ink on one of the royal carpets.

'This is one of the privileges(?)' noted Agnes Carey wryly, 'of living in a house belonging to Queen Victoria.'

Another disquieting feature of such a stay was that it was extremely difficult to keep anything secret from the Queen. If one did anything of which she might possibly disapprove— even something as apparently harmless as an island excursion— she invariably found out about it. Thus, when Eugenie wanted to take a couple of her companions on a walk through the old town of West Cowes, she had to do so before the Queen herself arrived on the island. The Empress was obliged, says Agnes Carey, 'to make hay while the sun shines, for on Tuesday the Queen arrives, and she would be horrified, and would positively veto for the Empress a trip on foot through the long, narrow, straggling street which constitutes the town'.

Worse still was the necessity for everyone, other than the Empress and one or two long-established members of her Household, to keep out of the Queen's sight. Victoria had an almost pathological dislike of meeting people unexpectedly. For all her dignity and sense of position, she was still an extremely shy person (Lady Lytton noticed how she always gave a quick, nervous laugh on meeting anyone new) and, like many who have learnt to control their shyness, an unexpected encounter was likely to reveal it. The Queen was particularly anxious to avoid chance meetings with acquaintances. With complete strangers, or with what the Victorians airily called 'the poor' she was better, but those whom she did not know really intimately—or even those whom she did—were advised to keep well out of her way.

This led to many bizarre incidents. One afternoon Agnes Carey and two other girls, related to the Empress, were strolling back to Osborne Cottage. As they turned a corner they saw, ahead of them, another party making its way back to the cottage. The party was made up of Princess Beatrice's husband, Prince Henry of Battenberg, the Queen's son, the Duke of Connaught, together with their aides and two senior members of the Empress's Household. The girls, not wanting to intrude on the more illustrious party ahead, slackened their pace. They wanted to allow the two princes time to take leave of their companions in the front porch. Suddenly, to their dismay, the girls spotted, in the distance, certain all-too-familiar white ponies and outriders. The Queen, having taken the Empress for a drive, was bringing her back home. 'Caught between the fires', as Miss Carey puts it, the girls chose the lesser blaze: they dashed towards the cottage. Forcing their way through the royal group saying their leisurely farewells in the porch, the girls disappeared into the house. The princes were anything but annoyed. Realizing what was happening (by now hoofbeats were audible), they left their conversation unfinished and followed the scurrying girls. Prince Henry, knowing his way about the cottage, ran straight through it, making his escape by way of the back door, the garden and the back gate. But the Duke of Connaught, less familiar with the house, turned frantically to Agnes Carey, begging 'piteously' to be shown a way out. In a matter of seconds the quick-witted Miss Carey had bustled him through the house and out of a french window. Her last view was of him careering across the lawn with his desperate aides-de-camp panting close behind. A few seconds later his mother's carriage drew up at the door.

When, at dinner that evening, the girls told Eugenie the story, she was very amused. Her eyesight being better than the Queen's, she had noticed the two men dashing across the garden. Very wisely, she had not drawn the Queen's attention to the singular sight. She told the girls that she had often seen even the Prince of Wales hiding behind the shrubbery in the grounds of Osborne House when he thought that his mother might be coming that way.

The Queen's actual visits to Osborne Cottage were even more unnerving. Her first call would always be a formal one. A mounted messenger would arrive at the cottage to announce the forthcoming visit. From then on the Household would be on tenterhooks. Everyone, except those whom Victoria had specifically asked to meet, had to keep out of sight. As to be seen hurrying away was almost worse than to be seen at all, Eugenie insisted that those not asked for were closeted in their rooms well before time. This could mean a two-and-a-half-hour wait. On the first occasion the uninitiated Miss Carey was imprisoned in her room for almost three hours with nothing whatsoever to occupy her. She dare not even tip-toe out of the room to fetch a book or a piece of sewing. What made things worse was that the Queen might change her mind and ask to have one of those prisoners presented to her after all: one's confinement was thus never free of a certain feeling of apprehension.

By the time the Queen arrived the house would be as quiet, and as cold, as the grave. The Empress always entertained the Queen alone in the drawing-room. Even such senior members of the Household as the Duke de Bassano were denied the honour of taking tea with Queen Victoria. Only close relations, such as Princess Beatrice and her husband, were allowed to remain in the Presence during tea. The Queen's ladies and gentlemen were obliged to wait in the dining-room with the members of the Empress's Household. Here the conversation would be conducted in little more than whispers. If the Queen did ask for some member of the Empress's suite to be presented, the introduction would not last for more than a few moments. After an agonizing week of waiting for a summons from the Queen, the Empress's two girl relations were sent for. They were back in a flash, having made their curtsies and kissed the royal hand. They found Her Majesty 'very simple, gracious and kind', reports Miss Carey.

The first formal visit over, Victoria was likely to drop in at any time of the day. This proved most agonizing of all. Accompanied by one of her grandchildren and with a collie dog frisking about her skirts, the squat black figure would make her way slowly through the grounds of Osborne House and cross the road to the cottage. A key turning in the lock of the gate in the side garden would be the first indication of the royal presence. It was up to Agnes Carey, whose bedroom window was directly opposite the gate, to spread the alarm.

'The Queen!' she would hiss, and there would be an undignified
flurry as aristocratic old ladies and venerable old gentlemen
scrambled to their rooms to leave the coast clear. This *sauve
qui peut* over, the Empress alone would prepare to welcome her
guest.

Eugenie was often invited to dine with Victoria at Osborne
House. Sometimes she went alone ('Her Majesty finds it too
hot for large parties just now,' reports one of her circle) and
sometimes she was accompanied by one or two of her suite.
After the Prince Imperial's death, the Queen had relaxed her
cast-iron rule of a low neckline at night with regard to the
Empress, allowing her to wear instead what was known as an
open bodice. She had adopted the same style herself. Recently,
however, the Queen had resumed the regulation low neckline
and short sleeves, and Eugenie, not wanting to be the exception, had also taken to wearing full evening dress. The Empress
looked, writes Miss Carey, 'so *distinguée*, her soft grey hair so
prettily dressed and so wonderfully young looking. Her youth-
fulness was accentuated by her simple black dress with only a
suggestion of jet trimming, her short sleeves and low bodice
showing to perfection her still beautiful arms and shoulders....
I do not wonder people raved about her when she was younger,
for she is still so charming and withal so majestic.'

This low bodice, insisted on by the Queen, was all very well,
but, when coupled with her insistence on open windows, the
results were often disastrous. One evening, during one of the
Queen's dinner parties at Osborne, one of the Empress's ladies
fainted at table. 'You see, Beatrice,' cried the Queen, rounding
triumphantly on her daughter, 'you will keep the rooms so
warm!' So, in spite of the fact that a chill wind was already
blowing across the lady's bare shoulders, more windows were
flung open and the company subjected to a further drop in
temperature.

Agnes Carey has left an interesting portrait of the Queen
during the middle years of the 1880s. The contrast between
Victoria's small stature and her immense dignity never ceased
to amaze the girl. 'It seems strange that a woman of her build,
verging on extreme old age, bereft of many former physical
attractions and unbecomingly dressed, should have such a

dignified bearing, and be able to impress everyone who comes in contact with her by her queenly personality and charm. Her delightfully modulated voice and sweet genuine smile have, I think, much to do with it: and her strong sterling qualities of mind and heart make themselves felt in spite of the somewhat plain exterior. The Queen's memory for names and places is something marvellous. Like the Empress she also takes a great, though impersonal, interest in people whom she has never seen and probably never will see; makes enquiries into incidents of their lives; and years after, surprises her hearers by her remembrance of the details which have been given her. . . .'

2

Of the many young women with whom the Empress Eugenie delighted to surround herself, few were more engaging than Ethel Smyth, afterwards Dame Ethel Smyth, the well-known musician. Eugenie first met this struggling but determined young woman during the 1880s and was immediately attracted by Ethel's vigorous and unaffected personality. Ethel might not have had the Empress's beauty and grace but she had something of her unquenchable spirit. Before long, and despite the fact that she knew very little about music, Eugenie had fallen into the rôle of a patroness.

Ethel had written a Mass while staying with the Empress at Cap Martin, but, as she seemed to be having some difficulty in getting it produced, Eugenie decided to bring the young composer to the attention of the Queen. A little royal patronage, she thought, might do her friend the world of good. Accordingly, when the Empress went north in the autumn of 1891 to stay at Birkhall near Balmoral, she invited Ethel to spend a few days with her. As Miss Smyth's talents as a writer equalled, if not outshone, her talents as a musician, she has given a delightful account of her stay.

Evidence of the nature of the friendship between the Queen and the Empress was apparent from the very start of the visit. Ethel was welcomed at the door of the house by the Empress herself wearing, much to her guest's surprise, 'a little erection

215

of black lace on her small, beautifully poised head'. Knowing the Empress's loathing for caps, the forthright Ethel immediately tackled her about it. It seemed that the Queen did not approve of 'capless old ladies' and the Empress had compromised with this little lace confection. *'Si cela fait plaisir à votre Reine!'* she said smilingly to the head-shaking Miss Smyth.

On the day after Ethel's arrival, the Connaughts and Prince Henry of Battenberg came to pay their respects to the Empress. Ethel was duly asked to sing for them. The royal guests obviously approved of her efforts for, later that day, a message arrived to say that when the Queen paid her visit the following afternoon, Miss Smyth was to be presented.

A storm of so violent a character was raging the next day that Ethel imagined that no one, especially no old lady, would ever venture out in it. She was wrong. No only did the Queen arrive, but she arrived in an open carriage unprotected by any rugs or wraps. Her Majesty never caught cold. 'Some of her ladies,' noted Miss Smyth, 'were old and frail, but the rigours of a Scotch "waiting", including a north-east wind *with rain*, were evidently nullified by the glow of loyalty within their bosoms. On the other hand, dread of displeasing "the dear Queen" . . . may have had something to do with it.'

The Queen arrived punctually at three. For an hour beforehand, the Empress had been scouting in corridors and peering into the storm-lashed garden to make sure that Victoria would not come across any stray people. When she did arrive, the house, which accommodated a considerable body of people, was as quiet and deserted as a churchyard. The red carpet, hastily rolled out to the steps of the Queen's carriage, was sopping wet before she had time to set foot on it. The Queen, the Empress and Princess Christian disappeared into the drawing-room; the less important were relegated to another part of the house.

Presently the Empress emerged from the drawing-room and beckoned Ethel to join them. She entered the Presence.

The Queen was seated in a small cane chair. On her head was a white straw hat; its only concession to the tempestuousness of the day being a black ribbon securing it firmly under the chin. Ethel found the Queen dignified, imposing and so awe-inspiring that she would have been terrified had it not been for Victoria's 'wonderful, blue, child-like eyes, and the sweetest, most entrancing smile' that she had ever seen.

Eugenie had warned her friend that, although the Queen had chronic sciatica and walked with a stick, she objected strongly to being helped out of her chair. It was all that Ethel could do not to rush forward and help her as she now, surprisingly, rose to greet her. Victoria lifted herself, she says, 'with a sort of one, two, three, and away movement'.

'It was not the Queen's way,' continued Ethel, 'and not according to the tradition she had been brought up in, to put you at your ease, as some Sovereigns do, and bring about anything distinctly approaching conversation.' So while Victoria sat in silence, the Empress ('the most socially competent of beings') and Princess Christian kept the talk flowing.

Inevitably, Ethel was asked to sing. As she never lacked confidence, she was soon banging away at the piano, choosing, with uncharacteristic subtlety, a selection of German songs. These so delighted the Queen that the Empress took the opportunity of suggesting that Ethel perform some of her Mass. Victoria agreed, and the room reverberated to the sound of Miss Smyth not only playing the piano, but singing the chorus, the solo parts, and 'trumpeting forth orchestral effects' in between. The Queen, the Empress afterwards assured her young friend, was much taken with this 'novel experience'. Eugenie's own opinion of the performance one does not know. It was bound to have been favourable: the Empress might have had no ear for music but she could always appreciate *élan*.

The recital over, the performer was dismissed. She retired to another room to join the rest of the company for tea.

Throughout the entire visit, said the Empress afterwards, the Queen made not the slightest reference to the tempest raging outside. Only when a gillie came banging on the drawing-room door, telling her that she would have to go as the horses could stand it no longer, did she rise to leave. John Brown was dead by now, but the Queen still allowed herself to be spoken to by her gillies in a fashion which would have earned anyone else, including her children, a very sharp rebuke.

The rain, which had been falling ceaselessly all afternoon, now began to pour down with even more vehemence. It was descending, says Ethel, like one continuous waterfall. Raising her voice above the noise of the storm, she asked one of Victoria's ladies whether the Queen would have the carriage closed going home. By leaning well towards her, Ethel was just able to catch what she called her serene reply. 'Oh dear no,' said the lady-in-waiting, 'I think not.' And as Ethel watched the departure from behind one of the firmly closed windows of the house, she saw that this 'incredible prediction' was fulfilled.

With back erect and head held high, the plump little figure of the Queen of England was borne away in an open barouche through the blinding cascade of October rain.

A few days later Ethel was commanded to dine, with the Empress, at Balmoral. With Ethel's taste in clothes being distinctly masculine, Eugenie was obliged to enliven the effect of her friend's dress with a few jet trimmings and to arrange, in her somewhat haphazardly styled hair, a 'grand jet serpent'. Eugenie, of course, looked superb. Together the incongruous-looking pair set out for the castle. On arrival there, the Empress was directed into the Queen's presence, while Ethel was obliged to dine with the Household in another room. Dinner over, the dining-room doors were flung open by two scarlet-liveried footmen and the company ushered into the drawing-room.

There now occurred what Ethel has described as 'one of the most appalling blunders I ever committed in my life'.

As the only woman guest present, Ethel headed the procession of lesser fry into the Queen's drawing room. Her mind, she says, was 'innocently set on making myself agreeable when I should get there'. The room into which she so confidently led the Household was a large one and, at the far end of it, standing on a tartan hearthrug, were the Queen and the Empress. They were chatting together rather animatedly, noticed Ethel; a good dinner obviously had its effects on even this unfrivolous Court.

Between the door by which she had entered and the hearthrug on which stood the two sovereigns, was an avenue of royal persons, ranged—Ethel was only afterwards to discover—in strict order of precedence. The most illustrious were standing nearest, but not on, the hearthrug, and the mere ladies and gentlemen of the Court were gathered at the end of the avenue nearest the door. What Ethel should have done was to take her place among the maids of honour huddled near the entrance and remain there until noticed.

What she did was to advance swiftly and purposefully up the avenue with the honest intention of saying a cheery 'How do you do' to Her Majesty the Queen.

'If a young dog strays up the aisle during church, no one says anything, no one does anything,' wrote Miss Smyth after it was all over, 'but, none the less, he soon becomes aware that something is wrong.' It was even so with her. As she strode in her unselfconscious, slightly hoydenish fashion towards the hearthrug, Ethel gradually sensed that something was indeed wrong: 'my cheerful confidence waned,' she said, 'and my step faltered'. But it was too late to stop. In a stunned silence she moved on, more hesitantly now, towards the hearthrug.

As she reached it, the Queen turned her head slightly and looked at her for a second. Then Her Majesty turned away and resumed her conversation with the Empress. 'If I had been a Brobdingnagian spider as big as a Newfoundland she would not have acted differently,' claims Ethel. Eugenie, unable to shriek, '*Mon Dieu, n'avancez pas!*' stood quite still, wishing, she afterwards admitted, that the earth would open up and swallow her.

At the very moment that Ethel, numb with fright, reached the hearthrug, Princess Christian stepped forward and quickly offered her hand. Then, tactfully but firmly, she drew her back into the crowd.

Later that night Eugenie explained to her friend about the hearthrug. 'It was,' she learnt, 'as sacred a carpet as exists outside Mohammedanism.' Only crowned heads could stand on it as a right but sometimes, as a supreme honour, some favourite minister might be allowed to set foot on it. It was not, however, for the likes of Ethel Smyth.

When the time came for Ethel to be greeted by the Queen— at the Queen's pleasure—Victoria was all graciousness. She had obviously forgiven her for her blundering behaviour. Indeed, the Queen asked her to perform some more of her Mass.

When Ethel asked whether the music was to be rendered as before, as at Birkhall ('a proceeding which seemed unthinkable in these surroundings') the Queen assured her that she would like exactly that rendering. It had been 'so very interesting'. So, undaunted by the ring of frozen faces about her, the resilient Ethel set to. Once again a room echoed to the sound of Miss Smyth emulating chorus, solo parts and orchestra. Nothing, not even trumpet calls, were missed out; with a free foot she thudded out 'certain drum effects'. Never, she claimed, 'did I get through one of these performances better or enjoy doing it more'.

The singular display over, Ethel glanced at what she calls the 'Madame Tussaud-like' faces of the members of Victoria's Court; not one revealed the slightest flicker of emotion. The Queen, however, was full of admiration. She hoped, she said to Ethel, that she would one day see her at Windsor.

After the Queen had said goodnight to the assembled company, she and the Empress left the room by a special royal exit. Despite the fact that Eugenie would be going home in the same carriage as Ethel, it would never have done for them to have left by the same door. 'This was lucky,' says Ethel, 'for I now had the chance of witnessing a wonderful bit of ritual.'

As the two royal ladies arrived on the threshold, the Queen motioned the Empress to pass before her. This Eugenie gracefully declined to do. They then turned to each other and curtsied. Crippled though the Queen was, her curtsey was surprisingly elegant and dignified. And the Empress was renowned for her curtsey. Although almost seventy at the time, Eugenie made 'such an exquisite sweep down to the floor and up again, all in one gesture', that the observer could only compare it to a flower 'bent and released by the wind'. Then they passed together out of the door, shoulders touching, but with the Empress—as the visiting sovereign—being allowed to precede the Queen—the home sovereign—by one inch.

Ethel saved the Empress one piece of humiliation that evening. The 'grand jet serpent' which Eugenie had arranged in her friend's hair did not collapse in coils over her face during the singing of the Mass. It did so only in the carriage on their way home.

3

A much more exotic setting for these meetings of the two sovereigns was the South of France. In the closing years of the nineteenth century Queen Victoria went, each spring, to Cimiez, above Nice. As the Empress's villa at Cap Martin was a mere carriage-drive away, Victoria would sometimes drive over to see her. The Empress had called her house Cyrnos—the Greek name for Corsica; in atmosphere, this holiday home was quite different from the massive, memory-steeped mansion at Farnborough. Situated on a pine-covered slope, with the Rock of Monaco behind and a view of the shimmering Mediterranean all around, it was a white, cheerful-looking villa. On its sunny terrace, the Empress spent a great deal of her time.

Victoria, accompanied by the inevitable and, by now, widowed Princess Beatrice and a couple of ladies, would drive over from Cimiez to arrive at Cyrnos a little before luncheon. If the day were hot, the Queen might find the drive tiring (she was nearing eighty by now) but she usually bore it very well. The carriage would wind up through the grounds planted with dark, bitter-scented trees and draw up at the main entrance. Here the Empress would be waiting to welcome them. 'She is certainly a most fascinating woman,' wrote one of Victoria's ladies of Eugenie at the time, 'so wonderfully graceful, and those beautiful features will be the same to the end.' If only, she complained, the Empress would not paint her eyes and eyebrows. With Eugenie always looking so much younger than her age, her erect bearing and nimble movements made a sharp contrast to the heaviness and slowness of the Queen. It was a contrast of which Victoria, only half a dozen years older, was well aware. 'The Empress was . . . wonderfully well,' she wrote rather wistfully on one occasion. 'The cure at Bath has made her quite active again. If only I could become so too.' It was unfortunate, she added, that she could not *stand* baths.

The visitors would lunch alone with the Empress and then go strolling through the sun-drenched garden. 'The afternoon was radiant and mild as a June morning,' wrote a guest of such a walk through the grounds, 'the sky milky blue, and the air seemed to quiver in the exquisite light. Close to the house, thousands of flowers, yellow, blue, pink, white, mauve and scarlet, waved in the sunlight. In the rest of the park the vegetation is of a sterner sort, cypresses, pines, oaks, laurels, acanthus, rock-roses, stocks and myrtles. . . .'

The two sovereigns would move slowly along the paths, the Empress walking, the Queen being wheeled in her chair, until they reached a narrow terrace overlooking the sea. Here, in the shelter of a clump of flowering shrubs, the party would settle down in a semi-circle of armchairs. This was Eugenie's favourite corner; she never tired, she would say, of this view of the jagged coastline.

With their grey heads tilted towards each other, the two old ladies would sit chatting in the spring sunshine. They had known each other for such a long time by now. Over forty years had passed since Victoria had first welcomed 'the very gentle, graceful and evidently very nervous Empress' to Windsor; it was almost as long since Victoria's ecstatic visit to Napoleon III's Paris. Over a quarter of a century ago the Queen had gone to Camden Place to see the Empress after the fall of the Second Empire; and it was almost twenty years since the terrible night that Victoria had received the news of the Prince Imperial's death. A second and a third generation had grown up since the time that they had first met; they were two relics from another age.

But they were both still women of unbroken spirit and strong opinions. Their talk was by no means confined to the past. These were the years during which France was being racked by the Dreyfus affair; both women were firmly pro-Dreyfus. To the Queen this victim of French anti-semitism was always a 'poor martyr'; and the Empress, contrary to what many may have believed, was in opposition to the majority of royalists on this matter. It was Eugenie, who had always been accused of being clerical and reactionary, who supported Dreyfus, while Plon-Plon's sister, the free-thinking Princess Mathilde Bonaparte, sided with the militant Catholics, the chauvinists and the anti-semites.

The conversation could take a lighter turn as well. Once, while Victoria was on holiday at Cimiez, she visited a private zoo belonging to a certain Countess de la Grange. The Countess was said to be a retired cocotte. Delighted by the Queen's visit, the notorious Countess presented her with an ostrich egg on which she had scrawled her name. Exactly, declared the startled Queen, 'as if she had laid it herself'.

After an hour or so on the terrace above the glittering sea, the party would return to the house. The Queen, having climbed painfully into the carriage, would take her leave. Eugenie, a lone, black-clad figure at the door of the villa, would stand looking after her until the carriage had swung into the dark shadows of the pines and out of sight.

CHAPTER EIGHTEEN

Entente Cordiale

1

As the friendship between the Queen of England and the ex-Empress of the French continued to flourish, so was there a steady deterioration in the relations between England and France. The last decades of the nineteenth century saw the development of a fierce colonial rivalry between the two nations. The points of conflict were innumerable: France was superseded by Britain in Egypt, the British forced the French to withdraw at Fashoda, France championed the Boers against the British in South Africa. By the 1890s French resentment of perfidious Albion was stronger than ever it had been during the most Anglophobe period of the Second Empire.

By few would this ill-feeling between the nations have been regretted more keenly than by the Empress Eugenie. She had always believed in an Anglo-French alliance. In this, she had the full support of the Prince of Wales. Bertie's affection for France—whether Empire or Republic—had remained constant. Ever since he had first set eyes on Paris, during that spectacular royal visit of 1855, he had been drawn to France and the French; now he longed for a return to the days when France and Britain had stood together as friends and allies. During his frequent visits to Paris he did what he could, by way of personal contact, to pave the way for a better understanding between the two nations. His calls on the Empress Eugenie would not have been unconnected with this. She too, with her enduring interest in foreign affairs, was not without contacts or influence. Although the eventual improvement in the relations between the two countries might well have been achieved without the efforts of the Prince of Wales, there is no doubt that he, encouraged by the Empress, did everything in his power to foster it.

If relations between France and Britain were to improve, relations between France and Germany remained as stormy as they had been since the Franco-Prussian war. Queen Victoria's grandson, the showy, neurotic, vainglorious Wilhelm II, was now German Emperor and his persistent sabre-rattling did nothing towards easing the tense situation. Yet the Empress Eugenie was on the friendliest terms with the Kaiser's mother, the widowed Empress Frederick. So much had happened to Vicky since the days of the Franco-Prussian war, when she had dashed off those triumphant letters to Queen Victoria. Her own life, since then, had almost matched Eugenie's for tragedy. A British liberal amongst Prussian reactionaries, Vicky had always been extremely unpopular in Germany. Her husband's reign, which was to have seen the inauguration of her passionately expressed ideals, lasted for ninety-eight days only: Frederick III died, in June 1888, of cancer of the throat. On the accession of their son, Wilhelm II, with whom Vicky had always been at loggerheads, she retired from public life. She now lived, in embittered and frustrated obscurity, at Friedrichshof, near Cassel. A woman of considerable intellect and vitality, the Empress Frederick delighted in the company of the equally lively Empress Eugenie. She often visited her at Farnborough.

It was almost half a century since, as a girl, Vicky had idolized the beautiful young Empress of the French. Of this admiration, something still remained. 'Receiving is a talent and an art like everything else . . .' Vicky once wrote to her daughter Sophie, Crown Princess of Greece. 'I have no right to preach, I know how gauche and awkward I am in such things, not possessing any social talent at all! The perfection of a hostess was the Empress Eugenie, no one ever came up to that. . . .'

In 1900, when the Empress Frederick was herself suffering from cancer, Eugenie offered her her villa at Cap Martin for the winter. 'If I had been well I should have accepted it gladly,' Vicky wrote to Sophie. 'Her kindness touches me so much, it is just like her. She does not stop to ask whether it will do her good or harm in the eyes of her Party in France, but follows the dictates of her kind heart.'

With the Empress Frederick's son, Kaiser Wilhelm II, the Empress Eugenie had very little contact. Although he often visited Queen Victoria (could not a hint be dropped, the Queen once asked, to the effect that the ebullient young man need not come to England *every* year?) the Kaiser did not meet the Empress until 1894. On that occasion the Duke of Connaught brought him to Farnborough Hill. The visit appears to have been a great success. The Kaiser, who could be charming, was fascinated by this great figure from the past.

Another of Queen Victoria's children with whom the Empress had remained on especially friendly terms was Princess Beatrice. In the years following the death of her husband, Prince Henry of Battenberg, in 1896, the Princess and her children often visited the Empress at Farnborough. Eugenie was godmother to Princess Beatrice's only daughter; indeed, the baby had been christened Victoria Eugenie. Always known as Ena, the young, fair-haired Princess was a great favourite with the Empress. At Farnborough Ena met many of the Empress's Spanish relations, among them young men who were friends of Spain's boy King, Alfonso XIII. And in 1905, Ena was to meet the King in person. A year later she would marry him and become Queen of Spain.

While Queen Victoria considered it perfectly natural that the ex-Empress of the French should associate so freely with the various members of her family, she was certainly not prepared to accept the present heads of the French nation on anything like the same terms. To the Queen, royalties were a race apart. That Eugenie was a parvenue, the wife of a popularly elected Emperor, she conveniently ignored. Thus when Felix Faure, the President of the French Republic, visited the Queen at Cimiez in 1898, Victoria was determined that he should not be received as an equal. Fortunately, her age and infirmity ruled out any question of her going downstairs to receive him; *he* would have to come upstairs to see *her*. However, as the Prince of Wales had come over from Cannes for the Presidential visit, his presence raised the same problem. The Queen was not going to have her heir demean himself by meeting the visitor at the door, nor was Bertie himself at all anxious to do so. On the other hand, one could hardly plead ill-health as an excuse in his case. After much discussion, a compromise solution was agreed upon. The President would be met at the door by the Household, and the Prince of Wales, pretending to be late, would come hurrying down to meet the President *half-way* up the stairs. This way, honour would be saved all round.

The President, however, proved no less resourceful. Being as conscious of his dignity as was the Queen of hers, he refused to remove his hat on being received by the members of the royal Household. Only on actually meeting the Prince of Wales on the stairs did he condescend to remove it. Not until that moment, reckoned the President, had the visit really begun.

2

The summer of 1900 was the last time that Victoria and Eugenie saw each other. The Empress had declined the Queen's customary invitation to spend the autumn in Scotland the year before ('it is too cold and I am not well enough,' Eugenie had written to a relation) but the following year she spent some time aboard her yacht, *Thistle*, off the Isle of Wight. She visited Victoria at Osborne and it was with considerable difficulty that she dissuaded the Queen from returning the call: 'nothing is more dangerous at sea,' cautioned the Empress, 'than transferring from one boat to another'.

A final glimpse of the two friends is provided by Madame Waddington, who, despite the fact that her husband was no longer French Ambassador, was received by both the Queen and the Empress that summer.

Eugenie received her aboard the *Thistle*. Madame Waddington had been warned by one of the Empress's ladies that Eugenie had a very bad cold; she had been forbidden to come up on deck or to talk. Nevertheless, Eugenie had agreed to receive her guest. Mary Waddington was led below and urged not to stay long on account of the Empress's voice.

'She was standing in her cabin,' wrote Madame Waddington, 'still a handsome, stately figure, with beautiful brow and eyes, and a charming manner, more animated than I had imagined. She was very well dressed in black.' The Empress would have been seventy-four at the time.

Eugenie invited her guest to sit down and promptly launched

into a stream of talk. It was all about Paris and mutual friends. She talked at such length, in fact, that the visitor began to worry about her throat. Surely the Empress was tiring herself out? Twice an agitated *dame d'honneur* appeared to suggest that Eugenie dismiss her guest and twice Eugenie waved her away. When she finally said goodbye, it was with many regrets for the brevity of the visit and with the expressed hope of seeing her guest soon again. *'Je ne dirai pas adieu, mais au revoir,'* shouted the Empress after her.

On the following day, wearing her best black taffeta and with a white aigrette sprouting from her toque, Madame Waddington was received by the Queen at Osborne House. Here, in contrast to the relaxed air of the *Thistle*, all was dignity and restraint.

The Queen, dressed in black, was seated in the middle of the room facing the door. When the visitor had made her curtsey, Victoria motioned her to sit close beside her. 'I thought she looked extremely well,' wrote Mary Waddington of the eighty-one-year-old Queen, 'of course, I couldn't tell if her sight was gone, as she knew I was coming and I sat close to her. Her eyes are blue and clear, and her memory and conversation quite the same.'

They spoke, first in French and then in English, of many things, but they spoke chiefly of France and the French. With the Boer War in progress, there was a great deal of ill-feeling in France against British aggression in South Africa. The Queen herself had not been spared by the French Press. She now spoke, 'very moderately', says her guest, of the 'caricatures and various little incidents that had occurred in France'. Madame Waddington hastened to assure her that the French public were most indignant at these attacks on the Queen. Victoria believed this to be true. Whenever she had been in France, she said, she had always been made to feel happy and comfortable. She could never forget the kindness of the French nation. She hoped that they realized this.

After a while Victoria dismissed her guest. Holding out her hand, the Queen said, 'I hope you will come back to England, and whenever you do I will be very glad to see you.'

'I suppose,' mused Madame Waddington at the end of the visit, 'I shall never see the Queen again. . . .'

3

That Christmas of 1900—the last of her long life—Queen Victoria did not write her usual letter to the Empress Eugenie. Too exhausted to make the effort, she dictated it to Princess Beatrice. On New Year's Day, 1901, some three weeks before her death, the Queen sent her friend a card; on it was inscribed, said the Empress, 'one almost illegible word'. The past year had been a terrible one for the Queen, wrote Eugenie to her nephew's wife, the Duchess of Alba. So many things had saddened her: the Boer War, the deaths of her son Prince Alfred and of her grandson Prince Christian Victor, the illness of her daughter the Empress Frederick. The Queen herself referred to it as a 'horrible year'.

Queen Victoria died on 22 January 1901. Her death saddened Eugenie immeasurably. 'It is an *immense* loss to me,' she wrote on the day of the Queen's death; 'she was a friend close to my heart, always good and affectionate, a support in my chequered life. I have never felt more strange or alone in this country; I am profoundly sad and dispirited. . . .'

Suffering from bronchitis herself, the Empress was unable to go to Osborne to see the Queen's remains nor to Windsor to attend the funeral service. 'Nothing,' she wrote, 'can give you an idea of the sense of desolation felt by great and small in this country, in the whole world, I should say, at the death of the Queen.'

From the new King, Edward VII, to whom the Empress sent a message of sympathy, she received a touching reply. 'I knew how deeply Your Majesty would sympathize with us all in our profound grief,' he wrote. 'Our dear mother was deeply attached to you.'

4

The long friendship between Queen Victoria and the Bonaparte family had come to its end. Of what value had it been? What were its enduring effects on the life of the Queen and on the politics of her country?

On a personal level, the association brought Queen Victoria into contact, throughout the greater part of her adult life, with a family that was refreshingly different from Europe's other royalties. Into the Queen's often staid, predictable and circumscribed life, the Bonapartes brought a breath of another world. All three of them—the Emperor, the Empress and the Prince Imperial—were exotics: they never quite rid themselves of their slightly unconventional air. Adventurers, parvenus, cosmopolites, the Second Empire Bonapartes radiated an aura of romanticism to which Queen Victoria's ardent nature was quick to respond. Her long association with them might not always have been harmonious but it was never dull. Time and again she found herself caught up in their turbulent careers.

In the beginning she had all but fallen in love with the bewitching Napoleon III; later she had seen him as a dire threat to her country and to Europe; after the cataclysmic fall of his Empire she had reverted to her previous political opinion of him. With the dramatic death of the Prince Imperial, she had been intimately concerned. Indeed, the tragedy had revealed the Queen at her most admirable: compassionate, practical, loyal and stubborn in her determination to put personalities before politics. Her unwavering championship of the dethroned, exiled and bereaved Eugenie was equally endearing and no less characteristic.

Without her involvement in the affairs of this tragic and colourful family, Queen Victoria's life would have been considerably poorer.

The political importance of the relationship is more difficult to assess. Although the actual Anglo-French alliance lasted for less than half-a-dozen years, the friendship, and the subsequent cooling of relations, were to have long-lasting effects. It is easy to overestimate the significance to nations of friendships between their rulers, yet, in this case, both Napoleon and Victoria were in positions in which they were able to ally friendship to foreign policy. He was an autocratic sovereign; she, although a constitutional monarch, was encouraged by Prince Albert to play a positive role in foreign affairs. There is no doubt that the Queen's early passion for the Emperor strengthened the Anglo-French *entente* and that her disenchantment with him helped weaken it.

For this ebbing of her enthusiasm, Prince Albert was largely to blame. The Prince, with his exaggerated fear of Napoleon III's ambitions, always favoured a future German, as opposed to a French, alliance; once Albert died, his heartbroken widow was determined that his ideas—like flies in amber—be lovingly preserved. His plans, and his prejudices, must be firmly adhered to. Thus it was that, while Napoleon III gradually liberalized his regime, Queen Victoria continued to champion illiberal Prussia. She assumed that her daughter Vicky, together with her husband Crown Prince Frederick, would—in accordance with Prince Albert's enlightened teachings—encourage democracy in Germany when once they were in a position to do so. The Queen was not to know that Fritz and Vicky would have to wait for thirty years before becoming German Emperor and Empress and that, when they did, it would be too late for the introduction of their liberal ideals. The Emperor Frederick, dying of cancer, would reign for less than one hundred days.

If only Queen Victoria had not shut herself up for so many years after Prince Albert's death, if only there had been more contact between her and Napoleon III during the 1860s, the Anglo-French *entente* might have revived and flourished. With Prince Albert dead, the Queen might have looked more kindly (as she had done at the beginning and as she was again to do at the end) on Napoleon III. She might have come to a better understanding of his plans for liberalizing his regime; she might have appreciated, as did both he and Eugenie, the growing threat of Prussia. After all, the Queen had always thought highly of Eugenie's capabilities; she might well have seen things from her point of view more often. Had Victoria remained friendly with the imperial couple, had there been a frequent exchange of State and private visits during the 1860s, the Anglo-French alliance could well have endured. Other than during the period of his Italian campaign, Napoleon III had always been popular in England; there was a strong feeling of rapport between the peoples of the two nations, such as there never was between the British and the Germans. Even though, by that time, the Queen was no longer in a position to guide foreign policy, a lead from the Sovereign (such as was given by King Edward VII in later years) might well have kept the alliance alive. And if, by 1870, Britain and France had been closely allied, Bismarck would certainly have hesitated to pick his quarrel with France and the Franco-Prussian war might have been avoided.

As it was, Europe had to wait almost fifty years before the Anglo-French alliance was revived. In the spring of 1904, the *entente cordiale* was established between Britain and France. It was an agreement that paved the way for the Anglo-French alliances of the First and Second World Wars. For King Edward VII, whose influence on the affair had been considerable, it was the climax of his life-long sympathy with the French. And that sympathy had been rooted, very firmly, in the Second Empire of Napoleon and Eugenie.

Epilogue

Epilogue

The Empress outlived the Queen by almost twenty years. During Eugenie's extraordinary lifespan, not only Victoria's grandsons but her great-grandsons grew to manhood. Over a dozen of the Queen's great-great-grandchildren had been born by the time of the Empress's death in 1920. Born six years after the death of King George III, the Empress Eugenie was to die six years before the birth of Queen Elizabeth II. With the new King, Edward VII, the Empress remained on the friendliest terms. Indeed, it was imagined, by the suspicious Germans, that the two of them were not merely friends, but conspirators. Why, otherwise, should the King be in touch with so many of the Empress's friends in France? Had Eugenie, during her visit to Austria, paved the way for King Edward's visit the following year? For what reason had the Empress had her yacht fitted with wireless if not to transmit messages from the King? The establishment of the *entente cordiale* seemed to confirm such exaggerated suspicions. Although, in fact, the Empress Eugenie's influence on the realization of the alliance could have been only minimal, there can be no doubt that the *entente cordiale* would have given her great pleasure. It would have been an echo of that other alliance, signed almost exactly half a century before.

In 1910 King Edward died and in 1914, ten years after the creation of the *entente cordiale*, Britain and France stood together as allies against imperial Germany. It was sixty years since the two armies had fought side by side in the Crimea; now the aged Empress had the satisfaction of seeing them united against the Reich which had risen so triumphantly from the ruins of the French Second Empire. 'England and France are meant by nature to work together,' she said to someone during the war, 'for each of them possesses high qualities which the other lacks.

Combined they are invincible. In England you find wonderful endurance, great steadfastness and a determination that nothing can alter. In France you have the dash, the sanguine temperament, but, above all, you have *foresight*.'

The Allied victory in 1918 and the subsequent return of Alsace-Lorraine to France filled her with elation. She felt that at last, after almost half a century, the Franco-Prussian war had been avenged. 'It makes up for everything,' she exclaimed, 'it obliterates everything, it repays me all my grief, it allows me to die with my head held high, in peace with France, which will have nothing to reproach us for. . . .'

During the war the Empress had converted a wing of Farnborough Hill into a hospital for officers. Not only had she financed this entirely from her own pocket but she had taken a more than conventional interest in the welfare of the patients. For her unstinting efforts, King George V decided to award her the Grand Cross of the British Empire. His two eldest sons, the future Kings Edward VIII and George VI, came to Farnborough to invest her with the decoration. 'I owe this much more to the kindness of Your Majesty than to any merit of my own,' wrote the Empress to George V, 'and I appreciate this token of friendship very much.'

A few months later, in December 1919, the Empress left Farnborough for visits to the South of France and her native Spain. She had turned ninety-three earlier that year. While spending a few days in Paris on her way south, the Empress received Maurice Paléologue, the French diplomat with whom she had had occasional discussions during the past two decades. They had not met for six years and Paléologue was shocked by the change in her appearance. He saw at once, however, that 'this pitiful frame was still dominated by a spirit at once energetic, tenacious and proud'.

The Empress, says Paléologue, always had three photographs beside her: one of Napoleon III, one of the Prince Imperial and one of Queen Victoria. 'It goes everywhere with me,' the Empress once said of the Queen's portrait. Now, as the Empress and Paléologue discussed the Allied victory over Germany and, more especially, the return to France of Alsace-Lorraine, Eugenie again spoke to him of the Queen. 'Today I can under-

236

stand why God has made me live so long,' declared the Empress. 'My dear friend Queen Victoria, who had absolute trust in the Divine justice and goodness, used often to say to me: "What we do not understand now, we shall understand some day—in this life or the next. But we can be sure that the explanation will not be withheld." God has graciously given me the explanation while I can still rejoice in it here below. So I shall have the crowning consolation of seeing France re-established with her nationality intact!'

They spoke at length, claims Paléologue, of other matters, and then, without showing any signs of fatigue, the Empress dismissed him. She planned to go to Spain, she said as they parted for, although she felt more like a very old bat, she was determined—like the butterflies—to make for the sunlight. 'Besides,' she added, 'before death takes me, I want to see my Castilian sky once more!'

And it was under her Castilian sky, in the Palacio de Liria, home of her nephew the Duke of Alba, that she died. The day was Sunday, 11 July 1920, and she was in her ninety-fifth year. Her body was sent back to England for burial at Farnborough.

When, a century before, they had buried the first Napoleon on Saint Helena, he had been laid to rest, unmourned by his British captors, in an unmarked grave. But when Eugenie, the last Napoleonic Empress, was buried in the crypt of Saint Michael's Abbey at Farnborough, there stood about her coffin a group of British royalties, headed by the sovereigns, King George V and Queen Mary.

'Strange, incredible contrast,' as Queen Victoria used to say.

Notes on Sources
and
Bibliography

Notes on Sources

Unless otherwise indicated, all quotations from Queen Victoria are taken from the Queen's Letters and Journals, both published and unpublished. The hitherto unpublished extracts are from the Royal Archives at Windsor and are published here by gracious permission of Her Majesty Queen Elizabeth II. The published extracts are taken from the three following sources:

The Letters of Queen Victoria; A Selection from Her Majesty's Correspondence. First Series, 1837–61, edited by A. C. Benson and Viscount Esher; 3 vols. John Murray, London, 1907. Second Series, 1862–85, edited by G. E. Buckle; 3 vols. John Murray, London, 1926. Third Series, 1886–1901, edited by G. E. Buckle; 3 vols. John Murray, London, 1930.

Leaves from a Journal. Edited by Nicolas Bentley. André Deutsch, London, 1961.

Napoleon III in England. By Ivor Guest. British Technical and General Press, London, 1952. (This book contains many extracts from Queen Victoria's *Journals.*)

CHAPTER ONE

Napoleon III's comment ('How long does perpetuity . . .'), Cheetham, *Louis Napoleon and the Genesis of the Second Empire.* All quotations from King Leopold are from *The Letters of Queen Victoria.* Lord Cowley's reports, *The Paris Embassy during the Second Empire.* Victoria's opinion of Princess Adelaide ('so pretty . . .'), H. Albert, *Queen Victoria's Sister.* Malmesbury on marriage question, *Memoirs of an ex-Minister.* Adelaide's mother ('Oh! if we . . .'), H. Albert, *Queen Victoria's Sister.* Victoria on Eugenie ('beautiful, clever . . .'), *Further Letters.* Countess de Montijo ('Sire, it cannot . . .'), Kurtz, *The Empress Eugenie.* Lady Augusta Bruce on wedding, *The Letters of Queen*

241

Victoria. Albert and Ernest on Napoleon III, Martin, *Life of the Prince Consort*.

CHAPTER TWO

Eugenie on Felix ('I hope he . . .'), Fleury, *Memoirs of the Empress Eugenie*. Greville, *The Greville Diary*. Albert on Napoleon III, Martin, *Life of the Prince Consort*. Lady Clarendon and the Duchess of Cambridge, Villiers, *A Vanished Victorian*. Napoleon in tights ('did not appear . . .'), Vizetelly, *The Court of the Tuileries*. Clarendon on Garter, also 'At last . . .', Villiers, *A Vanished Victorian*. Albert on imperial Court ('strictly kept . . .'), Martin, *Life of the Prince Consort*.

CHAPTER THREE

Froude and Carlyle from Froude, *Carlyle's Life in London*. Captain Fraser ('The head of . . .'), Guest, *Napoleon III in England*. Greville, *The Greville Diary*. Countess von Bernstorff, Guest, *Napoleon III in England*.

CHAPTER FOUR

Clarendon and Cowley, Cowley, *The Paris Embassy*. Viel-Castel, *Memoirs*. Victoria's ladies, Augusta Stanley, *Letters*. Albert on Neuilly, Martin, *Life of the Prince Consort*. Marion Ellice, Cohen, *Lady de Rothschild and her Daughters*. Mary Bulteel ('I regret to say . . .'), Stanley, *Letters*. Clarendon ('The unaccountable . . .'), Villiers, *A Vanished Victorian*. Mary Bulteel ('hesitant . . .'), Ponsonby, *Henry Ponsonby*.

CHAPTER FIVE

Albert ('Tomorrow . . .'), Martin, *Life of the Prince Consort*. Vicky, ('The English ones . . .'), Saunders, *A Distant Summer*. Fat official ('I would give . . .'), Villiers, *A Vanished Victorian*. Clarendon ('the assassin . . .'), Mary Ponsonby, *A Memoir*. Thackeray, *The Second Funeral of Napoleon*. Bertie ('You have a nice . . .'), Saunders, *A Distant Summer*. Albert on Bertie, Martin, *Life of the Prince Consort*. Bertie ('Not do without us . . .'), Greville, *The Greville Diary*. Victoria asks for Napoleon's opinion of her, Cowley, *The Paris Embassy*.

NOTES ON SOURCES

CHAPTER SIX
Albert ('a veritable . . .'), Longford, *Victoria R.I.* Palmerston on French alliance, Thompson, *Louis Napoleon.* Napoleon on 'rare qualities', *Letters of Queen Victoria.* Victoria on Castiglione, Kurtz, *The Empress Eugenie.* Clarendon and Albert on Napoleon's visit, *The Letters of Queen Victoria.* Vicky and the Empress, Corti, *The English Empress.* Conversations between Napoleon and Albert, Guest, *Napoleon III in England.* Clarendon on Napoleon's letter, *The Letters of Queen Victoria.*

CHAPTER SEVEN
Eugenie and Napoleon on Orsini incident, Kurtz, *The Empress Eugenie.* Greville, *The Greville Diary.* Victoria to Cowley ('unfortunate acquittal . . .'), Cowley, *The Paris Embassy.* Malmesbury and Disraeli reports to the Queen, *The Letters of Queen Victoria.* Albert on Cherbourg, Martin, *Life of the Prince Consort.* Victoria ('The nice caps . . .'), Martin, *Life of the Prince Consort.* Decorations on *Bretagne*, Mary Ponsonby, *A Memoir.* Napoleon's speech, Fleury, *Memoirs of the Empress Eugenie.* Victoria ('the dreadful . . .'), Martin, *Life of the Prince Consort.* Life Light, Malmesbury, *Memoirs of an ex-Minister.* Albert ('The war preparations . . .'), Martin, *Life of the Prince Consort.* Malmesbury on war rumours, *Letters of Queen Victoria.* Napoleon to Cowley ('I have done . . .'), *Letters of Queen Victoria.* Albert ('the old Italian . . .'), Longford, *Victoria R.I.* Albert ('At the Court of Napoleon . . .'), Martin, *Life of the Prince Consort.*

CHAPTER EIGHT
Cobden, Thompson, *Louis Napoleon.* Eugenie on Mexico (*l'accomplissement . . .*'), Paléologue, *Les Entretiens.* King Leopold, *The Letters of Queen Victoria.* Clarendon ('I am sure . . .' and 'with unbounded pleasure . . .'), Kennedy, *'My dear Duchess'.* Hardman, *A Mid-Victorian Pepys.* Napoleon to Victoria, *Letters of Queen Victoria.* Victoria to the Queen of Prussia, *Further Letters.*

CHAPTER NINE
Buckingham Palace ('commanding premises . . .'), Longford, *Victoria R.I.* Ponsonby ('there were prolonged . . .'), Ponsonby,

Henry Ponsonby. Prime Minister's comments on Balmoral, Ponsonby, *Henry Ponsonby.* Napoleon ('One of the first duties . . .'), Fleury, *Memoirs of the Empress Eugenie.* Empress ('literally cuirassée . . .'), Hegerman-Lindencrone, *In the Courts of Memory.* Life at Fontainebleau, Filon, *Souvenirs sur l'Impératrice Eugénie.* Victoria ('that Sodom . . .'), *Dearest Mamma.* Bertie in Paris, Cowley, *The Paris Embassy.* King Leopold on Alix, Battiscombe, *Queen Alexandra.* Victoria on Alix, Magnus, *King Edward the Seventh.* Victoria ('very satisfactory . . .'), *Dearest Mamma.* Vicky on Paris, *Letters of Queen Victoria.* Elphinstone, McClintock, *The Queen thanks Sir Howard.* Alice in Paris, *Letters to Her Majesty the Queen.* Lord Derby, *Letters of Queen Victoria.*

CHAPTER TEN

The Empress ('But it was the way . . .'), Oman, *Things I have seen.* Clarendon ('won't have the Holy . . .'), Cowley, *The Paris Embassy.* Disraeli ('our dear Peeress . . .'), Longford, *Victoria R.I.* Queen of Holland, Burghclere, *A Great Lady's Friendship.* Cowley ('sore at heart . . .'), Newton, *Lord Lyons.* Gladstone ('Your Majesty will . . .'), *Letters of Queen Victoria.* Crown Princess ('The King and everyone . . .' and 'What suffering . . .'), *Letters of the Empress Frederick.* Victoria ('the poor French . . .'), Longford, *Victoria R.I.* Granville, *Letters of Queen Victoria.* Lyons ('much pluck . . .'), Newton, *Lord Lyons.* Crown Princess on Sedan, *Letters of Queen Victoria.*

CHAPTER ELEVEN

Burgoyne's letter, *Letters of Queen Victoria.* Marie de Larminat ('She seemed unable . . .'), Des Garets, *L'Impératrice Eugénie en exile.* Filon ('They were very different . . .'), Filon, *Souvenirs.* Crown Princess and Granville on screen, *Letters of Queen Victoria.*

CHAPTER TWELVE

Napoleon on exile, *Revue des Deux Mondes.* Malmesbury, *Memoirs of an ex-Minister.* Eugenie on Napoleon, Paléologue, *Les Entretiens.* Cricket match, etc., Guest, *Napoleon III in*

England. Prince Imperial at Bath, Filon, *Memoirs of the Prince Imperial.* Stone ('the size of . . .'), Cope, *A Versatile Victorian.* Telegram, *Letters of Queen Victoria.* Bertie ('One cannot be wrong . . .'), Lee, *Edward VII.* Gladstone on Bertie, Magnus, *King Edward the Seventh.* Eugenie to Victoria, *Letters of Queen Victoria.*

CHAPTER THIRTEEN
Louis's looks ('In features . . .'), Forbes, *Souvenirs of Some Continents.* Victoria and Louis ('Good heavens . . .'), Ponsonby, *Henry Ponsonby.* Louis to Victoria (*'Rien ne pouvait . . .'*), *Letters of Queen Victoria.* Elphinstone, McClintock, *The Queen thanks Sir Howard.* Bertie on Louis, Lee, *Edward VII.* Marie de Larminat, Des Garets, *L'Impératrice Eugénie.* Eugenie to Victoria ('Tears came rushing...'), Kurtz, *The Empress Eugenie.* Louis to Duke of Cambridge, Filon, *Memoirs of the Prince Imperial.* Disraeli ('Well, my conscience . . .'), John, *The Prince Imperial.* Louis's will, Filon, *Memoirs of the Prince Imperial.* Victoria's telegram to Eugenie, Kurtz, *The Empress Eugenie.*

CHAPTER FOURTEEN
Victoria and news of Louis's death, *More leaves from a Journal.* Empress and news of Louis's death, Kurtz, *The Empress Eugenie.* Court Martial, Filon, *Memories of the Prince Imperial.* Victoria ('Terrible evidence of want of . . .'), Ponsonby, *Henry Ponsonby.* Salisbury ('National self-reproach'), Kurtz, *The Empress Eugenie.* Disraeli, *Letters of Disraeli.* Eugenie on Plon-Plon ('by leaving him . . .'), Eugenie, *Lettres Familières.*

CHAPTER FIFTEEN
Eugenie on Carey, *Letters of Queen Victoria.* Eugenie's plea ('The one earthly . . .'), Des Garets, *L'Impératrice Eugénie.* Eugenie to her mother, *Lettres Familières.* Eugenie ('Why cannot he leave . . .'), *The World.* Carey to the Empress, John, *The Prince Imperial.* Marie de Larminat, Des Garets, *L'Impératrice Eugénie.* Victoria ('a great deal . . .'), *More leaves from a Journal.*

Victoria ('She has benefited . . .'), *Further Letters*. Lady Wolseley, *Letters of Lord and Lady Wolseley*. Eugenie in Zululand, Filon, *Souvenirs*. Dean of Westminster ('chiefly anonymous . . .'), Ponsonby, *Henry Ponsonby*. Eugenie to Borthwick, John, *The Prince Imperial*.

CHAPTER SIXTEEN
Publicity-shy Empress ('When Eugenie . . .'), Carey, *The Empress Eugenie in exile*. Eugenie's manner with the Queen, Smyth, *Streaks of Life*. Eugenie's fear of Queen, Ponsonby, *Henry Ponsonby*. Eugenie and Plon-Plon, Filon, *Souvenirs*. Victoria on Bonapartism, Mallet, *Life with Queen Victoria*.

CHAPTER SEVENTEEN
Quotations from Agnes Carey, *The Empress Eugenie in exile*. Quotations from Ethel Smyth, *Streaks of Life*. Eugenie's looks, ('She is certainly . . .'), Mallet, *Life with Queen Victoria*. Cyrnos ('The afternoon was . . .'), Paléologue, *Les Entretiens*. Ostrich egg, Mallet, *Life with Queen Victoria*.

CHAPTER EIGHTEEN
Vicky on Eugenie ('Receiving is . . .'), Victoria, *The Empress Frederick writes to Sophie*. Eugenie ('it is too cold . . .' and 'nothing is more . . .'), *Lettres Familières*. Waddington, *Letters from a Diplomat's Wife*. Eugenie on Victoria's death, *Lettres Familières*. King Edward VII's telegram to Eugenie, Kurtz, *The Empress Eugenie*.

EPILOGUE
Eugenie on England and France, and on Grand Cross, Kurtz, *The Empress Eugenie*. Eugenie ('It makes up for everything...'), Aubry, *Eugenie, Empress of the French*. Paléologue, *Les Entretiens*.

Bibliography

Albert, Harold A.: *Queen Victoria's Sister.* Robert Hale, London, 1967.

Albert, Prince: *Letters of the Prince Consort, 1831–1861* (edited by Dr Kurt Jagow). John Murray, London, 1938.

—— *The Prince Consort and his brother.* Two hundred new letters (edited by H. Bolitho). Cobden Sanderson, London, 1933.

Alice, Grand Duchess of Hesse: *Letters to Her Majesty the Queen.* John Murray, London, 1885.

Anon: *The Empress Frederick: A Memoir.* James Nisbet, London, 1913.

Antrim, Louisa Countess of: *Recollections.* John Murray, London, 1937.

Aubry, Octave: *Eugenie, Empress of the French.* Cobden Sanderson, London, 1939.

Barkeley, Richard: *The Empress Frederick.* Macmillan, London, 1956.

Barthez, A. C. E.: *The Empress Eugenie and her circle.* T. Fisher Unwin, London, 1912.

Battiscombe, Georgina: *Queen Alexandra.* Constable, London, 1969.

Bellessort, André: *La Société Française sous Napoléon III.* Perrin, Paris, 1932.

Benson, E. F.: *Queen Victoria.* Longmans, Green and Co., London, 1935.

Bicknell, Anna: *Life in the Tuileries under the Second Empire.* The Century Co., New York, 1895.

Bonnin, Georges (Editor): *Bismarck and the Hohenzollern Candidature for the Spanish Throne.* Chatto and Windus, London, 1957.

247

Burghclere, Lady: *A Great Lady's Friendship: Letters to Mary, Marchioness of Salisbury, 1862–1890.* Macmillan, London, 1898.

Carey, Agnes: *The Empress Eugenie in Exile.* Eveleigh Nash and Grayson, London, 1922.

Cheetham, Frank H.: *Louis Napoleon and the Genesis of the Second Empire.* John Lane, London, 1909.

Cohen, Lucy: *Lady de Rothschild and Her Daughters.* John Murray, London, 1935.

Cook, Sir Edward: *Delane of the Times.* Constable, London, 1916.

Cope, Vincent Zachary: *A Versatile Victorian.* Harvey and Blythe, London, 1915.

Corley, Thomas A. B.: *Democratic Despot.* Barrie and Rockliff, London, 1961.

Corti, Count Egon: *The English Empress.* Cassell, London, 1957.

Cowley, Baron Henry Wellesley: *The Paris Embassy during the Second Empire.* Butterworth, London, 1928.

Delord, Taxile: *Histoire du Second Empire.* 6 vols. Baillière, Paris, 1869–75.

Des Garets, Marie Comtesse (de Larminat) de Garnier: *Souvenirs d'une Demoiselle d'Honneur: Auprès de l'Impératrice Eugénie.* Calmann-Levy, Paris, 1928.

—— *Souvenirs d'une Demoiselle d'Honneur: l'Impératrice Eugénie en exile.* Calmann-Levy, Paris, 1929.

Disraeli, Benjamin: *Letters of Disraeli to Lady Bradford and Lady Chesterfield.* Ernest Benn, London, 1929.

—— *Letters from Benjamin Disraeli to Frances Anne, Marchioness of Londonderry.* Macmillan, London, 1938.

Du Camp, Maxime: *Souvenirs d'un Demi-Siècle.* Hachette, Paris, 1949.

Duff, David, *The Shy Princess.* Evans, London, 1958.

Eugénie, Empress of the French: *Lettres Familières de l'Impératrice Eugénie.* 2 vols. Le Divan, Paris, 1935.

Evans, Thomas W.: *Memoirs of Dr Thomas W. Evans.* T. Fisher Unwin, London, 1906.

Filon, Augustin: *Memoirs of the Prince Imperial.* Heinemann, London, 1913.

—— *Souvenirs sur l'Impératrice Eugénie.* Calmann-Levy, Paris, 1920.

Fleury, Comte Maurice: *Memoirs of the Empress Eugenie.* D. Appleton and Co., New York, 1920.

—— and Sonolet, Louis: *La Societé du Second Empire.* A. Michel, Paris. (N.D.)

Forbes, Archibald: *Memoirs and Studies of War and Peace.* Cassell, London, 1895.

—— *Souvenirs of Some Continents.* Harper and Bros, New York, 1885.

Fraser, Sir William: *Napoleon III; My Recollections.* Sampson Low, London, 1895.

Frederick III, German Emperor: *Diaries of the Emperor Frederick* (translated by Frances A. Welby). Chapman and Hall, London, 1902.

Froude, J. A.: *Carlyle's Life in London.* Longmans, Green, London, 1890.

Fulford, Roger: *The Prince Consort.* Macmillan, London, 1966.

Gooch, G. P.: *The Second Empire.* Longmans, London, 1960.

Gorce, Pierre de la: *Histoire du Second Empire.* Paris, 1896.

Greville, Charles: *The Greville Diary* (edited by P. W. Wilson). 2 vols. Heinemann, London, 1927.

Guedalla, Philip: *The Second Empire.* Hodder and Stoughton, London, 1932.

Guest, Ivor: *Napoleon III in England.* British Technical and General Press, London, 1952.

Hardman, Sir William: *A Mid-Victorian Pepys.* Cecil Palmer, London, 1923.

Hegerman-Lindencrone, Lillie Moulton: *In the Courts of Memory.* Harper and Bros, New York, 1912.

Herrison, Comte M. d'Irisson: *Le Prince Impérial.* P. Ollendorff, Paris, 1890.

Holden, W. H. (Editor): *Second Empire Medley.* British Technical and General Press, London, 1952.

Hubner, Count: *Neuf ans de souvenirs d'un Ambassadeur d'Autriche.* 2 vols. Paris, 1904.

Jerrold, Blanchard: *The Life of Napoleon III.* 4 vols. Longmans, Green, London, 1874–82.

John, Katherine: *The Prince Imperial.* Putnam, London, 1939.

Kennedy, A. L.: *'My dear Duchess'.* John Murray, London, 1956.

Kurtz, Harold: *The Empress Eugénie*. Hamish Hamilton, London, 1964.

Langtry, Lillie: *The Days I knew*. Hutchinson, London. (N.D.)

Lee, Sir Sydney: *King Edward VII*. 2 vols. Macmillan, London, 1925.

Legge, Edward: *The Empress Eugénie, 1870–1910*. Harper and Bros, London, 1910.

—— *The Comedy and Tragedy of the Second Empire*. Harper and Bros, London, 1911.

—— *The Empress Eugenie and her son*. G. Richards, London, 1916.

Loliée, Frederic: *The Life of an Empress*. Dodd, Mead, New York, 1909.

Longford, Elizabeth: *Victoria R.I.* Weidenfeld and Nicolson, London, 1964.

Lytton, Lady Edith: *Lady Lytton's Court Diary* (edited by Mary Lutyens). Rupert Hart-Davis, London, 1961.

Magnus, Sir Philip: *King Edward the Seventh*. John Murray, London, 1964.

Mallet, Marie: *Life with Queen Victoria* (edited by Victor Mallet). John Murray, London, 1968.

Malmesbury, James Howard Harris, Earl of: *Memoirs of an ex-Minister*. Longmans, London, 1884.

Martin, Sir Theodore: *The Life of His Royal Highness the Prince Consort*. 5 vols. Smith, Elder and Co., London, 1877–80.

Maxwell, Sir H. (Editor): *Life and Letters of the Fourth Earl of Clarendon*. Edward Arnold, London, 1913.

McClintock, Mary Howard: *The Queen thanks Sir Howard*. John Murray, London, 1945.

Metternich, Princess Pauline: *Souvenirs 1859–71*. Plon, Paris, 1922.

Monypenny, W. F., and Buckle, G. E.: *The Life of Benjamin Disraeli*. 2 vols. John Murray, London, 1929.

Morley, John: *The Life of William Ewart Gladstone*. 2 vols. Macmillan, London, 1905.

Newton, Lord: *Lord Lyons*. 2 vols. Edward Arnold, London, 1913.

Nicolson, Harold: *King George the Fifth*. Constable, London, 1952.

North Peat, A. B.: *Gossip from Paris during the Second Empire*. Kegan Paul, London, 1903.

Oman, Sir Charles: *Things I have seen*. Methuen, London, 1933.

Paléologue, Georges Maurice: *Les Entretiens de l'Impératrice Eugénie*. Plon, Paris, 1928.

Ponsonby, Arthur: *Henry Ponsonby: His life from his letters*. Macmillan, London, 1942.

Ponsonby, Sir Frederick: *Recollections of Three Reigns*. Eyre and Spottiswoode, London, 1951.

Ponsonby, Mary: *A memoir, some letters and a Journal* (edited by Magdalen Ponsonby). John Murray, London, 1927.

Saunders, Edith: *A Distant Summer*. Sampson Low, Marston and Co., London, 1946.

Sencourt, Robert: *The Life of the Empress Eugenie*. Ernest Benn, London, 1931.

—— *Napoleon III: the Modern Emperor*. Ernest Benn, London, 1931.

Smyth, Dame Ethel Mary: *Streaks of Life*. Longmans, London, 1921.

Stanley, Lady Augusta: *Letters* (edited by the Dean of Windsor and Hector Bolitho). Gerald Home, London, 1927.

Thackeray, W. M.: *The Second Funeral of Napoleon*. John W. Lovell Co., New York, 1883.

Thierry, Augustine: *Le Prince Impérial*. Grasset, Paris, 1935.

Thompson, J. M.: *Louis Napoleon and the Second Empire*. Blackwell, Oxford, 1954.

Tisdall, E. E. P.: *The Prince Imperial*. Jarrolds, London, 1959.

Vandam, Albert: *An Englishman in Paris*. Chapman and Hall, London, 1893.

Victoria, German Empress: *Letters of the Empress Frederick* (edited by Sir Frederick Ponsonby). Macmillan, London, 1929.

—— *The Empress Frederick writes to Sophie* (edited by A. Gould-Lee). Faber and Faber, London, 1955.

Victoria, Queen of Great Britain: *Leaves from the Journal of our Life in the Highlands, 1848–1861*. Smith Elder and Co., London, 1868.

Victoria, Queen of Great Britain; *More leaves from the Journal of a Life in the Highlands, 1862–1882.* Smith Elder and Co. London, 1884.

—— *Letters of Queen Victoria: A Selection from Her Majesty's correspondence, 1837–1910.* 9 vols. John Murray, London, 1907–30.

—— *Further Letters: From the Archives of the House of Brandenburg-Prussia.* Thornton Butterworth, London, 1938.

—— *Leaves from a Journal* (edited by Nicolas Bentley). André Deutsch, London, 1961.

—— *Dearest Child: Letters between Queen Victoria and the Princess Royal* (edited by Roger Fulford). Evans Bros, London, 1964.

—— *Dearest Mamma: Letters between Queen Victoria and the Crown Princess of Prussia* (edited by Roger Fulford). Evans Bros, London, 1968.

Villiers, George: *A Vanished Victorian.* Eyre and Spottiswoode, London, 1938.

Viel-Castel, Comte H. de: *Memoires du Horace de Viel-Castel.* 6 vols., Paris, 1883–4.

Vizetelly, E. A.: *The Court of the Tuileries.* Chatto and Windus, London, 1912.

Waddington, Mary: *Letters of a Diplomat's Wife.* Smith Elder, London, 1903.

Wellesley, Sir Victor, and Sencourt, Robert: *Conversations with Napoleon III.* Ernest Benn, London, 1934.

Wolseley, Lord: *The Letters of Lord and Lady Wolseley, 1870–1911* (edited by Sir George Arthur). Heinemann, London, 1922.

Wood, Sir Evelyn: *From Midshipman to Field Marshal.* Methuen, London, 1906.

NEWSPAPERS AND PERIODICALS

Paris: *Le Temps, Figaro, Moniteur, Revue des Deux Mondes.*

London: *The Times, Daily News, Morning Post, Graphic, Punch, Illustrated London News, The World.*

Index

Abdul Aziz, Sultan of Turkey, 118–120
Abdul Karim, 25
Abergeldie, 185, 186, 188, 190, 205
Adelaide of Hohenlohe-Langenberg, Princess, 12–15
Alba, James, 15th Duke of, 15
Alba, James, 16th Duke of, 237
Alba, Paca, Duchess of, 15, 103, 107
Alba, Rosario, Duchess of, 229
Albert, Prince Consort, 5, 7–9, 13, 17, 19, 21–24, 26–28, 32, 34–36, 40–44, 46, 47, 50, 54, 55, 58–60, 67, 72–77, 79, 81, 82, 84, 87, 91–96, 101, 102, 104, 109, 116, 141, 145, 159, 173, 185, 186, 188, 199, 208, 230; visits Boulogne, 18; welcomes Napoleon III at Dover, 20; distrust of Napoleon III, 28–29, 65–66, 80, 83, 93, 98, 105–106, 147, 231; death, 106–107
Alexander II, Tsar of Russia, 75
Alexandra, Queen of England. As Princess of Wales, 114–116, 131, 133, 162, 177, 204
Alfonso XIII, King of Spain, 226
Alfred ('Affie'), Prince, Duke of Edinburgh, 117, 155, 179, 193, 229
Alice, Princess, Grand Duchess of Hesse, 118, 131, 140
American Civil War, 106
Arthur, Prince, Duke of Con-

naught, 22, 28, 33, 74, 116, 117, 140, 162, 179, 212, 216, 226
Augusta, German Empress, 155; as Princess of Prussia, 29, 54, 75; as Queen of Prussia, 107
Austerlitz, battle of, 6, 10, 65

Balmoral Castle, 73, 109, 110, 132, 171, 172, 185, 188, 205, 210, 215, 218
Bassano, Duke de, 113, 149, 172, 213
Battenberg, House of (*see* also Henry), 25
Beatrice, Princess, 78, 139, 140, 157, 171, 177, 180, 195, 202, 204, 212, 213, 214, 221, 226, 229;
and Prince Imperial, 163–166
Bernard, Dr, 88, 89
Bernstorff, Countess von, 43
Bigge, Arthur (afterwards Lord Stamfordham), 190–191, 206, 207
Bismarck, Otto von, Prince, 68, 115, 128–131, 145, 150, 161, 232
Boehm, Johannes, 193
Boer War, 228, 229
Bonaparte, House of (*see* also Napoleon, Louis, Jerome, etc.), 10, 11, 47, 125, 133, 177, 178, 180, 230
Bonapartists, 4, 153, 155, 156, 159, 160, 206, 207
Borthwick, Algernon, 192, 195

Bourbon, House of, 89
Brigg, Mr, 194
Brown, John, 26, 110, 124, 161, 171, 186, 217
Bruce, Lady Augusta (afterwards Stanley), 15, 16, 52, 53
Buckingham Palace, 37, 39, 51, 87, 108, 109, 119, 151
Bulteel, Mary (afterwards Lady Ponsonby), 52, 53, 57
Burgoyne, Sir John, 137–138
Byng, Sir Henry, 205

Cambridge, Duke of, 17, 22, 34, 43, 160, 167–169, 175, 182, 184, 190
Cambridge, Duchess of, 32
Camden Place, 138–140, 142, 143, 146–149, 151–153, 155, 157, 158, 160, 163, 168, 169, 172, 177, 184, 185, 187, 189, 199, 222
Campbell, the Hon. Mrs, 190
Canrobert, General, 57
Carbonari, the, 89
Cardigan, Lord, 33
Carey, Agnes, 211–215
Carey, Captain, 174–175, 181–185, 187
Carey, Mrs, 181
Carisbrooke, Marquess of, 166
Carisbrooke Castle, 78
Carlyle, Thomas, 38, 39
Castiglione, Countess de, 76, 78, 92
Chamberlain, Joseph, 194
Charles of Brunswick, Duke, 25
Charles of Leiningen, Prince, 22
Charlotte, Empress of Mexico, 102, 123
Chelmsford, Lord, 167, 169, 174, 175, 183, 189, 190
Chesterfield, Lady, 177, 180
Chiswick House, 138
Christian, Prince, 155
Christian, Princess, 216, 217, 219
Christian Victor, Prince, 229
Churchill, Lady, 53
Clarendon, Lord, 15–17, 19, 20,

26, 34, 46–48, 56, 57, 60, 63, 72, 74, 75, 77, 81, 84, 104, 106, 122, 126
Clarendon, Lady, 32
Claridge's Hotel, 103, 104
Clothilde, Princess, 95
Cobden, Richard, 100–101
Coburg, House of (see also Leopold, etc.), 5, 13, 14, 102, 164
Compiègne, Palace of, 111–114, 200
Connaught, Duke of, see Prince Arthur
Constantine, Bishop of, 179
Constantine, Grand Duke of, 75
Corvisart, Baron, 172
Cowley, Lord, 9–11, 14, 16, 19–21, 36, 46–48, 72, 74, 76, 89–90, 96, 98, 105, 110, 114, 117, 124, 125
Cowley, Lady, 12, 72
Crimean War, 17–19, 31, 35, 73, 235
Cromwell, Richard 6
Crystal Palace, 41
Cyrnos, 221

Danube, S.S., 170
Decamps, 58
Delacroix, 58
Delane, J. T., 38
Demidoff, Prince, 62
Derby, Lord Edward, 88, 91, 97, 98, 118, 119
Deutscher Bund, 54
Dilke, Charles, 194
Disraeli, Benjamin, 25, 27, 89, 123, 124, 169, 173, 176, 177, 180, 184, 194
Dreyfus, Colonel, 222

Edinburgh, Duke of, see Prince Alfred
Edward VII (Bertie), King of England, 229, 232, 235; as Prince of Wales, 22, 23, 33, 46, 58, 62, 65, 68, 71, 92, 106, 117, 138, 151, 153, 159, 177, 179,

Edward VII—*cont.*
183, 193, 204, 208, 212, 226, 227; love of France, 66–67, 114–115, 224, 232; and Franco-Prussian War, 131–133; Napoleon III's funeral, 155–156; relations with Prince Imperial, 162–163; and *entente cordiale*, 67, 224, 232, 235

Edward VIII, King of England, 236

Elan, the, 208

Elizabeth II, Queen of England, 235

Ellice, Marion, 56

Elphinstone, Sir Howard, 116, 117, 162

Ely, Lady Jane, 149, 154

Elysée Palace, 124, 125

Entente cordiale, 5, 67, 101, 224, 232, 235

Ernest of Saxe-Coburg, Duke, 18, 87

Eugenie, Empress of the French, 19–21, 28, 36, 47, 50, 58, 63, 66–68, 71, 74–77, 89, 96, 101, 107, 129, 131, 132, 146, 147, 150–152, 160, 161, 163; courtship and marriage, 14–16; at Windsor, 22–24, 29–33; in London, 39–41, 43–44; pregnancy, 46, 47, 56; and Queen's visit to Paris, 56–57; at Osborne, 78–84; Orsini attempt, 87; at Cherbourg Fêtes, 92; visits Scotland, 102–105; Court of the Second Empire, 109, 111–114; visits Victoria at Osborne, 121–124; calls on Victoria at Paris Embassy, 124–127; flees Paris, 133; flight to, and arrival in, England, 137–138; receives Queen at Camden, 139–140; and death of Emperor, 154–159; quarrels with Plon-Plon over will, 158–159; Louis and Beatrice, 164–166; and Louis's plan to go to Zululand, 167–170; hears news of Louis's death, 171–172; receives Victoria, 172–173; Louis's funeral, 180; and Captain Carey, 174, 181–185; at Abergeldie, 185–188; pilgrimage, 188–192; Louis's memorial, 192–195; builds mausoleum, 199–200; life in exile, 200; friendship with Queen, 200–205; 'last political act', 205–207; and French sailors, 208–209; at Osborne Cottage, 210–214; and Ethel Smyth, 215–220; in South of France, 221–223; friendship with Queen's relations, 224–226; last meeting with Victoria, 227; receives Mary Waddington, 227–228; death of Victoria, 229; value of friendship, 230–232; and *entente cordiale*, 235; last years and death, 236–237

Evans, Dr T. W., 137–138, 140

Exposition Universelle de 1855, 46, 58–62, 66, 69

Exposition Universelle de 1867, 118

Eylau, battle of, 65

Farnborough Hill, 199, 200, 206, 207, 210, 221, 225, 226, 236, 237

Faure, Felix, 226, 227

Félix, M., 23–24

Ferdinand, Duke d'Orleans, 55

Fidelio, 40, 42

Filon, Augustin, 143, 191

Fitzmaurice, the Hon. Major, 94

Flahaut, Charles de, 35

Fleury, Count E., 35

Fontainebleau, Palace of, 68, 100, 111–114, 124–127

Franco-Prussian War, 129–133, 139, 143, 145, 146, 148, 150, 165, 225, 232, 236

Franz-Josef, Emperor of Austria, 102, 200

Fraser, Captain, 39

Frederick III, German Emperor, 225, 231; as Prince Frederick Wilhelm of Prussia, 43, 81; as Crown Prince, 127, 128, 132, 144, 150, 231
Frere, Sir Bartle, 191
Friedrichshof, 225
Froude, 38

Galerie des Glaces, 68, 145
Gambetta, Léon, 206
George III, King of England, 17, 29, 32, 235
George V, King of England, 62, 191, 236, 237
George VI, King of England, 236
Gladstone, W. E., 130, 132, 151, 155, 194
God save the Queen, 65
Grange, Countess de la, 223
Granville, Lord, 129, 132, 138, 144, 145, 155
Grey, General, 123
Greville, Charles, 26, 41, 88, 182
Guildhall, 39, 40
Gull, Sir William, 153

Ham, fortress of, 4, 5
Hapsburg, House of (*see* also Franz-Josef, Maximilian, etc.), 102
Hardman, Sir William, 105
Harrison, Colonel, 175, 183
Haussman, Baron Georges, 42
Henry of Battenberg, Prince, 204, 212, 216, 226
Hohenlohe-Langenburg, Duchess of (*see* also Adelaide), 14
Hohenzollern, House of, 128
Hohenzollern-Sigmaringen, *see* Leopold, Prince
Holland, Queen of, *see* Sophie
Hortense de Beauharnais, Queen of Holland, 4, 75

Imperial, Prince, *see* Louis
Ingres, J. A., 58

Iphigénie, the, 208
Isabel II, Queen of Spain, 31, 128
Isandhlwana, battle of, 167, 175, 189
Italian campaign, 94–98, 231
Invalides, Hôtel des, 63, 64, 199

Jane Eyre, 92
Jenner, Dr, 119
Jerome Bonaparte, King of Westphalia, 31, 47
Joinville, Prince de, 63
Josephine, Empress of the French, 4
Juarez, Benito, 101, 102

Kent, Duchess of, *see* Victoria
Kirchbach, General, 143
Kirkpatrick, William, 15

La Bretagne, 93
Langtry, Lillie, 163
La Reine Hortense, 84, 124
Larminat, Marie de, 142, 165, 167, 185–188
Leaves from the Journal of Our Life in the Highlands, 162
Lebreton, Madame, 138, 140
Leopold I, King of the Belgians, 3, 5–11, 16, 24, 29, 50, 51, 53–56, 60, 73, 80, 91, 95, 96, 98, 102–104, 115, 153
Leopold, Prince, Duke of Albany, 23, 110, 193
Leopold of Hohenzollern-Sigmaringen, Prince, 128–129, 140
Life of the Prince Consort, 162
Liria, Palicio de, 237
Louis, Prince Imperial of France, 97, 103, 107, 112, 116, 117, 131, 138–141, 143, 146, 148, 151, 153, 187, 199, 201, 206, 207, 214, 222, 230, 236; birth, 74–75; escapes to England, 137; goes to Woolwich, 152; and father's death, 155–159; career and personality, 160–163; and Princess Beatrice, 163–166; arranges

Louis, Prince Imperial of France
—*cont.*
to go to Africa, 167–170; news
of his death, 171–174; and
Carey, 174–175, 181–185; funeral, 176–180; Eugenie's pilgrimage, 188–192; memorial to,
192–195
Louis Bonaparte, King of Holland,
4
Louis Philippe, King of the
French, 4–7, 9, 20, 51, 55, 63, 64
Louvre, Palace of the, 47, 60, 140
Lyons, Lord, 124, 126, 132, 207
Lytton, Lady Edith, 211

McNeill, Miss, 205
McNeill, Sir John, 205
Magenta, battle of, 96
Malmesbury, Lord, 9, 10, 13, 14,
89, 90, 92, 94, 95, 149
Marie Amélie, Queen of the
French, 20, 54, 55, 59
Marie-Antoinette, Queen of
France, 51
Marlborough House, 162, 190
Martin, Theodore, 159, 162
Mary, Queen of England, 62, 237
Mary of Cambridge, Princess, 62
Mathilde Bonaparte, Princess, 47,
50, 56, 57, 61–63, 65, 178, 222
Maximilian, Emperor of Mexico,
102, 121, 123
Meissonier, Ernest, 58
Melbourne, Lord, 25
Metternich, Princess Pauline, 113
Moniteur, 88
Montijo, Count de, 15
Montijo, Countess de, 14, 15, 183,
185
Morning Post, 192, 195
Morny, Count de, 75, 88
Mouchy, Duchess de, 180
Murat, Joachim, 35

Napoleon I, Emperor of the
French, 4–7, 10–12, 31, 34, 47,
50, 61, 63–65, 83, 90, 95, 97,
100, 146, 157, 167, 178, 237
Napoleon II, Duke of Reichstadt,
4, 10
Napoleon III, Emperor of the
French, 137, 139, 141, 145, 161,
162, 165, 166, 169, 173, 178,
182, 199, 200, 201, 204, 208,
222, 226, 230–232, 236; birth
and early career, 3–7; *coup
d'état*, 3, 7–10; assumes title of
Emperor, 10; approaches to
Queen Victoria, 11–14, 17–20;
marriage, 14–16; State Visit,
Windsor, 20–37; charms the
Queen, 24–29, 41, 45, 53, 68–
70, 71–72, 147; Investiture,
33–34; in London, 38–45;
arranges State Visit to Paris,
46–48; plays host at St Cloud,
48–57; in Paris, 58–72; at
Napoleon's tomb, 63–65; Peace
of Paris, 73–75; and Castiglione,
75–76; visits Osborne, 77–84;
Orsini attempt, 87–89; Italian
question, 89–90; Cherbourg
Fêtes, 91–94; Italian War, 94–
99; China and Mexico, 100–
102; and Eugenie's visit to
Scotland, 102–105; and Prince
Albert, 105–107; Court of the
Second Empire, 108–120; and
Eugenie's visit to Osborne, 121–
124; and Victoria's visit to
Paris, 124–127; Franco-Prussian
War, 127–132; Sedan and the
fall of the Empire, 132–133;
arrives in England, 146; visits
Victoria at Windsor, 147;
receives her at Camden, 148–
149; his stoicism, 149–150; life
in exile, 151–153; illness and
death, 153–154; funeral, 155–
156; Queen visits Camden, 157–
159
Napoleon, Prince Jerome (Plon-
Plon), 31, 47, 49, 50, 58, 61–63,

Napoleon, Prince Jerome—*cont.*
65, 71, 73–77, 95, 153, 158, 159,
178–180, 206–207, 222
Neuilly, Palace of, 55
Ney, Marshal, 35
Nicholas I, Tsar of Russia, 11
Nieuwerkerque, Count de, 63
Normanby, Lord, 7, 9
Normanby, Lady, 7

Orleans, House of (*see* also Louis
Philippe, Ferdinand, etc.), 8,
13, 54, 55, 125, 159, 202, 207
Orontes, H.M.S., 174, 177
Orsini, Felice, 88–90
Osborne Cottage, 210–214
Osborne House, 3, 9, 46, 76–84,
91, 109, 110, 119–121, 153, 161,
185, 204, 210–214, 227–229
Osborne, the, 208

Paléologue, Maurice, 236, 237
Palmerston, Lord, 7, 8, 20, 63, 74,
81, 83, 88–90, 98, 101, 105
Paris, Congress of, 73
Paris, Count de, 55
Partant pour la Syrie, 22, 37, 44,
83
Pélican, the, 20
Pélissier, Marshal, 90, 91
Persigny, Count de, 81, 83, 90
Phipps, Sir Charles, 114
Pietri, Franceschini, 154
Plon-Plon, *see* Napoleon, Jerome
Ponsonby, Sir Henry, 110, 137,
138, 151, 161, 164, 166, 167, 191,
194, 205
Ponsonby, Lady Mary, *see* Bulteel
Pope Pius IX, 97, 103, 122
Punch, 91

Queen's Cross, 191, 192

Rothschild, Lady de, 56
Rubens Room, 24
Russell, Lord John, 6–8, 98

Saint Cloud, Palace of, 49, 50, 52,
53, 58, 60, 61, 111–113, 127,
131, 143, 204
St George's Chapel, 194, 195
St James, Court of, 35, 90, 115
St Mary's, Chislehurst, 156, 157,
176, 199
St Michael's Abbey, 166, 199, 237
St Paul's Cathedral, 151
Salisbury, Lord, 176
Saul, 179
Schiller, 18
Scott, Dr, Frederick, 190
Sebastapol, battle of, 54, 73
Sedan, battle of, 132, 137
Slade, Lt, 190
Smyth, Dame Ethel, 215–220
Solferino, battle of, 96
Sophie, Queen of Holland, 122,
125, 126
Sophie, Crown Princess of Greece,
225
Stamfordham, Lord, *see* Bigge
Stanley, Colonel, 166
Stockmar, Baron Christian von,
53, 54, 67, 91
Summer Palace, Peking, 100
Sweden, Prince Royal of, 179
Sydney, Lord, 171, 172
Sydney, Lady, 149

Teck, Duke of, 62
Tennyson, Alfred, 195
Thackeray, W. M., 64
Thérésa, Mlle, 113
Thistle, the, 227, 228
Thompson, Sir Henry, 153
Times, The, 38, 92, 93, 103, 126,
129, 130, 145–147
Torrington, Lord, 205
Triquetti, M., 55
Tuileries, Palace of the, 17, 46,
60, 64, 66, 69, 70, 71, 74, 111,
113, 115, 133, 137, 140, 147–
149, 200, 206

Vaillant, Marshal, 35

Vernet, Horace, 58
Versailles, Palace of, 55, 59, 63, 68, 145, 148
Victor Bonaparte, Prince, 178, 206
Victor Emmanuel, King of Sardinia (afterwards King of Italy), 95
Victoria, Queen of England; reaction to *coup d'état*, 3–10; acknowledges Napoleon III, 11; and Napoleon's marriage plans, 12–14; and Emperor's marriage to Eugenie, 14–16; wary of meeting Napoleon, 17–19; agrees to receive Emperor, 20; meets Napoleon and Eugenie, 22; State Visit to England: Windsor, 21–37, Buckingham Palace, 38–45; charmed by the Emperor, 24–29, 41, 45, 53, 68–70, 71–72, 147; first impressions on meeting Eugenie, 24, 29–32, 43; and arrangements for State Visit to Paris, 46–48; arrives in Paris, 49; at Saint Cloud, 50–57; in Paris, 58–72; visits Napoleon's tomb, 63–65; leaves France, 71–72; first disenchantments, 73–77; receives Emperor at Osborne, 77–84; and Orsini attempt, 87–90; at Cherbourg Fêtes, 91–94; Italian War, 94–97; exasperation with Emperor, 98–99, 105–106, 129–130; Mexican adventure, 100–102; and Eugenie's visit to Scotland, 102–105; death of Albert, 106–107; widowhood, 108–113; opinion of Paris, 114–115; childrens' visits to Paris, 115–118; receives Abdul Aziz, 118–120; with Eugenie at Osborne, 121–124; passes through Paris, 124–127; Franco-Prussian War, 127–133; hears of Eugenie's escape, 137–139; visits Camden Place, 139–140;

welcomes Eugenie to Windsor, 140–143; and screen, 143–145; receives Napoleon at Windsor and returns visit, 146–150; and Prince Imperial, 151–152; and death of Napoleon III, 153–156; visits Camden, 157–159; and Louis's career, 160–163; Louis and Beatrice, 163–166; and Louis's plan to go to Africa, 166–170; hears news of Louis's death, 171–174; and Carey, 174–175, 181–185; at Louis's funeral, 177–180; invites Eugenie to Abergeldie, 185–188; and Eugenie's pilgrimage, 188–192; Louis's memorial, 192–195; friendship with Eugenie, 199–205; Eugenie's trip to Paris, 205–207; reviews fleet, 208–209; entertains Eugenie at Osborne, 210–215; and Ethel Smyth, 215–220; in the south of France, 221–223; and relations with France, 224–226; last meeting with Empress, 227–228; death, 229; significance of friendship, 229–232; Eugenie's memories of, 235–237.
Victoria, German Empress; as Princess Royal, 22, 23, 33, 43, 46, 58, 66–68, 71, 80, 81, 83, 87; as Crown Princess, 96, 106, 115–116, 129–133, 140, 143–145, 150, 190, 204, 231; as Empress Frederick, 225, 229
Victoria, Duchess of Kent, 15, 94
Victoria Eugenie, Queen of Spain, 226
Victoria and Albert, the, 48, 71, 91, 94
Viel-Castel, 47
Vienna, Congress of, 11
Ville,-Hôtel de, 47, 60, 61, 118, 133, 148

Waddington, Mary, 208, 227–228

Walewski, Count Alexandre, 7, 8, 13, 14, 19, 81
Walewska, Countess Marie, 7
Walewska, Madame, 92
Waterloo, battle of, 5, 17, 98
Waterloo Gallery, 32
Westminster Abbey, 192–195
Westminster, Dean of, 193, 195
Wilhelm I, German Emperor, 145; as King of Prussia, 106, 115, 123, 128, 129, 131, 144
Wilhelm II, German Emperor, 204, 225, 226
Wilhelmshohe, Palace of, 133, 139, 141, 146

Windsor Castle, 16, 17, 20, 21, 23, 24, 28–32, 35, 37, 39, 46, 6ϡ, 74, 102–104, 109, 114, 139–141, 147, 151, 169, 180, 189, 194, 195, 202, 210, 220, 222, 229
Windsor, Dean of, 9
Winterhalter, F. X., 18, 24, 58
Wolseley, Sir Garnet, 190, 191
Wolseley, Lady, 190
Wood, Sir Evelyn, 189, 190
Wood, Lady, 190
World, the, 164

Zulu War, 167–170, 171, 174–175, 189, 193